Principles of Group Treatment

PRINCIPLES OF GROUP TREATMENT

ERIC BERNE, M. D.
McAuley Neuropsychiatric Institute
San Francisco

GROVE PRESS, INC., NEW YORK

To the 202 members
and all others
who understand Martian

Foreword

There are three reasons for writing this book:

1. It deals with group "treatment" rather than with group "therapy." These two approaches are sufficiently different to warrant a separate consideration for the former.

2. There is no other systematic treatise on the use of transactional analysis in groups.

3. A large number of people who have observed the writer's groups or have heard him discuss them want more information about why he does what he does, especially when he does what other therapists would not do, or does not do what other therapists would.

The book is based on more than twenty years of experience in practising group psychotherapy in a variety of settings, and in supervising, advising, training, and observing other group therapists in hospitals and clinics, in private, public, and governmental agencies, and in private practice. Most of the ideas, as used by the writer and his colleagues, have been under continuous and fairly ruthless scrutiny at the San Francisco Transactional Analysis Seminars, and have been subjected to healthy destructive criticism when formally presented elsewhere in teaching courses or at society meetings. The organization of the book is based on experience in teaching transactional group treatment primarily in the San Francisco Bay area: at the Veterans Administration Mental Hygiene Clinic, Langley Porter Neuropsychiatric Institute of the University of California Medical School, the Stanford–Palo Alto Psychiatric Clinic, Mount Zion Hospital, the McAuley Neuropsychiatric Institute of St. Mary's Hospital, the Child Guidance Clinic at Children's Hospital, and the San Francisco Transactional Analysis Seminars. The author has kept in mind the questions most commonly asked by beginners in this field.

His formal experience in group treatment began in an army hospital during World War II. Liquor was forbidden on the premises and the soldiers were in the habit of buying large quantities of shaving lotion and secreting it in various places, to be drunk when opportunity arose. Hence it was necessary to institute a mattress check every morning, during which two orderlies lifted the mattress off each bed to see what was concealed on the springs. Large quantities of bottled toxic substances were thus uncovered. In desperation, the writer called a meeting of the patients in the day-room to discuss the pharmacological properties of shaving lotion. The patients liked the meeting so well that they requested a daily opportunity to continue these discussions. Shortly thereafter group therapy came into favor with the War Department, and the writer was thus enabled to continue his policy with official encouragement and has been meeting with patients in groups ever since.

ACKNOWLEDGMENTS

What is written here has been learned from the hundreds of students who have attended the writer's seminars and the hundreds of patients who have attended his treatment groups, and he is grateful to all of them. Perhaps the outstanding individuals in this respect have been the active members of the San Fran-

cisco Transactional Analysis Seminars (formerly the San Francisco
Social Psychiatry Seminars), but everyone who has presented
material for discussion has been in some measure stimulating.
The "old-timers," most of them now holding Clinical Membership in the International Transactional Analysis Association, have
been particularly helpful in testing the transactional approach in
practice. For the manuscript itself, my thanks go to my secretary, Mrs. Allen Williams. To Dr. Alfred C. Wood, Jr., of Philadelphia, I am indebted for his meticulous sentence-by-sentence
criticism of the semi-final draft; and I am most grateful to Dr.
Michael Khlentzos, Chief of the McAuley Neuropsychiatric Institute, for an opportunity to set up and carry out a systematic
training program in transactional group treatment for the residents and staff.

SEMANTICS

"He" is used as a common pronoun, and in an appropriate context means an individual of either sex. Where something is more
applicable to the female sex, "she" is used. "Is" refers to something that the writer is convinced of; "seems to be" or "appears
to be" refer to propositions he is not yet completely sure of.
"Group" is used in a specific sense which is discussed in the text.
In accordance with transactional usage, Parent, Adult, and
Child are capitalized when they refer to ego states; without capi-
tals, parent, adult, and child refer to actual people. For the sake
of simplicity of discourse, in describing certain personal experiences the writer will refer to himself as "Dr. Q." "Therapist" is used (since it is the only available term) to include both
those who are engaged in "group treatment" as described in this
book, and those who do "group therapy." "Group therapy" is
used in some contexts as a general term which includes "group
treatment." In other contexts where it is indicated, the two are
sharply distinguished.

The term "transactional analysis" as used here refers to the system described by the writer in his previous works cited in Chapter 10, which is based on a specific theory of personality first reported in 1956 (Berne, E. "Ego States in Psychotherapy." *Am. Jnl. Psychother.* 11: 293–309, 1957). Despite certain important similarities in outlook, there are decisive differences between this and the "transactional social work," "transactional research," and "transactional psychotherapy" of Grinker, which followed the work of J. P. Spiegel and F. R. Kluckhohn, and which are explicitly "based on operations derived from field, role, and communication theories rather than on a theory of personality." (Grinker, R. R. "A Transactional Model for Psychotherapy." In *Contemporary Psychotherapies,* ed. M. I. Stein, pp. 190–227. Free Press of Glencoe, New York, 1961.) Although both use the word "transactional," Grinker and his associates on the one hand, and this book and the International Transactional Analysis Association on the other, represent two distinct approaches in theory and application. But all, I think, would salute the relaxed or "cowboy" therapist who has permission to be happy himself and can transmit this license to his patients.

Carmel, California   E. B.
July, 1965

Contents

II Transactional Analysis

Figures

Introduction

It was the custom at a large metropolitan hospital for the members of the psychiatric staff—psychiatrists, psychologists, and social workers—to sit together at lunch in the hospital dining-room. Occasionally a surgeon, internist, or other member of the medical staff would take a seat at the same table. Then it sometimes happened that the newcomer was jokingly greeted as a "real doctor." Behind this joke lay some unspoken ideas about what distinguished a "real doctor" from a "nonreal" (or even "unreal") doctor. These distinctions seemed to be as follows:

1. A "real doctor" is specifically oriented throughout his training toward curing his patients, and that is his overriding consideration throughout his practice.

2. A "real doctor" can plan his treatment so that at each phase he knows what he is doing and why he is doing it.

3. A "real doctor" clearly distinguishes research and experimentation from good medical or surgical care, and the former is always subsidiary to the latter.

4. A "real doctor" takes sole and complete responsibility for the welfare of his patients.

This book is written for those who wish to become "real doctors" or the equivalent thereof. Some years of experience in training group therapists has emphasized the need for teachers in this discipline to be clear and forthright and to take full responsibility for their opinions. At every step the student should be required to compare himself—his attitude, his aims, and his procedure—with the best tradition of the ancient healing arts, so that in due time he can take his place at the table with the other real doctors.

Principles of Group Treatment

"A group in its very concept is the untruth. . . . The falsehood first of all is the notion that the group does what in fact only the *individual* in the group does, though it be every *individual*. For "group" is an abstraction and has no hands: but each individual has ordinarily two hands. . . . The group is untruth. Hence none has more contempt for what it is to be a man than they who make it their profession to lead the crowd. . . . The witness to the truth is to engage himself if possible with all, but always individually, talking to every one severally on the streets and lanes . . . in order to disintegrate the crowd, or to talk even to the crowd, though not with the intent of educating the crowd as such, but rather with the hope that one or another individual might return from this assemblage and become a single individual."

S. KIERKEGAARD
That Individual

"To the corkscrew, the knife is crooked."
CYPRIAN ST. CYR
Letters to My Wife's Maid

"Man cannot live only by knowing the score."
CHARLES MC CABE
San Francisco Chronicle

I
Basic Principles

1
General Considerations

The term "group treatment" is used in this book to refer to the treatment of psychiatric patients when the leader meets in a specified place for a specified period of time with a small number of them, usually not exceeding eight or ten. It is assumed that the leader of such a group is a trained group psychotherapist or a properly prepared trainee under adequate supervision, and that his declared purpose is the alleviation of psychiatric disabilities.

Group treatment is thus distinguished on the one hand from individual therapy, in which a single patient is seen by the therapist at a private session, and on the other hand from large group meetings which are attended by a large number (from twenty to five hundred) of patients or clients. It is also distinguished from meetings of small groups which are held for purposes other than the alleviation of psychiatric disabilities, or whose leader is not trained or in training as a psychotherapist; and from therapeutic communities in which patients live in an artificial co-operative society. Group treatment, however, may be part of the program of a therapeutic community. Experimental groups, discussion groups, alternate meetings, ward

3

meetings, multiple therapy, and group work are allied activities which must be clearly differentiated from treatment groups and group treatment as the latter terms are intended here.

The present discussion will be confined to one type of psychotherapeutic treatment group, the sedentary social group of adults, which is the commonest type in clinical practice. "Sedentary" means that for the most part the patients stay in their seats; "social" means that the only way they can legitimately structure their time is by talking; and "adult" means that they are postpubertal. Such groups are commonly included under the label "group therapy." "Group therapy," however, is sometimes concerned with matters that are peripheral to the central aim of curing patients. The use of the term "group treatment" (or "treatment in groups") frees the therapist from these peripheral issues, so that he can focus his undivided attention on the specific primary therapeutic goal. The nature of the difference between group therapy and group treatment will be further clarified in later sections.[1,2] In some contexts, however, where there is no special reason for distinguishing the two, the term "group therapy" will be used loosely to include group treatment, just as the word "therapist" will be applied to all psychotherapists, regardless of which particular approach they are using.

SELECTION OF PATIENTS

The term "selection of patients" raises two different problems: first, which patients are suitable for group treatment; and second, which patients should be assigned to a specific group. In practice, however, almost any patient can be introduced to a treatment group after proper preparation (the nature of which will be discussed later), so that it is only necessary to consider here the problem of assignment.

There are two types of groups in this respect, homogeneous and heterogeneous. Homogeneity may be a matter of specific planning or of personal policy. A planned homogeneous group is one which is designed to deal with a specific kind of patient: schizophrenic, mentally retarded, alcoholic, stuttering, psychosomatic, delinquent, parent of delinquent. In fact, any condition which is thought to be amenable to psychotherapy lends itself to the formation of a special group. The homogeneity demanded or preferred by some therapists as a matter of policy is in a different category. It is usually based on personal prejudices, supported by rationalizations which may be become untenable in the face of systematic criticism. Some of the homogeneities often sought for, such as age, psychiatric diagnosis, attitude ("passivity," "dependence," etc.), and cultural, racial, or economic background, are only as relevant to the prognosis of well-planned ongoing group treatment as they would be to the prognosis of appendicitis.

The real issue in this connection is not the one commonly debated, "What are the criteria for the selection of patients?," but the underlying, usually unstated assumption "Criteria for selection are good." There are strong theoretical and practical reasons, as will be demonstrated later, for saying that in most situations, and with a few dramatic exceptions, "Selection of patients is not good"; in fact, it may be deleterious to the progress of treatment. The best policy is to pick patients at random or in order of application, or in some other fashion which is likely to increase the heterogeneity of the group.

Covert snobbishness is often a basis for rejecting candidates for a given group, typical premises being "How can I put this uneducated bohemian in with this group of cultured well-to-do ladies?" or "How can I put this mentally backward farmer in with this group of highly educated professional men?" If the therapist can allow himself to experiment in this respect, he may discover that often the previously derogated patient turns out to have better psychological insight than the other members of his group and gets better faster, thus at first earning their respect and later evoking their chagrin. The good group therapist never misses a chance to learn, and he will not fail to do so if he challenges himself by relaxing his criteria for selection. Such relaxation has the added advantage that it frees his time and attention for more important issues.

It is a good thing to remember that neither the patient's behavior in a group nor the group's reaction to a patient can always be reliably predicted. A depressed patient who has hardly spoken or smiled for months may find himself joking and laughing heartily at his first meeting, while one who is elated and voluble in individual therapy may become thoughtful and silent. Such reactions depend largely on the skill of the therapist, which can only be tested by actual confrontation in the group situation.

In general, then, the preferable basic position should be "Criteria for selection are not good, except under special circumstances." Some of the exceptions will be discussed in the next chapter.

NEW PATIENTS

There is no reason why new patients, after they are properly prepared, should be excluded from already established treatment groups. Their introduction may benefit all concerned: the new patient sees and is encouraged by the obvious progress made by the older ones; the older patients, noting the naïveté of the newcomer, feel both gratified and helpful. If the newcomer is sharp, there is no harm done either.

PHYSICAL ARRANGEMENTS

The less distraction from the physical surroundings, the more energy that can be devoted to therapy. The meeting-place should be selected with some care to keep external disturbances at a minimum. If the room is assigned rather than chosen, the supervisor should extend himself to see that the group has the same degree of physical comfort and privacy that any other form of medical treatment would require, and the therapist is entitled to request this courtesy, together with any special equipment he desires, such as a blackboard or a tape recorder.

The group should meet at a regular time for a specified period, and should begin promptly and end promptly. Tardiness on the part of the therapist, of course, is not to be tolerated. This does not mean that he is the first one there, but that he arrives at the time he has set for himself: perhaps five minutes after the appointed hour, to allow time for the members to get settled. The expectation of promptness throws into bold relief a patient who has a special problem with punctuality. At the other end, a habitually prompt termination uncovers the patient who insists on having a "private interview" at the end of each session. It should be understood that all problems of each patient are the concern of the whole group, so that a persistent demand for a private interview after the meeting is then unmasked as a maneuver in violation of the stated policy. More important, a prompt beginning and ending enable the therapist to structure the proceedings to the best advantage of the therapeutic plan.

The commonest excuses for terminal private interviews are finances and prescriptions. A fee schedule should be set for each patient according to his means, and adhered to. The manner of payment should also be agreed upon, together with a delinquency date for those who pay monthly. Repeated irregularities and delinquencies then stand out clearly and can be investigated for their possible psychological significance. Although the basic postulate of a therapy group is that any subject whatsoever can be broached, it is often found that the question of fees is implicitly regarded as an exception. Sex and hostility are freely discussed to give the illusion of liberty, but financial problems internal to the group may be veered away from as though by common consent. In most such cases, the patients have taken their cue from the therapist, and the first thing to question if

money is not discussed in the group is his own attitude about
it. Once it is established that money is no more obscene than
sex, and if the medical therapist also takes the trouble to bring
his prescription blanks to the meetings, it will be found that
most of the terminal private interviews have been eliminated.
By discussing prescriptions during the session, the therapist also
brings into the open "games" revolving around medication.

THERAPEUTIC GOALS

The therapist should have his goals clearly defined in his own
mind and preferably also in the mind of each patient according
to his need. The ideal situation is to have a therapeutic contract
with each patient so that both patient and therapist know what
they are aiming for. Popular goals nowadays are psychodynamic
reorganization of the patient's personality, symptomatic remission or cure, increased and more satisfying socialization, increased control of feelings and behavior, or the abandonment of
stereotyped relationship patterns. In order to avoid mere opportunism, fuzzy thinking, and therapeutic ecstasy, these goals
should be regarded as distinct from each other, or at least
thought through separately and ordered systematically, in a
well-planned therapeutic program. Such terms as "sharing,"
"integration," "maturity," and "growth" (if used at all), should
be carefully defined in accordance with the strictest, rather than
the loosest, methodological principles.

METHOD

The goals or the succession of goals having been decided, the
therapist must then choose the method best adapted to the
attainment of each one. He has at his disposal three kinds of
techniques: borrowed, opportunistic, and indigenous. The beginner generally borrows methods familiar to him from his train-

ing in individual therapy, such as the psychoanalytic approach, being constrained to order the phenomena he observes in the group according to the hard-earned vocabulary learned during his residency. Much of the current literature on group therapy encourages this tendency. These methods may not always make the best use of the specific advantages offered by the group situation because they are not primarily designed for it.

As he gains confidence, the therapist senses this and begins to branch out in an opportunistic way, trying first one thing and then another as the occasion seems to warrant in his search for improvement. At this stage there is a temptation to relinquish his clinical orientation in favor of a sociological or even metaphysical interest in the group as a whole, as a kind of entelechy. The elaboration of this interest gives rise to the systems included under the rubric of "group analysis."

The indigenous methods fall into two categories, both making specific use of the inherent richness of the group situation and the factors that differentiate it from the more circumscribed relationship of the individual interview. The first category includes the group analytic methods, those approaches treating the group as a whole. The second makes direct clinical application of the actual occurrences in the group as they affect or reveal the idiosyncracies of each member as a person in his own right. The analysis of transactions, for example, offers a way of breaking down complex, many-handed transactions into individual components.

Once a method is selected, it should be adhered to firmly, and the best guarantee of good results is a clear commitment on the part of both therapist and patients to the method chosen. This, however, does not exclude an occasional opportunistic advance through the use of some other approach if sound indications arise, but never at the expense of the chosen therapeutic program; after such digressions, the group should be quickly brought back to the main issues. The therapist should know, preferably in advance, each step he plans to take with each patient. As soon as one phase has been completed, he should know exactly how to move on to the next one, and each phase should be oriented toward the stated therapeutic goal.

COMBINED THERAPY

It is best to have at least one preliminary individual session (and more if indicated) with each patient before he enters the group. During this session the history can be obtained, the patient and therapist can have a chance to look each other over, and the therapeutic goals and other pertinent matters can be discussed and decided upon. If the therapist feels that group treatment is the method of choice in a given situation, there should be an agreement that when either the therapist or the patient feels it is indicated, each of them should feel free to suggest an individual interview. In any case, for most patients whose treatment is primarily in a group, an individual interview every eight or ten weeks is usually a good idea. In other cases, group treatment is ancillary to individual therapy, the patient being introduced to a group, for example, at a certain stage of psychoanalytic therapy.

Sometimes a patient is referred to a group therapist while he continues in individual treatment with someone else. If the group therapist is clear about his goals this need cause no complications, and it may not even be necessary to have lengthy discussions with the referring practitioner as long as there is a good initial understanding. The luncheon hours thus saved can be spent to good advantage listening to anthropologists, sea-captains, endocrinologists, neurosurgeons, and other companions suitably instructive for a psychotherapist. The first two will educate him in group dynamics, and the others will increase his knowledge of psychopathology. A competent medical group therapist might be able to make a psychopathological diagnosis of carcinoma of the thyroid. After he visits the patient on the surgical ward a week later and the pathologist shows him the slides, he will have the thrill of knowing that now he can eat with the real doctors.

ATTENDANCE

The promulgation of rules regarding attendance will have little effect on the actual results, which are determined by other factors. Any apparent effect may be regarded as a statistical accident, since the mean attendance for large series of groups of different types and different degrees of compulsion shows surprisingly little variation. For example in one study, total attendance at all schools in the United States (under legal compulsion), all Rotary Clubs in the United States (under social pressure), and a series of psychotherapy groups (with free choice, remission of fees for absence, and financial obligation for attendance) were each 88.8 per cent with a maximum deviation of only 1.5 per cent.[3] Spontaneous attendance should be taken as a measure of the therapist's skill, and, indeed, this is one of the clearest and most objective criteria in the whole field of therapy. A good rule of thumb is based on the ratio (Total actual attendances/Total possible attendances) over a period of three to six months as shown by actual records. If this exceeds 90 per cent, the therapist is doing a superior job. If it is below 75 per cent, something is wrong and immediate corrective measures are indicated; these are best prescribed by a consultant. A refinement of this is to subtract from the total number of absences all those clearly due to unavoidable external circumstances; the remaining absences are regarded as being due to psychological factors. If the "psychological" absences exceed 15 per cent of the total possible attendance, a review of the therapeutic approach should be undertaken.

The therapist should formulate a policy either for his whole practice or for each individual patient as to whether the patients pay when they miss a group meeting. The basic policy should be that they do not pay, and exceptions to this rule should be carefully considered. A simple way to avoid the issue is to charge the patient a flat monthly rate, rather than having him pay for each session.

It is of no particular value to spend time during the group session discussing why a patient is or was absent unless it can be demonstrated in an individual case that this is directly related to the therapeutic goal for that patient. The same applies to long discussions about who is sitting in which chair. Such pedantry is the hallmark of the unprepared therapist.

INFORMAL MEETINGS

Some groups evolve an external social life; for example, going to coffee after each meeting. Initially, a laissez-faire policy is best in this regard. But if after six months or so the patients do not at least stand on the corner and gossip after the meeting, this may indicate that the therapist is too rigid in some respect. On the other hand, if they start going to a saloon instead of to a coffee shop, or if there is an extra-mural affair blossoming, the therapist's first reaction should be to look for his own contribution to this over-activity.

It is not unusual in some parts of the country to set up an "alternate meeting" during the week, when the patients meet without the therapist. The clinician with a few years of experience behind him may want to experiment with this idea, having one group meet by themselves between formal sessions, and other groups not, to see the difference. His own experiments in this direction will be much more convincing to him, one way or the other, than what he reads in the literature on this subject.

TERMINATION

Termination may be accidental, resistant, or therapeutic. The commonest termination of group methods of treatment occurs by accident: that is, the patient moves away or some external force over which he has no control makes it necessary for him to withdraw from the group. The next commonest is the resistant termination by plausible excuse or unexplained and unannounced withdrawal; such terminations are based on fear, dissatisfaction, or triumph, and indicate that the therapist has overlooked something. Each such occurrence, therefore, should prove instructive and add to his knowledge and experience. If he cannot understand clearly what happened, the other members of the group may be able and willing to enlighten him. Their observations in this regard are a good test of how well he is doing his job of increasing their perceptiveness.

Therapeutic termination occurs when the therapist and the patient agree that the planned therapeutic goals have been attained, and that either an interruption or a final termination is in order. The consensus of the group lends force to this, although the other members may have to overcome a tendency to get angry with anyone who gets better, since many of them are there in the first instance to prove that the therapist cannot help anybody; thus, for someone to get better is from that point of view a kind of cheating. Sometimes the therapist feels apologetic too, and if he presents the case, he may "modestly" gloss over the fact that the patient recovered. Some of the reasons for these paradoxical phenomena will become clear in the following chapters.

REFERENCES

For further discussion of most of the topics treated in this chapter, the reader is referred to the following books. The first two were written by thoughtful therapists of long experience, who differ in some instances from the views presented here.

1. Mullan, H., and M. Rosenbaum. *Group Psychotherapy, Theory and Practice*. Free Press of Glencoe, New York, 1962.
2. Wolf, A., and E. K. Schwartz. *Psychoanalysis in Groups*. Grune & Stratton, New York, 1962.
3. Berne, E. "Group Attendance: Clinical and Theoretical Considerations." *Int. J. Group Psychother.* 5:392–403, 1955.

2
Preparing the Scene

The group therapist is subject to the same two types of contracts as the practitioner in any field of treatment: one referring to organizational practice, the other to private practice. The complexities of organizational practice will be considered first. The organizational therapist has a double responsibility — on the one hand to his organization and on the other to his patients. Each of these aspects should be clarified separately before a synthesis is attempted.

The Administrative Contract If the therapist or his organization proposes to do group therapy, the first step is to have an understanding as to the occasions for and purposes of the project and the organizational goals. In some agencies these are stated in writing and perhaps set forth by law. During the preliminary discussions, the law or other directives should be read aloud in the presence of all those interested in furthering the project. A personal, detailed knowledge of all pertinent directives may avoid later difficulties with supervisors or higher authorities. If there are no written directives, then the supervisor should be persuaded to make a formal, unequivocal statement of the purpose of the project. This basic discussion may employ terms which are essentially sociological, such as "rehabilitation" and "remission," and the local understanding of those terms should be elucidated. There should also be a clear understanding and firm commitments concerning problems of finance, personnel, facilities, and equipment.

The Professional Contract After the administrative aspects are settled, the next problem is the professional goal of the therapy, which will be stated in psychiatric terms such as "symptomatic cure," "personality reorganization," "social control," "reorientation," or "psychoanalysis." The local meaning of such terms should again be agreed upon even at the risk of appearing pedantic, for this is preferable to being vague at this point.

The Psychological Contract This concerns personal needs of supervisors, superiors, and colleagues, of which they themselves may or may not be aware, but which it is within the professional province of the therapist to assess. It is of decisive importance for the therapist to formulate these factors to himself, drawing upon his personal knowlege of the individuals concerned, but he must not of course refer aloud, even jokingly, to this aspect, except to people who are fully competent and fully prepared to understand its significance. The meaning of the psychological contract will be clearer later after the reader becomes familiar with some of the "games" commonly played by the staff members of clinical agencies. For the present, a provocative paradox will serve to illustrate the point. A very effective therapist who discharged his patients much more rapidly than any of his colleagues did, might be disappointed to find that instead of being congratulated on all sides, he was regarded as a "controversial figure," even though the administrative and professional contracts explicitly encouraged effective therapy. They might treat him as though he had broken some unspoken "gentleman's agreement" which was different from and perhaps even in conflict with the stated goals. As one hard-headed therapist put it: "My problem is, how effective can I be without getting fired?" [1] By this he meant that in his new job the unstated psychological contract must be considered along with the stated "job description."

Organizational Needs   In this area also lies the problem of how conservative or daring the therapist should be in his therapeutic efforts in a given organization. If he is too daring, he may have a high withdrawal rate and more "incidents," and this may arouse uneasiness in his superiors and bring censure on himself, even though he might get quicker and better results with a larger proportion of patients than his more conservative colleagues do.

The Authority Diagram   In order to consider systematically these three aspects of the organizational contract — the administrative, the professional, and the psychological — the therapist should draw an informal "authority diagram" such as that shown in Figure 2B (Chapter 6), including everyone inside the organization and as much of the external hierarchy (the Mother Group) as possible. For example, a complete authority diagram of a federal agency would start with the elevator operators and receptionists (who might be giving various patients friendly advice from time to time), go up through the medical staff and director, and then jump to the hierarchy in Washington right up to the President (to whom a patient might appeal by letter or through an interested organization). In the case of a state hospital, the authority diagram should include the state department of mental health, and above that, the governor. The therapist should surmise which aspects each person in this hierarchy would consider the therapist's responsibility, and what each of them would (and would not) expect from the group therapy program. He should then formulate plans for meeting or dealing with these expectations.

While at first sight such thoroughness might seem to be superfluous, anyone who recalls vividly the many sensational occurrences and investigations in mental health agencies in recent years will appreciate its value. Any unfortunate happening in a public agency may be subjected to pitiless and often unsympathetic scrutiny by a crusading press. A certain type of oversight on the therapist's part, taken together with other oversights in other programs of the same agency, might result in someone in the hierarchy losing his job. The therapist must therefore consider all these possibilities and clarify for himself where his responsibilities lie and what compromises he is willing or unwilling to make in balancing rapid therapeutic progress against other factors.

The Therapist-Patient Contract   The therapist's contract with the patients [2,3] will have the same aspects as the organizational contract — administrative, professional, and psychological. At the administrative level, he should explain to the patients the relationship between himself, the organization, and themselves. He should consider not only what he intends to convey to them, but also how they are likely from their side to understand his organizational role and responsibilities.

At the professional level, the most acute question is whether the therapeutic goals will conflict with the patient's understanding of the administrative contract, particularly if he is receiving material aid from the agency or from some other agency. He may be in a dilemma between getting better and losing the material aid, or staying sick in order to continue receiving it. This dilemma strongly influences the psychological aspect of the therapist-patient contract, the "games" which are likely to be played in the group. There are often good grounds for doubting whether the patients will be able to adhere consistently to their declarations of good faith. This dilemma may require a frontal attack before therapy can proceed. Similar considerations apply in hospitals and clinics of the armed services, where the question of returning to duty, whether hazardous or not, becomes a decisive consideration in the patient's mind; and obversely, in correctional institutions where the patient's release is the critical item.

It is, therefore, important in such situations that the therapist-patient contract be clarified realistically, first in the therapist's mind and then with the patients. The therapist's commitment to them ("My job here is to . . .") and their commitment to him ("My reason for coming to this group is to . . .") should be stated unequivocally, so that any shilly-shallying on either side can immediately be brought into question as a possible breach of good faith, with the focus on the hidden ambiguities which now stand revealed. If such clarification is made a bilateral obligation, the therapist may be pleasantly surprised at how much he can learn about his own motivations under the critical scrutiny of patients who are thus put on their mettle.

Unless all three aspects of these two contracts — that with the organization and that with the patients — are considered beforehand, the therapist may find himself taken by surprise at a later date, with the loss of a considerable investment of time and energy. At this initial stage, above all, there is no place for naïveté and uncritical acceptance of unspecific assurances of good will. The therapist should stand skeptically, even cynically, aloof until he has used his clinical knowledge to assess the real goals of all the parties concerned, including himself. Only after he has attained full awareness of the possibilities can he afford the luxury of being a good fellow.

Private Practice In private practice the situation is different. There the responsibility of the therapist is almost exclusively to the patient; the possible impact of authorities external to the group itself is so unlikely that no reasonably circumspect practitioner need take them into account under ordinary conditions. There is essentially no organizational contract beyond that contained in his Code of Ethics, unless fees are paid by an outside organization, in which case their regulations may prove hampering in some respects. In such cases, the contract with the intruding organization should be treated like any other organizational contract. In "pure" private practice, the contract with the patient is favorably influenced by the fact that the patient is seeking treatment on his own initiative, and his overt motivation at least — the alleviation of his suffering — is usually in good faith.

Even in "pure" private practice, however, the therapist should examine the contractual situation carefully. If the patient's bills are being paid by another individual (as in the case of minors, for example) or he comes for treatment under pressure (as is frequent in cases of impending divorce or excessive drinking), the therapist may find himself involved in a "three-handed game" in which he may end up holding the busted hand and lose not only the patient but his fees as well. He should therefore make sure that all parties directly concerned understand clearly both the practical demands of the therapeutic situation (the administrative contract) and the limitations and potentialities of what his treatment has to offer (the professional contract). In this way the therapist is least likely to be hurt professionally and financially and is more free to devote himself to the psychological aspects of the contract which become part of the therapeutic struggle.

THE THERAPIST

The conscientious group therapist will prepare himself in two ways: professionally and personally. Professionally, he will not undertake therapeutic programs for which he is not qualified, unless he is under adequate supervision. He will not, for example, attempt psychoanalytic therapy, transactional analysis, or psychodrama unless he has had approved training in those fields * or is able to find a qualified supervisor. Personally, he will examine his motives and fortify himself against temptation or exploitation of his weaknesses.

* If he lives in a remote area where none is available, he is reduced to assiduous reading and prudent experiment until he can take time off to obtain the necessary education.

Education Ideally he will have had preliminary training in psychoanalytic theory and practice, transactional analysis, the principles of group therapy, and group dynamics. The training in group dynamics should come from a competent source, since this is the area in which most clinicians are weakest. It is a current fashion to consider that a knowledge of individual psychodynamics and some experience with therapy groups somehow qualifies people as group dynamicists. This is not so. Group dynamics is a special branch of science requiring serious study in order to attain the degree of understanding necessary for the effective leadership and control of a therapy group. In this area neither the assumptions current in clinical literature nor the basic principles of Freudian group psychology are sufficient equipment for clinical competence. Unfortunately, the modern "research" approach of social psychology and sociology is of limited value for the group therapist. Far more pertinent and realistic is the work of the older thinkers (1500–1800) as summarized by Otto Gierke [4] in 1883.* For a more thorough clinical preparation, he should also have some acquaintance with existential therapy, gestalt therapy with its laudable emphasis on observation, modern Jungian psychology, psychodrama, and the ideas of Trigant Burrow. Further discussion of this literature, with a bibliography, will be found in Chapter 9.

Self-Examination Optimally, the therapist should have had not only didactic training, but also personal experience as a patient in both individual and group therapy. These are the best preparations for attaining the degree of self-awareness necessary to have a full grasp of what is happening in his groups. Why is it, for example, that the same patients are more excitable or impulsive with one therapist than with another? Even if the therapist has not had an opportunity for extensive personal therapeutic experience, however, he can prepare himself if he

---

* The present writer's book on group dynamics [5] is also directly relevant to the problems of group treatment.

subjects himself to a sufficiently ruthless self-examination. In fact, personal analysis or group therapy is not enough and must be supplemented by a more specific appraisal.

This specific preparation will consist of an examination of his motives for starting group therapy. First, he should be clear as to why he is using the group instead of individual therapy for his patients. It is good practice for him to write down three reasons for this choice. In most cases, these will be appropriate and convincing, and constitute the rational or Adult aspect of his motivation. Once this is settled, he should write down a fourth and fifth reason. These may be more revealing of important influences which might not otherwise be brought into the open. Some beginners discover that they are dazzled by the prospect, or that it is an act of compliance or bravado, or that it offers a unique arena for therapeutic ardor. Ambitious and "parental" drives should be dissected out as forming the Parental aspect of his motivations. Finally, he should search assiduously for archaic needs which he is "unconsciously" (in reality usually preconsciously) planning to satisfy through manipulation and exploitation. These form the Child aspect of his motivations, which is not only the most difficult to get at, but is the most important because it in the long run will usually determine the outcome of his therapeutic efforts.

Self-Correction   The Parent and Child aspects of his motivations (Chapter 10) influence the therapist much more systematically and pervasively than he may realize. It may take him several months to perceive that he is consistently acting like a jerk, a slob, or worst of all, a sulk, in his interventions. It may take even longer to become clear that almost everything he says has the exploitative quality that is characteristic of a game leading to a masked ulterior goal. In any case, the more productive question is not "Am I playing a game?" but rather "What game am I playing?" When it is discovered through supervision, for example, that a group therapist is engaged in a particular set of subversive maneuvers, this should not be a matter for surprise nor should it be taken to mean that he is unusual; rather it should be taken as a challenge and a matter for concern if a given therapist's game cannot be unmasked quickly so that self-corrective measures can be applied.

The therapist's attitude in this regard should be that of the professional rather than the amateur. He should not assume that until proven otherwise his behavior will be irreproachable, but should find out ahead of time in what respects it is likely to depart from the ideal, so that he can correct for them from the beginning. His position is analogous to that of a navigator: it is only the amateur who expects his compass to point due north; the professional assumes that there will be a deviation and wants to know what correction he should apply every time he takes a reading. In this sense the therapist before undertaking group therapy, should "calibrate" himself so that at all times he knows in which direction he should make corrections.

THE ASSISTANT THERAPIST

The presence of a second professional person in a treatment group may be part of the contract, and such an arrangement should be scrutinized with the same uncompromising forthrightness as the other terms of the contract if administrative difficulties and therapeutic obscurities are to be obviated.

The Co-Therapist The second professional person can be fairly called a co-therapist only if he is both administratively and professionally a peer of the therapist. This situation rarely occurs in actual practice. When it does, the question still arises as to whether a group functions better with two leaders. Often the second professional person is there because the primary therapist is reluctant to take full responsibility. Such arrangements are only exceptionally found in other branches of treatment; one hears of co-surgeons, for example, only in unusual cases, because experience has shown that an operating room works better if it is clearly understood by all concerned who is in charge of the operation.

The evasion of responsibility implied by having a co-therapist is often rationalized by saying that one represents a father and the other a mother. This kind of statement is subject to considerable criticism on both theoretical and clinical grounds; theoretically it is presumptuous and clinically it is naïve. Even if it were defensible, the practical advantages of such an arrangement remain to be explained. It is difficult enough to grasp what is going on in a therapy group anyway, and an ill-understood complication of the situation may obscure many issues which are perhaps more important. Experience indicates that what the presence of a co-therapist contributes in dynamic confusion usually outweighs what he offers intellectually or therapeutically.[6]

If, however, after due consideration of the drawbacks, the therapist feels that he wants to share the responsibility of leadership with an administrative and professional peer for personal or experimental reasons, then the second professional person may be validly called a co-therapist. This situation may arise in the case of two friends or two residents at the same stage of training. If the idea of the dual project comes from the administrative or supervisory level, then the supervisors should be careful that the two therapists chosen are actually peers. Too often the co-therapist is only given that title as a matter of courtesy. The patients soon become aware of the hypocrisy involved, and may conclude that it signifies that hypocrisy is permissible in that particular group. Such an impression, of course, should not be encouraged.

There is an occasional anomalous situation where the title of "co-therapist" is justified even though the two professional people are not peers. In one training center, a social worker who was experienced in group therapy was periodically assigned a green psychiatric resident for a limited period of training. The social worker was responsible for the continuity of the group and its ongoing therapeutic program, while the resident was responsible for the over-all psychiatric care of the patients. It was thought desirable to delineate clearly the responsibility that each carried during the actual sessions of the group and to make this division of labor known to the patients. Since each had well-defined duties which the other did not encroach upon, while they acted jointly in deciding the admission and disposition of patients as far as the group was concerned, they could fairly be called co-therapists. Even here, there was potential trouble whenever there was a clash of professional pride between a newly assigned resident and the social worker. Such a clash can easily be exploited by adroit patients, and calls for decisive handling by a tough-minded supervisor.

The Assistant Therapist There are, however, some legitimate functions which a second professional person can perform in a therapy group. The situation is clearer to the patients if the second professional is both administratively and professionally junior to the therapist, thus avoiding the drawbacks, difficulties, delicacies, and hypocrisies outlined above. It is also easier with such an arrangement for the therapist to understand what is going on. If the feelings of the second person are hurt by his being given the subordinate title of "assistant therapist" rather than the status of "co-therapist," perhaps he should be relieved of his assignment and transferred to the surgical service for re-education.

The willing assistant therapist, promoted perhaps from the role of observer if he shows sufficient promise, can learn much during his apprenticeship and can be of considerable help by attending to certain routine duties, leaving the therapist free to concentrate on the actual proceedings of the group. In effect, he can act as the group's "apparatus" (Chapter 6) while the therapist acts as its leader. That is the administrative function of an assistant therapist. His intuitive keenness and his talents as a clinical observer and thinker can be exercised in the informal post-group discussions which follow each meeting, and he may be able to make himself very useful to the therapist by pointing out things the therapist has missed, or by exploring further possibilities in unresolved situations. That is his professional function. By his presence in the group, he offers the same temptations to the patients as a co-therapist does, and that is his personal or psychodynamic function. In this area, variations in the sexes of the two therapists offer possibilities for minor experiments. In general, however, the object is to get on with the therapy as effectively as possible, and such "experiments" should be left to nonclinical workers unless the therapists feel an irresistible urge to write papers.

The Observer   Observers are of three types: critics, trainees, and visitors. The critic is a supervisor or other professional person whose job it is to point out things the therapist has overlooked or to raise questions regarding technique. A trainee observer is a colleague with less experience than the therapist to whom the therapist points out what has happened, after the meeting is over, and whose questions he answers as definitely as possible. A visitor is a colleague who comes only once or twice to see what he can learn or contribute. A true observer will remain completely silent during the meetings week after week as long as he is invited to stay. If addressed by a patient, he should answer courteously and unambiguously but he should not encourage the patients to include him in their conversation, although they may (but need not) talk freely about him. He should be introduced by name and organization, and his relationship to the therapist should be stated succinctly and honestly, e.g. "He is my immediate supervisor," "He is one of my pupils," or "We interned together at Yale and he wants to see what I'm doing these days."

The Recorder   A stenographic recorder is detrimental to a group and should be dispensed with unless the group is officially designated as an experimental group. All over the country there are institutions that have filing cabinets crowded with notes of group therapy sessions which will probably never be examined systematically. The same applies to tape recordings. The assumption that patients get used to human and tape recorders and are not significantly influenced by their presence should be treated with caution. Many patients also "get used to" inlying catheters or continuous intravenous drips, but what a relief when they are taken away! Most patients who move from a recorded group to an unrecorded one express their relief after a few weeks. They feel more like real people and less like "subjects" privileged to play the role of "patient."

STAFF ORIENTATION

While an administrative and professional contract with those immediately concerned in the project is necessary, orientation of the staff as a whole has little to recommend it.

Preliminary Discussions Extensive preliminary discussions with irrelevant staff members tend to increase the therapist's external responsibilities needlessly and may lead him to make superfluous commitments or half-commitments which he may later have cause to regret. It puts him on the spot more than is necessary. His basic needs are simply a quiet room with some patients and the possibility of replacing patients who have withdrawn; as long as the staff is not actively hostile to group therapy he can usually obtain these requirements.

Clinical Conferences As a matter of conscience and "public relations" the therapist may want to present occasionally at a clinical staff conference. This gives his colleagues an opportunity to judge his work on its merits and progress rather than on his promises and intentions, and it gives him a chance to find out how they really feel about what he is doing. In order to avoid pe-

dantic rehashing or veering with the wind which may result from
an overly co-operative atmosphere, such presentations should be
spaced at least six weeks apart. The weekly conferences with
the group therapy supervisor should be adequate to take care
of any therapeutic problems that arise. Presentations to the staff
at large should be regarded as an educational service to them
rather than as an opportunity for the therapist to do missionary
work with them, or on the other hand, for inexperienced people
to convey their prejudices to the therapist.

Skeptical Colleagues For some therapists at least, having a
few skeptical or even hostile people around is beneficial. It tends
to keep the therapist on his mettle and improve his craftsmanship. In a clinic, the people he really needs on his side are the
intake social worker, who will supply him with patients, the
head of the clinic, who will see to it that he has proper facilities
to work with, and his supervisor, who will assist him in time of
need. If the other members of the staff are skeptical, so much
the better perhaps. After all, they may be right. The evidence
that group therapy is invariably or even frequently superior to
individual therapy is still debatable. For this reason, their skepticism should be respected.

SELECTION OF PATIENTS

As previously noted, the deliberate selection of patients in order
to have a so-called homogeneous group is often deleterious to
therapeutic progress. The contrary view is held by many therapists on grounds which are not clear either theoretically or
clinically. The positive reasons for considering heterogeneity
desirable will be discussed in Chapter 10. On the negative side,
in brief, homogeneity may tend to set up a massive *folie à tous*
under the supervision of the therapist.

Special Groups In certain organizations, an outward homogeneity results from the nature of the situation, as in an alcoholic

clinic or adolescent service, where all the patients will be heavy
drinkers or teen-agers. In a general clinic or agency the therapist
may decide to set up criteria for selection as an experiment or
even as a matter of policy. In order to avoid the unwarranted
implications and unstated assumptions contained in the word
"homogeneous," groups that are selected according to specific
or intuitive criteria should be called "special groups." Groups
to which patients are assigned without any clinical or social
criteria for selection may be called "general groups." Any group
in a specialized agency will automatically fall into the category
of special groups, and if there are additional criteria for selection
after intake, they may be called selected special groups.

Assignment of Patients   In practice, one of the simplest ways
to end up with as heterogeneous a group as possible is to have
the patients assigned by someone not professionally connected
with the group therapy project; for example, every third patient
applying to the clinic may be referred for group therapy by
the intake social worker. Another way is to assign every patient
to a therapy group sooner or later; in private practice, for example, each patient after proper preparation may be put into
whichever group happens to have an opening at the time. Heterogeneity can also be attained by assigning patients opportunisti-
cally: for example, a patient may be assigned to whichever
group meets at the time most convenient for him. Assignment on
the basis of such extrinsic factors makes it easier for the patient,
and relieves the therapist of the obligation of going through
complicated technical rationalizations for assigning the patient
to one group or another.

Exceptions   Some of the extremes which arise from such
policies should, it is true, be carefully considered. Putting a
teen-age girl in the same group as two sexual psychopaths might
better be avoided, partly on clinical grounds and partly because
of the extra work entailed in dealing with apprehensive staff
members and relatives of the patient. There is no particular ad-

vantage in such an assortment of patients, and transferring the
young lady will save the therapist time and energy which he
can better apply to other matters. Putting elderly people suffering from senile parenchymal deterioration, cerebral arteriosclero-
sis, Pick's or Alzheimer's disease, or other essentially irreversible
conditions in with younger people with more potentiality and
flexibility is another situation that might be regarded as experimental. Special groups may be indicated for severe epileptics,
deaf people, and some stutterers.

Very rarely, special conditions have to be considered. A patient who is faced with a contested divorce suit or damage suit
may properly be advised for legal reasons to withdraw from
group therapy, or to postpone his introduction to the group until
after the case has been settled in court. The same may apply to
a patient under suspicion or indictment for a felony. It is probably also unwise to take professional gangsters into therapy
groups outside correctional institutions. A professional stool-
pigeon who earns his living by being a police informer or a
criminal with a record of blackmail should not be put, without
careful thought, in with a group of vulnerable citizens. Siblings,
parents, spouses, lovers, and rivals of patients can be included
in the same group, and the therapist should not share the patient's misgivings in such cases without a fair trial. The only
set of people which is perhaps too difficult to handle in the
present state of knowledge are relatives and friends of the
therapist himself. It is probably better on the whole, for the time
being at least, to refer such intimates to some other therapist.

There is one clinically valid criterion for selection which depends on choice of therapeutic method. It appears that some
recovering schizophrenics do better for the first six or twelve
months in a group in which the therapist uses a supportive or
Parental approach to supplement a psychodynamic or transactional Adult method. The therapist, therefore, may have a special

group into which such patients are put for a preparatory period before they are transferred to one of his general groups.

An Illustrative Anecdote   The following anecdote will illustrate some of the principles at stake in patient selection.

For some years the writer had been conducting a group for the mothers of disturbed children at a large metropolitan clinic. The mothers were referred by the intake social worker of the Children's Service, whose ideas about the aims and values of group therapy were different from the writer's. (For ease of expression, in recounting such personal experiences the writer will henceforth refer to himself as "Dr. Q".) He took every mother that she referred, without exception.

On one occasion a colleague friend asked Dr. Q if he would try one of his "clinical experiments" and take into this group (since it was the only group Dr. Q had at that particular clinic) a thirty-year-old man, Mr. P, who suffered from severe cerebral palsy. Mr. P had had many different kinds of treatment: neurosurgery, drugs, occupational therapy, and psychotherapy in succession with a social worker, a psychologist, and a psychiatrist. Dr. Q interviewed Mr. P and decided that he was quite unsuitable for group treatment, and especially for the mothers' group, on the grounds that his athetotic movements, inco-ordination, and speech impediments were too severe. The patient appeared greatly disappointed when Dr. Q told him that the group was not suitable for him and suggested to Mr. P that he go back to his psychiatrist or seek therapeutic assistance from the Cerebral Palsy Foundation. When Dr. Q recounted this to one of his students, the student reproached him, saying: "You are the one who says there shouldn't be any criteria for selection."

Dr. Q, of course, had as a matter of good faith either to accept this challenge or abandon his teaching of nonselection. He called Mr. P's social worker and asked her to inform Mr. P that he need not take Dr. Q's word for it, but could come to the next meeting of the group and see for himself that it was unsuitable. Mr. P in turn accepted the challenge. True, as Dr. Q had anticipated, the mothers were at first frightened by Mr. P's hyperactivity, but contrary to his expectations, their fear lasted not several weeks or months, but only about five minutes. When after ten minutes Mr. P dropped his newspaper on the floor and none of the women offered to pick it up, leaving Mr. P to do it for himself, Dr. Q knew that everything was going to be all right. At the very first meeting it became apparent to everyone present that many of Mr. P's random or "uncontrollable" movements were really transactional in nature. Once this was established and worked over in detail, rapid improvement ensued, so that by the end of eight weeks Mr. P was able to do many things which he had never before in his life attempted, such as traveling for a whole week end by himself. All present agreed that this was one of the most exciting experiences they had had in that group, and for Dr. Q it was one of the most gratifying improvements in his whole career as a group therapist.

In this case the tendency to exclusion and selection was based on the therapist's well-rationalized anxiety, ignorance, and snobbishness. Few people but his own students would have criticized him for rejecting such an extreme case of motor disturbance under the circumstances, particularly since Mr. P's admission in prospect seemed to threaten the relatively smooth course of improvement of the other members of the group. The fact that the patient's exclusion would have been forgivable, however, did not as it turned out mean that it was either well advised or clinically justifiable.*

In summary, then, the therapist should be prepared to take into any group any patient whatsoever; no patient should be excluded from any group until after the therapist's ostensible

---

* Mr. P stayed in the group for about two years, and three years after he left he was found working as a junior executive in a sheltered workshop.

reasons have been subjected to the severest examination by himself and others.

Reading Charts and Histories　After a patient has been referred and his name put down to be included in a specific group, the therapist will be confronted with the clinical chart or the referring practitioner. It is probably best for the beginner to read the chart or listen to the description of the patient offered by the referring agency, as this will leave him in a less vulnerable position if difficulties arise. In principle, however, this is undesirable. The patient should be allowed to present himself as he sees fit, and the therapist should examine this presentation in the light of his own personal impressions of the patient. Charts and verbal reports present someone else's picture of the patient, which is based on the way the patient chose to present himself to the previous therapist. In a sense reading the chart is subversive because it introduces an artifact into the patient's relationship with the therapist, somewhat analogous to reading the psychiatric chart or a private detective's report on one's fiancée. There is a minimum of essential items, however, which must be inquired into: whether the patient has any current or past physical disabilities which affect his prognosis or of which the progress must be observed; whether he is taking drugs, and which ones; and whether he has had shock treatment or brain-cutting. In private practice the first can be taken care of by referring the patient elsewhere for a complete physical examination. In any case, before or soon after entering a group, every patient who has not had a thorough physical examination during the past year should be referred for a careful checkup.

Illustrative Anecdotes　Dr. Q never read the charts of any of the women referred to the mothers' group, and he avoided unnecessary discussion of any of them with the therapists assigned to their children; to this self-discipline he attributes the smoothness of his relationships with the mothers in the group, and their satisfactory progress without blood and sweat and with a minimum of unnecessary tears. It should be noted that the group meetings were open to qualified visitors, but none of the children's therapists availed themselves of this accessibility. The decisive point about this lack of communication is that it worked to the satisfaction of everyone concerned, therapists and patients alike.

Similar considerations apply to other outside sources of information which might contaminate the relationship between the patient and the therapist. The husband of a prospective patient in private practice told Dr. Q that his wife had had a laparotomy for gonorrheal salpingitis. Week after week passed without the patient mentioning this; she talked about her laparotomy once or twice, and when asked the reason for it stated that it was some ovarian condition. The therapist began to distrust her, and had the option of continuing to harbor his distrust or confronting the patient, both of them undesirable alternatives. Although he was in a difficult position, eventually he did confront her, and the matter was settled temporarily at least, but both he and the patient were left feeling a little unpleasant about the situation. (She maintained that the operation was for an ovarian cyst.) The patient was untrustworthy in many respects, which became apparent early in her treatment, but this instance could have been handled much more gracefully if it had been a matter between herself and the therapist without the intervention of her husband.

Mr. B, a Navy veteran who had had several courses of shock treatment, presented himself as a schizophrenic in remission. About six months after treatment began, the relatives telephoned Dr. Q in some agitation to report that Mr. B had been drinking again and had got into some minor difficulty with the police. When the initial psychiatric history was taken, Mr. B had mentioned that he drank occasionally but did not consider this a serious problem. The telephone call was the first inkling that drinking was a more critical activity than the patient cared to admit at that time.

The call was mentioned at the next interview, "hoisted on the flagpole to see if he would salute it," so to speak, but he chose to minimize the situation, and the therapist followed his wishes. There were further calls during the next two or three years, each duly reported casually to Mr. B as a matter of good faith and as an opening for further exploration if he seemed prepared for that, but each time he brushed it off and the therapist did not push the confrontation. Eventually he brought the subject up himself, presenting it rather differently, however, than the relatives had. This patient progressed steadily during the years and had no recurrence of his schizophrenia. Dr. Q is quite convinced that the gratifying outcome of this case, and the patient's ever increasing insight, stem from the therapist's respect for the way Mr. B wished to present himself from one epoch to another. Mr. B was grateful to Dr. Q for not allowing information obtained from external sources to influence their relationship. Even favorable reports are sometimes open to objection in this respect.

Many therapists will agree that listening to outside informants (or informers) too often means being provoked by a third party into a game of "Let's You (the therapist) and Him (the patient) Fight." Even if the outside intervention is warranted, it may so discomfit the therapist that he is no longer free to form his own picture of the patient. If he allows himself to be influenced by outside sources, his own intuition and experience are to that extent nullified. Nevertheless, referring agents and agencies must always be listened to and answered with proper professional courtesy, and it is not necessary for them to become aware of the therapist's attitude. The position outlined requires a considerable degree of autonomy and a certain degree of courage, since it increases the therapist's vulnerability to criticism if anything should go wrong. For this reason it is doubly important for him to maintain good professional relationships with everyone concerned with his patients. Younger therapists whose careers are at stake cannot afford the luxury of getting a completely fresh view of their patients unless they have the full backing of their supervisors for pursuing this policy.

Much the same considerations apply to the not unusual device of having the patient write an autobiography. It is true that in this case the patient is presenting himself in writing to the group therapist and not to some other individual, but this may only becloud the issues. If such autobiographies are available they should be filed away until certain items of information in them become meaningful and worth thinking about. The properly trained clinician should be able to make his own independent judgments about the patient; other sources may then be consulted as bearing on the finality of his opinions. Information for its own sake when it has no contextual significance is an unnecessary burden and sometimes interferes with the clinical acuity of the therapist's personal observations.

Memorizing Histories   For example, if a woman is all mother, no one in the group is likely to forget that she has children. With other women it may happen that a therapist who is not paperbound has to ask several times in the course of a year how many children they have. This may be taken as a negative finding of considerable importance, reinforced by the fact that when such women do discuss their children on request, they often neglect to state the sex of their offspring, and even more often discuss them at length without bothering to mention their names. If the therapist has memorized the family histories of his patients, such curious deficiencies in maternal pride may never be brought to light. The negative effect which is brought into focus by the therapist's relaxed attitude about mnemonics may be of decisive importance for the progress of maternally inhibited women.

Information is of no value for its own sake, but only because of its personal significance to the patient. A formal description of someone's father may be hardly worth remembering until, for example, the patient has a dream about his father; then suddenly it becomes worthwhile to make inquiries and review the information on file, after which the therapist may never forget it. Even years later he may still remember it in detail, because it was fixed in his mind not mnemonically, but by its function in the whole psychodynamic gestalt of the patient. In fact, the situation is probably best summarized by saying that what has to be memorized is not worth remembering, and what is worth remembering will not have to be memorized. This applies, of course, only to the clinical situation and not to the staff conference, where the therapist must be prepared to be set upon by a horde of hobbyists and professional competitors who will test his memory to its utmost limits.

The time to consult the chart for clinical rather than administrative reasons is when the information it contains has already become meaningful in the light of the therapist's own observation of the patient.

TESTING AND RESEARCH

Psychological Tests   There are several questions to be raised about the advisability of psychological tests. They can be of value when a rapid diagnosis is urgently needed, or as an organizational procedure before a patient is assigned to therapy. But most psychiatrists seem to rely on their own diagnostic acumen with patients whom they are going to see in continued treatment. Tests are again in a sense an unfair assault on the patient's persona. They can never be adequately explained to the patient by the therapist, since he does not understand them clearly himself unless he is a trained psychologist. The patient, on the other hand, thinks the clinician knows all about them and therefore all about him. This gives rise to fantasies and inhibitions which may be time-consuming and difficult to resolve.

A sinister psychological diagnosis, however disguised and softened by evasive polysyllables, gives rise to apprehension in the therapist which he is almost certain sooner or later to communicate to the patient. If his own prognosis is better than the psychologist's, then he will be a little edgy for the next ten or fifteen years for fear the psychologist may have been right. If by chance the patient should ask if he is schizophrenic, it is much easier for the therapist to discuss this question honestly if the diagnosis is based on his own observation than if he is trying to conceal the fact that psychological tests indicate that the patient is schizophrenic. Both the therapist, and the patient if he should find out about it, will feel cornered by the mathematical machinery that the psychologist confronts them with; if this machinery is not taken seriously, there was, of course, no reason to have the tests done in the first place. On these grounds, psychological tests are not advised unless there is a clear indication for them in exceptional cases.

As a matter of fact, in many cases psychological tests are used for "protection" (that is, in case anything goes wrong, there will be someone else to share the blame with). A completely honest therapist might feel called upon to explain to the patient who was being protected from whom and what.

Hidden Research It should be apparent by now that research (in the academic sense) and therapy must be clearly separated. If so-called research is done subversively, as by undisclosed one-way mirrors or "bugs," it introduces an element of disingenuousness into the situation. A dishonest therapist can hardly demand that his patients be honest, and it is probable that honesty on both sides is desirable for the best therapeutic results. Hence it is likely that the dishonest therapist is giving his patients less than the best, and this should not be permitted.

Open Research If the research is done openly, then the therapist has to deal with the patient's fantasies of what is going to happen to the material. Since there is a little bit of paranoia in almost everybody, the risk of side effects is almost unavoidable. The therapist should therefore examine very closely his motives for doing research or for permitting intruders into his group. He should bear in mind again the warehouses full of tape recordings, movie films, and notebooks, whose significant contribution to the problem of how to cure patients more thoroughly or more quickly is so far almost imperceptible.* His own powers of observation and synthesis are much more important instruments in this respect, and he should not impair them by diverting their attention to artifacts.

For these reasons it is better not to introduce research into situations whose stated aim is therapy. A research group should be so designated, and any therapeutic results which are obtained should be regarded as secondary to the research.

An Illustrative Anecdote When Dr. Q wrote a book about psychotherapy, the publisher asked him to include some statistics to demonstrate the effectiveness of his approach. Dr. Q mentioned this in several of his groups, and the patients said they would be glad to co-operate. In the ensuing discussions, however, they began to question more and more both the value and the feasibility of obtaining such data. Whatever was proposed soon took on the aspect of an irrelevancy. A few patients challenged the problem with observations like the following: "Before I came up to the meeting today, I was sitting in the restaurant across the street drinking a cup of coffee. I looked at the coffeepot, and all of a sudden I could really see it. It was the first time in my life I had ever really seen a coffeepot. How are we going to make a statistic out of that?"

It was apparent to everyone present that this experience of "seeing" the coffeepot was important to the patient, but what tests would serve to evaluate or verify it after the fact for outsiders? One took her word for it and saw how her face lighted up when she told about it. At any rate, however disconcerting their conclusion was, none of the groups felt that figures could meaning-

---

* The excellent video tape studies being done by the Psychiatric Department of the University of Mississippi Medical School may turn out to be a gratifying exception to this pessimistic view.[7]

fully convey very much to an outsider about what had happened
to them in or as a result of the treatment group. But they all
offered to do whatever the therapist thought would be most
helpful to him. By this time, however, he had decided not to
make the attempt.

That is not the point of the story, however. The dénouement
occurred when Dr. Q related these experiences to a group of
colleagues. A research fellow in the social sciences asked: "Why
on earth did you tell them you were going to make statistics?"
The implication was that statistics should be made only behind
the patients' backs. Not only were the reasons for that policy
difficult for Dr. Q to accept, but it would have required him to
adopt a patronizing or exploitative attitude toward his patients,
which he preferred not to do. He would certainly expect them
to discuss it if they were making statistics about him.

In group treatment, then, no unilaterality is permissible which
is not explicitly stated in the contract with the patient, and at
least implicitly agreed to. (If the therapist wants to make statistics or tape recordings, the patients usually assume that they
are not expected to reciprocate.)

BRIEFING THE PATIENT

There are two different variables to be taken into account when
preparing the patient to enter a group: the therapeutic program
and the patient's attitude toward group treatment. Regarding the
therapeutic program, there are three common situations.

The Unprepared Patient   If the patient is taken into the group
without any formal intake or any individual interviews at all,
he can be gently introduced to the therapeutic plan in the course
of two or three meetings. Sometimes, however, the treatment
takes quite a different direction from what he anticipated, and
then his orientation may have to be postponed until the therapist
feels that he is properly receptive. For example, when a group

of parents of disturbed children is first activated, the members usually expect to talk about how to bring up children. It may take two or three months before they are ready to perceive that the most valuable function such a group can serve is self-examination, rather than examination of their children's behavior. Their stories about their children are highly colored, and there is no way for the therapist or their fellow members to find out what really happened; but their own behavior in the group can be observed firsthand. The therapist's task during the initial phase, therefore, is to break up the game of "PTA" as tactfully as possible and divert the members' attention to each other. If this is properly done, the parents, who may at first be disconcerted by the therapist's reaction, will not be long in expressing their gratitude to him for offering them something of greater cogency and value.

The corresponding task with a group of alcoholics is more difficult, since they are even more reluctant to talk about themselves rather than about their drinking. Perhaps most difficult of all is to wean a group of inmates in a penal institution away from their complaints about the staff in order to consider their own social and psychological operations. The therapist should remember that it is very doubtful that an alcoholic has ever been cured by repeatedly describing his wife's behavior, or that a prisoner has gone straight because his colleagues agree that a certain guard is misanthropic. He should not be afraid to wade in, after his patients are properly prepared, and break up the "Alcoholic" game or the prisoners' game of "You've Got To Listen."

The Single Interview If there is only one interview before the patient enters a group, a complete psychiatric history should be obtained, including family background, medical and surgical history, the course of any previous psychotherapy, and a general survey of the patient's current situation and symptoms. It is a good policy to ask the patient for any dream that comes to his mind, whether recent or old; this may serve many of the same purposes as a battery of psychological tests. A dream of world destruction or frank incest, properly evaluated in context, for example, may indicate a diagnosis of schizophrenia more clearly than any other single phenomenon.* The questioning should not be obtrusively systematic, but the therapist should make sure in this situation that he obtains by one means or another each item of information that he wants to have. If the patient is too discursive, the therapist may have to set aside the last twenty minutes of the interview for the specific purpose of filling in gaps.

Time should be reserved toward the end of the interview for outlining the therapeutic contract: what it is hoped to accomplish through group treatment, which symptoms will be of primary concern, and what the therapist has to offer. During this phase the patient may ask questions about the nature of group treatment, and the therapist should give him as much satisfaction as possible and advisable in this respect. The psychiatric pokerface should not be exploited at this critical time to conceal vagueness or lack of preparation for answering perfectly legitimate enquiries from the patient.

Combined Therapy   The third situation is where the patient is in individual treatment and at an appropriate time is introduced into a therapy group. Since such patients are already familiar with what the therapist has to offer, and the patient's history is well known to the therapist, it is only necessary here to answer the patient's questions about the advantages of group treatment, or for the therapist to explain why he is introducing the patient into a group at that particular moment.

In all three of these situations, the therapist's explanations will be influenced by the the patient's state of mind in regard to group therapy.

---

* This statement should not be misunderstood by readers who are not professionally trained to evaluate contexts.

The Unsophisticated Patient The inexperienced, untrained patient, still attributing magical powers to the therapist, and not yet awed by, resentful of, or disappointed by his real ones; unable, unready, or unwilling to distinguish an observation from a rebuke; and often still rash enough at times to interrupt his sagacious mentor — such people present a special problem. The reasons for using group treatment instead of or in addition to individual therapy should be clarified. The advantages of the group in giving the patient an opportunity to exhibit a wider repertoire of spontaneous behavior, and to see what he does to or with the other people in the group and what they do to or with him, may be mentioned. It may be indicated that this is not a social group, but a psychiatric group. It is surprising how often patients are unaware of rather obvious aspects of group treatment: for instance, whether the therapist himself will be present. The time of beginning and ending the meetings should be clearly stated for two reasons: first, for the patient's convenience in planning home and work schedules for the day; and secondly, to bring into sharp focus as quickly as possible any tendency to play punctuality games. The manner of payment of fees should be an equally explicit agreement for analogous reasons: budgetary for the patient, and technical for the therapist. Young divorced women are particularly apt to play a game of "Creditor" with a young male therapist, and he should make sure that the financial commitment in such cases is a realistic one for the patient; then any dilatoriness on her part is much more easily separated out as a psychological problem. The rule that the patient can say anything whatsoever with no exceptions should be clearly stated so that its subsequent interpretation by the patient can be legitimately investigated.

Aside from these three contractual necessities, it is unwise to state any further rules, since rules only serve to set up situations from which the patient can select an area of rebellion. Sometimes, however, it is necessary to tell very timid or very aggressive patients that while everyone is free to say whatever he likes, it is forbidden to strike anyone.

Sophisticated Patients Patients who have been schooled by months or years of therapy need only be told that the group offers an arena for a wider repertoire of behavior than is possible in individual therapy, and that in the group the therapist can get firsthand rather than secondhand information about the patient's proclivities.

The Skeptical Patient The patient may be an intellectual skeptic, or he may have seen "group therapy" on television or read about it in books. It should be made clear to him that the therapist's approach is different from what he imagines or from what he has seen on the screen or read about. Beyond that, the only persuasion that can legitimately be attempted is to say, "Well, try it and see. In my experience it takes about six weeks to feel at home in the kind of groups I conduct, so unless you're willing to try it for that long, I don't know if it will be worth your while." If the patient says he is only willing to try it for a week or two, there is no reason for the therapist on his own behalf to reject this offer, once he has made his preferences clear, but he has to consider the effect on the other patients in the group. With certain types of patients, an element of professional snobbishness may be indicated: "Well, you are describing the way they do it in New York (or Hollywood) because of the cultural lag in those two places, but you may find the modern approach more congenial."

The Receptive Patient If the patient is too receptive or eager, for instance if he calls on the telephone and says; "I hear you do group therapy, have you got a place in one of your groups for me?" the therapist must make it clear that group treatment is just as serious a medical procedure as any other. He should insist on a diagnostic interview in such cases, so that he can determine whether group treatment is the method of choice for the patient, and he should make it understood that he cannot let the patient prescribe his own treatment.

Referred Patients The referred patient should be treated with the same diagnostic care as the receptive patient. If he is to continue with another therapist for individual treatment, there should be some discussion of confidentiality and a clear contract in this respect. The group therapist may state his preference as to how much or how little he would like to confer with the individual therapist, but the final decision about confidentiality is up to the patient, and his decision should then be discussed with the other therapist. Conferences between the therapists have advantages, but these are often outweighed by the danger that the patient will provoke a three-handed game. If the therapists do not confer, the best the patient can do is two separate two-handed games, one with each therapist, and if the therapists are competent, they can take care of themselves. If the therapists do confer, the patient, being only human, can hardly resist the temptation to start a game of "Let's You and Him Fight," in which the therapists will be at a marked disadvantage because of the restrictions imposed by professional ethics and courtesy. The first move is for the patient to ask whether the group treatment will conflict with his individual treatment. The group therapist cannot answer this, but presumably the referring doctor is prepared to handle any conflicts which may arise, or he would not have made the referral, and the patient may be told this.

Therapists, however, are also susceptible to the attractions of this game. A lay therapist should be wary of accepting group therapy referrals from strange psychiatrists. Even friendly psychiatrists may turn out to be "Bessarabian friends" in such situations, according to the proverb "Whoever has a Bessarabian for a friend does not need any enemies." An equally loaded situation arises when a patient is in individual treatment with a lay therapist of unknown capacities and comes to a psychiatrist for group therapy. The psychiatrist may then find himself in a three-handed therapeutic situation which he does not entirely approve of, but professional ethics forbid him to voice any criticism of his lay colleague. To avoid such contretemps, which may be very distressing to a conscientious psychiatrist, it is advisable to tell the patient initially that he will be taken on for a trial period to see how it works out, and that if it works out satisfactorily they will continue. This gives the psychiatrist an opportunity to withdraw "without prejudice" if he finds it advisable.

The Reluctant Patient   If the patient is unwilling to go into a therapy group on grounds which he is unable to clarify at the moment, there is no harm in waiting until he is able to state his reasons clearly. It may be some archaic fear or embarrassment, or something more realistic. Perhaps a friend or acquaintance is in the group; the patient can be reassured that any hesitation he feels on this account will not interfere with the purpose of the group, which in a manner of speaking is the study of hesitations of whatever nature; and that in any case experience has shown that previous acquaintance may in the long run be helpful to group members and only rarely causes embarrassment after the first few meetings. Or he may be shy for business, professional, or political reasons; in that case he may be told that he is under no obligation to reveal his identity, and that in the past, membership in a therapy group has not been known to damage a member's career. But the therapist should not push a reluctant candidate, for if any adverse consequences did arise, the therapist might blame himself unduly. The fact is, however, that the writer has had no complaints from originally reluctant members who have remained with the group, and the improvements in business ability or political adeptness resulting from group treatment have nearly always been appreciated. Only if the member terminates his treatment prematurely is there likely to be a sour reaction, and there is no way to predict with complete certainty whether he will or not.

The Unready Patient   The patient may be willing to go into a therapy group on recommendation of the therapist, but may not be psychologically ready to deal with it. This particularly applies to psychotic patients, who should demonstrate some stability in their relationship to the therapist before being put into a group if the best results are to be obtained. If the patient has spontaneously revealed some intimate details of his inner sex life and fantasies he probably has enough confidence in the therapist to rely on him for protection if the going gets rough in the group (unless the revelations were part of a game of "Psychiatry").

The Group-Shy Patient If the patient objects that he never gets along well in groups, the obvious answer is that that is precisely why he might benefit from group treatment; the group is specifically set up to find out the sources of people's fears of groups. Another kind of group-shy patient is the one who says: "It's no use putting me in a group, because I'll just take over." This challenge can be gladly accepted by the therapist on behalf of his patients, but he should not show his skepticism. He merely says: "Well, let's try it anyway."

The Ineligible Patient It may happen on rare occasions that a patient has made himself ineligible for group therapy by some past action. He may have committed an undetected crime, he may be a bigamist, or he may have taken an oath of secrecy in the national interest. Many such patients are ineligible even for individual therapy unless some decisive step is taken to clear up the past. "Celebrities" are temporarily ineligible only if their lack of talent for anonymity will be disturbing to the other members of the group, or if they act coy. Otherwise there is no reason why they should not mingle with other responsible patients.

Provisional Fantasies It is of some interest to ask the patient, in terms that he can understand, to outline his fantasies or expectations of what will happen in the group. (This is the provisional group imago described in Chapter 6.) He may thereby give valuable indications of how he is to be approached in the group to his best advantage, and also as to the underlying motivations of his transactions with the other patients. Since the group will never be quite what he expects, and is often radically different, his statement may offer an opening wedge for discussing his fantasies about people, when the time comes for that. In transactional language, the provisional group imago helps the therapist anticipate what games the patient is most likely to play in the group, and he can use this information in formulating his therapeutic plan for that patient.

SUPERVISION

Ideally, supervision begins before the group meets. This policy has proved practical and beneficial over a period of several years at the San Francisco Transactional Analysis Seminars. The therapist presents the project in whatever form is most natural or comfortable for him; after that the consultant or seminar leader sets up the aspects which should be settled before the group is activated, and sees to it that the discussion does not wander off into irrelevant speculation and exchanges of "bright ideas."

The Organizational Aspects   The organizational and administrative background of the projected treatment group is discussed — as the therapist sees it, as the patients are likely to see it from their point of view, and as the discussants see it. A formal or informal "authority diagram" (Figures 2A and 2B, Chapter 6) is drawn, and an attempt is made to infer the expectations relating to the group of each person or bureau in the hierarchy. If the favorite games, ulterior motives, and ultimate responsibilities of each person in the hierarchy are known, these should be appraised realistically for their possible influence on on the project.

Therapeutic Aims   It is often a surprise to the prospective therapist himself to find how difficult it is for him to formulate, in the face of objective, disinterested questions and criticism, exactly what his therapeutic program consists of. Curiously enough, psychiatrists, in spite of their therapeutically oriented medical training, are often just as indefinite in this connection as nonmedical therapists.

The Therapist's Motivations The therapist's motivations and fantasies concerning the proposed group should be systematically elicited and broken down into four components: procedural artifacts and slogans based on reading, training, or the expectations of superiors (institutionalized component); directive, restrictive, or protective attitudes (Parental component); rational or intellectual plans (Adult component); and archaic, instinctual, or exploitative fantasies (Child component). As a courtesy, the last category may be excluded on request from the public discussion and left for the therapist to meditate about or to discuss in private with the supervisor. Both indigenous and exogenous games of the therapist are reviewed, and their possible effects on the prospective patients are carefully considered. Thus, the beginner may have a Parental "advisory" attitude, with an indigenous tendency to play "Why Don't You . . . Yes But." Exogenously, he may have learned to practice psychotherapy according to the rules of Professor K or group therapy according to the rules of Mr. Y. These influences may conflict not only among themselves, but also with the interests of effective therapy in some situations.

This preparatory enquiry helps the therapist to "calibrate" himself so that he can correct any persistent tendency to deviate from the true north of effective therapy before he finds himself veering toward right or left field.

Selection of Patients The therapist's criteria for selection are discussed, with particular attention to snobbish attitudes or undeclared anxieties. If the anxieties are open, the discussants may be able to help him deal with them.

Candidness It is best not to pull any punches during this preliminary survey, and the therapist may be driven very close to the ropes. The whole future of his group depends on what is elicited here and what decisions he makes in the light of what he hears. It is far better for him to have his feelings injured than to spend a year or two under the influence of unstated or vague assumptions or motivations which he is reluctant for personal reasons to have clarified. If the group project is seriously undertaken, the lives of the patients and their families are going to be strongly influenced, and there is no excuse for indulgence of the therapist's private proclivities at this point. Since the group has not yet begun, he has not yet committed himself in action, so that he has no real cause to be disturbed if some of his autistic or unexamined presumptions are critically regarded. If he is unable to tolerate or even welcome this type of inquiry, perhaps he is not yet ready to become a group therapist. In fairness to him, he may be given a week or two to think over what he has heard and then be offered an opportunity to present the project again, if he wishes, in the light of his revised thinking. Experience has shown that about one therapist out of five will go away from such a discussion so angry, embittered, or defensive that he will not return. The other four either appreciate immediately what has been offered, or regain their composure sufficiently after a week or two to express their gratitude for the survey. Those who return may profitably devote part of their second session to a discussion of how they are going to present their material: by tape recording, from notes, or from memory.

Tape Recording Some of the drawbacks of tape recording have already been noted, but for the beginner that may be the best way of learning. Tape recording is usually deleterious to really firstclass therapy, but the disadvantages may be outweighed by the benefits which the therapist, and hence the group members, derive from good supervision.

A special problem with tape in supervision is that the therapist naturally wants the consultant to hear the whole tape before forming his judgment, and there is not enough time to do that in a one-hour consultation. If the consultant hears only part of the tape, that is often unfair to everyone concerned. The therapist may have corrected an apparent error later in the meeting, or the consultant may make a suggestion at one point which the therapist has already carried out or invalidated later in the meeting. This difficulty can be overcome by either note taking or reporting from memory.

Note Taking The taking of detailed notes during the session distracts the therapist from what is going on. In fact, experience shows that the most copious notes are taken while very little of significance is happening; when something meaningful is taking place, there is a natural and beneficial tendency to forget the notes temporarily; hence notes taken during the session are apt to recount in the most detailed way the least important aspects of the meeting, while the substance is only sketchily outlined. Paradoxically, however, it sometimes occurs that a therapist will not take notes of something he describes as a "trivial" or "irrelevant" discussion. After he has finished his presentation, the consultant may be at a loss to account for what happened. If he then asks the therapist to fill in the details of the "trivial" or "irrelevant" episode, the whole thing becomes clear. In such cases, the episode was trivial only in the light of the therapist's knowledge, or irrelevant only to his fantasies rather than to the external realities; or for his own reasons he may have taken care not to listen closely. Conversely, at times what seems important to the therapist may be more important to his own fantasies than to the progress of his patients; this situation often leads to the publication of premature articles.

Notes written after the meeting are subject to the same criticisms in a diluted form. If the therapist is distracted during the meeting by trying to remember what he is going to put in his notes, to that extent his therapeutic efficiency is diminished, and probably his effectiveness also. Note taking during the

meeting by an assistant is, of course, even more disturbing to
the members than is the presence of a tape recorder, even though
they "adjust" to it.

Memory In reporting from memory the therapist selects unconsciously as well as consciously, so that he may omit significant material, particularly his own part in setting up games in
the course of the meetings. The consultant's comments, however, may and should serve to remind him of these and other
omissions. This should be understood from the beginning so that
both parties are relaxed. The therapist should not be disconcerted if after he presents what he thinks is the essence of a
session, a comment by the consultant causes him suddenly to
remember a whole segment that he has left out. This is the
natural course of events, which should be taken for granted and
used for its own value rather than causing any apologies or
exasperation.

Selection of Method Tape recordings are useful for beginners because the proceedings can be analysed transaction by
transaction, and the therapist can develop his skill in observing
and interpreting vocabularies, inflections, and nonverbal phona-
tions such as coughs, laughs, and grunts. For more advanced
students, notes taken after the session are most helpful because
it is possible within the supervisory hour to get a quick view of
the whole meeting so that games and other ongoing forms of
social action can be picked out. Third-year students, and teachers,
can often most profitably present by anamnesis, since they can
briefly summarize the action and then concentrate at length on
problems of special interest or difficulty.

Selection of Consultant The qualifications of a group treatment supervisor should be carefully evaluated by the organization and the therapist, since anomalous situations are common.
The consultant should have not only a practical clinical knowledge of group treatment, but also adequate training and experience in individual therapy and group dynamics, and prefer-

ably in clinical psychiatry as well, although, failing that, the services of an additional psychiatric consultant should be available on the premises. Formerly, and still to some extent, group therapy consultants have been more or less self-elected. At present, however, there are enough training centers and enough fully qualified and experienced group therapy supervisors to make a more careful selection possible. The *sine qua non* of an adequate supervisor is that he himself should be currently practising group treatment very actively (with the possible exception of a few experienced septuagenarians). If the therapist is working in an organization, it is an advantage to have a consultant from outside the organization. Otherwise the consultant will be constricted by the same institutional factors as the therapist, and they will in a sense be sharing a kind of *folie à deux*.

Frequency As in most other fields, it is an advantage to have regular supervision, preferably once weekly. Anything less than that becomes more or less episodic. It takes about six weeks for a beginner to understand the verbal meaning of the terminology, about six months for him to appreciate the clinical application of the principles, and another six months for him to gain some skill and confidence in applying them. Therefore, supervision once weekly for at least a year is advisable.

Private or Public Supervision in a seminar has the advantage that what one observer or listener may miss, another may pick up. It has the disadvantage that the consultant cannot concentrate nor speak as frankly to the therapist in front of others as he might do privately. On the whole, private supervision is usually preferable, since the seminar gives too much opportunity for others to introduce conflicting interpretations and theories, which confuse the therapist if he is friendly and co-operative. This weakens his commitment to his own therapeutic program, and since the commitment itself is an important therapeutic factor, such a weakening may have a deleterious effect.

SETTING UP THE FIRST MEETING

Having taken care of these preliminaries, the therapist is now free to consider the physical arrangements for bringing the patients together.

The Room   The room should be chosen for size, privacy, and sound-proofing. There should be enough chairs to accommodate the expected complement and one or two extra for unexpected additions. The room should not be bare to the point of asceticism, since that makes an unnaturally depressing atmosphere. Such a condition can be partly alleviated by investing in a few prints. On the other hand, there should not be so many objects as to distract the patients from the business at hand and invite them to evade pressing issues by discussing trivialities about furniture, fixtures, and decorations.

It is best for the patients to sit in a rough circle rather than in rows, except for experimental situations. Sitting around a table tends to dilute the proceedings because it encourages smoking, leaning, and other evasive maneuvers and also conceals from view the lower halves of the patients' bodies, removing certain stimuli which might otherwise provoke significant reactions, and makes it easy for the therapist to overlook such signs of tension as foot-twitching. It also deprives the patients of the possibility of physical exhibitionism, so that such tendencies may never come to the therapist's attention. But the very fact that a table supplies such comfort and protection to the patients and dilutes the proceedings, which in most cases hampers maximum therapeutic progress, may sometimes be turned to advantage in dealing with excited or unstable patients such as manics and schizophrenics. The beginner may wish to experiment for himself in this regard, using appropriate controls, for without them he will gain only clinical impressions rather than comparative results. He may have a series of meetings with a table and then remove it, or start in the open and then put in a table, or run two comparable groups, one with a table and one without. This particular experiment should not interfere materially with the therapeutic aims of his groups. A more advanced project which would be frankly experimental rather than therapeutic would be to conduct a group with the top halves of the members' bodies concealed by a curtain, contrasted with another group in which the bottom halves were concealed by a table.

Food   The effects of serving food are analogous to those of sitting around a table. The resulting rituals and activities offer a screen for patients to hide behind. In most cases this is deleterious, but with psychotics it may be desirable to provide an escape hatch. If food is served, the paternalism and symbolism involved should not be smugly accepted as clever thinking on the part of the therapist, but should be reconsidered and re-evaluated minute by minute in the light of every transaction that takes place during the eating period. If the therapist realizes seriously and conscientiously what a tremendous additional burden he imposes on himself by introducing such artifacts, he may think twice before he complicates further an already complex situation.

Seating Arrangements   The therapist should sit in a corner because a diagonal position usually offers the best vantage point for observing each patient at all times. A blackboard with an assortment of colored chalk should be within easy reach, and he should learn how to make the best use of it. In order not to have his visual acuity impaired, he should sit with his back to the window, or if this is convenient, the blinds should be drawn and the meetings conducted in artificial light. This arrangement should not be treated as a trick of the trade and imposed upon the patients without explanation, but the reasons for it should be stated concisely so that the matter can be dropped. Nor should a questionable sense of "consideration" for his patients restrain him from making sure that he is in a position to observe to the best advantage. It is just as important for him not to have the light in his eyes as it is for a surgeon, and any prolonged discussion of this matter (except by paranoid patients with a specific problem in this area) is just as much of a digression as it would be in an operating room.

The chairs should be arranged according to the size of the room so that no patient can "withdraw" from the group and so that it is difficult to make a "back row." Temporary exceptions to this rule can be made for timid schizophrenics. The therapist should be aware that there are certain critical distances between people which influence their behavior. The distance at which two people sitting side by side cannot touch each others' fingers by abducting their arms is too great for group therapy, since it constitutes psychodynamically an isolated position. The next significant distance is one arm's length. The next is that at which an individual crossing his legs has to be careful lest he touch his neighbor. With more crowding, people become cautious about moving their elbows. Of special dynamic significance in a therapy group is the distance at which people can see each other's faces with near vision, roughly about twenty inches. This marks perceptually the border of "intimacy." Within this distance patients looking at each other may be confronted with the experience of "eidetic perception," and that may be very disturbing to them if they allow it to happen. The distance which introduces the least ambiguity into the therapeutic situation is a little less than one arm's length. That constitutes "sitting beside" while at the same time leaving freedom for leg and elbow movements without other-consciousness.

If ideal facilities are not available, the therapist should approximate them as closely as circumstances permit. It is perfectly possible to hold a productive meeting in a hotel bedroom providing the therapist does not allow himself to be beguiled into a pseudo-psychoanalytic discussion of the furniture. The most distracting situation is where there is a relatively immovable desk in a small room, so that either the therapist or one of the patients has to sit behind it. Unfortunately, such layouts do occur in some institutions. No mercy should be shown to the desk if it is possible to move it out of the way.

Interruptions If a tape recorder is used, it should be set up and *tested* as a matter of courtesy before the patients arrive. If there is a locked door, as in an apartment house, it may be understood that the patient who chooses to sit nearest the entrance will act as a monitor to admit late-comers. The therapist should have no qualms about answering the telephone occasionally (nor more than twice an hour) during a meeting. If the telephone is in the same room, he can make it short, and such brief interruptions may elicit interesting reactions from the patients. If the telephone is in another room, an absence of two or three minutes may have even more interesting results. There is no evidence that therapists who shut off their telephones cure patients faster than those who do not, although patients and colleagues alike may want to argue the point. Sometimes it is even beneficial to the therapist to be interrupted, as he may discover meanwhile that he was more involved than he was aware of in something that was going on, and he may have some second thoughts by the time he gets back to the business in hand.

Introductions and Greetings One object of a therapy group is to find out how people go about presenting themselves to each other. If the therapist conducts an introduction ritual at the first meeting, or when a newcomer arrives, important observations will be forever lost. Such rituals serve to allay the therapist's anxiety, and if he asks himself what he is afraid will happen if he does not introduce the patients to each other, the answer may be instructive. When the patients are ready they will introduce themselves. If they fail to do so, that is a significant negative observation and an enquiry toward the end of the first meeting may prove enlightening. An interesting situation arises when a newcomer not only fails to introduce himself by the end of his first meeting, but the others fail to ask his name. The question should be raised quite bluntly in order to find out what lies behind this mutual exclusion.

Much the same considerations apply to greetings. An important function of greetings is to allay anxiety, and the therapist should be clear whose anxiety is being allayed. If he likes his patients and is glad to see them, they will ordinarily perceive that clearly enough without formalities, and if he does not, hypocritical greetings will not advance his cause. If they greet him first, he can return the courtesy if that is all it is; if it is more than that, the time will come when a confrontation is in order.

For certain schizophrenics and depressed people, introductions and greetings may have more than the usual significance, and clinical intuition will tell the therapist when exceptions should be made to the policies outlined above.

Termination Meetings should be terminated promptly. The patient who thinks of something important to say during the last five minutes and wants to run over is probably addicted to this maneuver and would do it no matter how long the meeting lasted. A patient who habitually tries to linger after the meeting should be deliberately called upon five or ten minutes before the time is up, thus impressing upon him and the group that all things pertaining to group treatment are the business of the entire group, the only exception being matters discussed in private sessions which the patient specifically requests the therapist not to divulge to the group, or which the therapist himself considers it would be untimely to bring up. But each such exception has to be resolved sooner or later, since it is unfair to the rest of the group for something pertinent to be concealed from them. The patient should be gently but firmly told that "private" problems concerning fees, medication, or unwanted pregnancies must sooner or later be brought up during the meetings, and cannot be used more than once or twice as excuses to corner the therapist afterward.

SUMMARY

The situation is now as follows. All preliminary matters have been clarified with the organization and with the patients, and the therapist has a clear understanding of what he is about to do and why he has chosen to do it. The patients are assembled in the therapy room and the therapist is ready to walk in and put his treatment plan into action. It is a good policy for him to come in five minutes after the appointed time at each meeting in order to give the patients a chance to settle down. He should not, however, commit himself by sitting down until at least three patients have arrived; otherwise there is a boring, inhibited, and unwieldy quarter of an hour as the late-comers get settled. Good group treatment should be crisp, and the therapist should not be a party to such soggy beginnings. If when he walks in he finds someone in the seat he has reserved for himself, he should politely request the patient to take another chair, and explain the reason.

Everything possible has now been done to prepare the scene; the patients are seated, and group treatment is about to begin. The therapist has chosen his method and will soon begin to exhibit his wares. But before he does that, he must make it clear to himself and the patients whether he intends to proceed in an institutionalized way or with more autonomous and relevant forthrightness.

REFERENCES

Special aspects of the therapist-patient contract have been discussed by the following writers:

1. Berne, E., R. Birnbaum, R. Poindexter, and B. Rosenfeld. "Institutional Games." *Transactional Analysis Bulletin* 1:12, 1962.

This journal is published quarterly by the International Transactional Analysis Association, P.O. Box 5747, Carmel, California 93921.

2. Johnson, J. A. *Group Therapy: A Practical Approach*. McGraw-Hill Book Company, New York, 1963, Chap 4.

3. Ormont, L. "Establishing the Analytic Contract in a Newly Formed Therapeutic Group." *British Journal of Medical Psychology* 35:333–7, 1962.

Other references in this chapter are:

4. Gierke, O. *Natural Law and the Theory of Society*. Ernest Barker, trans. and ed. Beacon Press, Boston, 1957.

5. Berne, E. *The Structure and Dynamics of Organizations and Groups*. J. B. Lippincott Company, Philadelphia, 1963.

6. Mullan and Rosenbaum (Chap. 1, ref. 1), p. 10, question the naïve assumption that co-therapists function as "father and mother." Beyond that, a consideration of simple group dynamics emphasizes the complications introduced by a co-therapist. With one therapist, the proceedings are divided into (a) Patient — Therapist (Major Process, $Major_1$) and (b) Patient — Patient (Minor Process, $Minor_1$). With two therapists, the aspects are (a) $Major_1$ (Patient — Both Therapists), (b) $Major_2$ (Patient — Therapist A), (c) $Major_3$ (Patient — Therapist B), (d) $Minor_1$ (Patient — Patient), (e) $Minor_2$ (Therapist — Therapist). (See Berne, Chap. 2, ref. 5, p. 81). Hence rigorous analysis of the proceedings with one therapist is analogous to solving a quadratic equation; analysis with two therapists is analogous to solving an equation of the fifth degree. The "two heads" rationalization for co-therapy is therefore equivalent to saying that two people *in medias res* can solve an equation of the fifth degree better than one person can solve a quadratic equation.

7. Moore, F. J., E. Chernell, and M. J. West. "Television as a Therapeutic Tool." *Arch. Gen. Psychiat.* 12:217–20, 1965.

3

The First Three Minutes

As the group therapist takes his seat before the assembled patients, his first concern should be to compose his mind for the task which lies before him. He should make a point of starting each new group, and ideally each new meeting, in a fresh frame of mind. It is evident that if he conducts his groups this year just as he did last year he has learned nothing in the meantime and is a mere technician. For the sake of his own development and self-esteem he should not allow such a thing to happen. He may set as a goal (which he may not always be able to attain) to learn something new every week — not something new out of books, nor some interpretive sidelight, but some more general truth which will increase his perceptiveness.

Physical Condition The first requisite for this fresh frame of mind is a physiological one which takes literally the word "fresh." The group therapist, like any physician, owes it to his patients to keep in good health, to get sufficient sleep during his work week, and not to arrive in his treatment room under the influence of medication, alcohol, fatigue, or a hangover. He should have a healthy and regular sex life such as marriage provides. Regular outdoor exercise will give him more respect for the benefits of physical vitality and for the health of the body, which is the only known vessel for the human psyche. He should not allow the skepticism of his more self-indulgent or lazier colleagues to interfere with this old-fashioned and healthful régime.

Psychological Attitude Psychologically, as the patients on their part compose themselves for the session with uneasy rustle, the therapist clears his mind of everything that has gone before in the way of preparation, of all that he knows about the patients, of all his personal problems, and of everything he has learned about psychiatry and psychotherapy. At his best, he becomes like an innocent new-born babe who has passed under the arch of his office doorway into a world he never made. Then on the *tabula rasa* of his unencumbered mind should appear three ancient slogans.

THERAPEUTIC SLOGANS

Primum non nocere The first concern of all healing arts is not to injure, to cut only when and where necessary, but then to cut cleanly and with clear knowledge of what is being cut into. The group therapist, then, must become aware of the possibilities of damaging his patients by bruising them, by misleading them (especially sinful and wicked toward the young), by opening up areas of pathology without proper preparation, or by losing them in such a way that they will be unable afterward to avail themselves of the services of other psychotherapists. Specifically, he should wield the interpretive knife gently, though firmly and steadily; he should avoid entering sequestered areas of psychosis until the patient has been fully prepared to meet face to face what he has so long sequestered; and he should be careful not to agree too quickly with derogatory statements of a patient concerning a parent or spouse. He should not poke into any traumatized areas until he is ready to finish what he begins and feels assured that the patient can survive the procedure. His first task, therefore, is to locate such areas and estimate their extent, in order to avoid them until the time has come for them to be explored.

Vis medicatrix naturae The patient has a built-in drive to health, mental as well as physical. His mental development and emotional development have been obstructed, and the therapist has only to remove the obstructions for the patient to grow naturally in his own direction. This means, among other things, that there is no such thing as a "weak ego," but only weakly cathected egos. The therapist's second task, therefore, is to locate the healthy areas in each patient's personality so as to nurture them and strengthen their potential.

Je le pensay, & Dieu le guarit * The therapist does not cure anyone, he only treats him to the best of his ability, being careful not to injure and waiting for nature to take its healing course. There is no need for false humility, but only for facing the facts: we treat them, but it is God who cures them. Hence in practice "curing the patient" means "getting the patient ready for the cure to happen today." We can be persistent, industrious, devoted, conscientious, and acute, but we must not be ardent. The professional therapist's job is to use his knowledge therapeutically; if the patient is going to be cured by love, that should be left to a lover. When the patient recovers, the therapist should be able to say, "My treatment helped nature," and not "My love overcame it" — a statement which should be reserved for the patient's intimates.

These are the first thoughts which run through the therapist's head as the patients wait for him to give them instructions, or begin to talk by themselves.

THE THERAPEUTIC RELATIONSHIP

Basic Questions His next step should be to ask himself some fundamental questions about the real meaning of the therapeutic

* This is the rendition, out of at least ten possible variants, suggested as the standard (from the 1585 edition of Paré's *Oeuvres*) by L. R. C. Agnew (*Jnl. History of Med.*, XVIII: 75–7, 1963). The reference was kindly supplied to me by Professor Ilza Veith of the University of California Medical School in San Francisco.

relationship. He may never be able to answer these definitively, but each time he asks them of himself he may come a little closer to a significant answer.

First, in regard to his own development, he should ask himself: "Why am I sitting in this room? Why am I not at home with my children, or skiing, or skin-diving, or playing chess, or whatever else my fancy might dictate? What will this hour contribute to my unfolding?"

In regard to his patients and their motivations, he should ask: "Why are they here? Why are they not home with their children, or doing what their fancy dictates? Why did they choose psychotherapy as a solution? Why not religion, alcohol, drugs, crime, gambling, or automobile racing? What will this hour contribute to their unfolding?"

Then in regard to his duties toward them and their expectations of him: "Why did they choose to come to me rather than to some other equally qualified person? What do they think I can do which someone else could not do as well or better? What makes them think I can do more for them than an experienced clergyman or scoutmaster could? Why did I get a doctor's degree? Of what value here are the hours I spent studying the surgical anatomy of the hand, the cross-section of the spinal cord, the pituitary hormones, the way of a rat in a maze, or the ethics of the slums?"

The Therapist's Assets During the time these questions are running through the therapist's mind, the patients have perhaps become restless. His preoccupation has prevented him from making premature interventions which might help them conceal their anxieties. Now when he turns his attention to the other people in the room, they are already, without unnecessary delay, offering samples of their behavior which may be significant and useful. At this point, after a few minutes have elapsed since he sat down, the therapist can give himself a partial answer to the question of what a well-trained group therapist has to offer that other types of group leaders do not: his special powers of observation, his willingness to be looked over without prejudice, and his ability to structure the group to the best therapeutic advantage. Against the background of his philosophical questionings and reservations, his clinical qualities now come to the fore: observation, equanimity, and initiative. He prepares to use these three interdependent faculties, based on his whole previous clinical training and experience, for the maximum benefit of his patients.

OBSERVING AND LISTENING

Like any good clinician, the group therapist should ideally use all five senses in making a diagnosis, assessing the situation, and planning the treatment: sight, hearing, smell, touch, and taste. As previously noted, he should sit in such a position that he can easily observe all his patients at all times, so that as far as possible not a single movement in the room escapes him; with enough experience, he can develop useful eyes in the back of his head. Similarly, his ears should be selectively open so that he misses no sound emitted by any patient, no matter what sounds of traffic and construction penetrate into his office. Good odors and bad odors should be noted, and this may require the resurrection of a sense of smell which has been severely suppressed by social training, especially in America. Generally speaking, touching patients is poor technique except for naturally exuberant people; but even the most reserved therapist should permit himself an occasional handshake, which may yield useful information. The sense of taste has become even more unfashionable as a clinical instrument than the sense of smell, even for diagnosing diabetes, and in group treatment there is seldom an occasion to use it unless the patient offers the therapist a candy, which may turn out to be sour or bitter.

Visual Observation Observation is the basis of all good

clinical work, and takes precedence even over technique. Any well-read student or properly programed computer can make correct interpretations, given properly weighted findings; the real skill lies in collecting and evaluating data. Observations in group treatment should be made on a physiological basis, although their interpretation will be psychological. The therapist should be aware of the probable physiological state of every one of his patients during every moment of the session. He should know when to look directly at a patient, when to be content with peripheral vision, and when to sweep the whole group with his gaze. He should note not only overt blushing, palpitation, sweating, tremors, tension, excitement, rage, weeping, laughter, and sexuality, but should also be able to detect each of these in their incipient stages before they come out into the open. In order to do this he must observe carriage, posture, movements, gestures, facial mimicry, twitches of single muscles, arterial pulsations, local vasomotor and pilomotor phenomena, and swallowing.

Facial Expressions   The most subtle and challenging of these manifestations are the semi-voluntary expressions of facial mimicry and gestures. There is a rule of facial mimicry which has played an important part in determining the destinies of individuals and even of nations. The therapist meets this in day-to-day practice if he becomes drowsy during an interview. He does his best, he thinks successfully, to conceal his condition from the patient facing him, but almost invariably he will find that the patient is fully aware of what is going on. The rule is as follows: the visual impact (on the onlooker) of small movements or small changes of the facial musculature is greater than their kinesthetic impact (on the subject). Very small movements of certain muscles such as the levator palpebrae superioris, which may seem insignificant to the subject or escape his attention altogether, may be very obvious to an onlooker. This can be easily tested by drooping the eyelids to what seems kinesthetically a negligible extent, and then examining the effect in a mirror. The experiment may be repeated by contracting the risorius or the orbicularis oris just a few millimeters. There is a surprising difference between the small kinesthetic impact of such minimal excursions, and the visual impact of the facial expressions they produce. Few people are aware of the visible extent of the changes in the chin muscles produced by putting the tip of the tongue between the teeth and either the upper or lower lip; in this case the changes spread even to the zygomaticus and temporalis.[1]

When people are preoccupied with other matters, they may be unaware of even more extensive changes in their facial expressions. This means that people (including parents and children) are continually giving themselves away without knowing it; sometimes when the therapist or another patient points out an inconsistency between verbal content and facial expression, the patient finds it hard to believe that he has made his "hidden" feelings so obvious. For a lesson in keenness of observation in such matters, Darwin's wonderful book *Expression of the Emotions in Man and Animals* should be consulted—it is worth missing a month of newspapers and journals in order to read it.

Gestures Another science which the group therapist should cultivate is that of pasimology, the science of gestures. For his purposes, gestures may be classified descriptively as symbolic, emphatic, exhibitionistic, or functional. A symbolic gesture is a conventional sign which is not directly related to the subject matter, such as the circle made with the thumb and forefinger that symbolizes "OK." An emphatic gesture is one which emphasizes a point and is in effect a nonverbal exclamation, such as knee pounding, finger-pointing, head-nodding, and simpering. An exhibitionistic gesture is one which the speaker is more conscious of than he is of the content of what he is saying; for example, a woman who raises her leg in a group to show a run in her stocking is often evidently more interested in how the men react to seeing her legs than she is in the condition of her stocking. Most interesting are the functional gestures. These are of an archaic nature and form a counterpoint to what the person is saying. They are characteristically idiosyncratic with the speaker, so that in order to understand them it may be necessary to inquire why certain gestures accompany certain words, since they do not seem to be directly related. Such cases give the effect of two messages coming at once, the verbal content and the more primitive and picturesque gestural accompaniment.[2]

Some gestures are sex-linked and constitute "trade secrets," as it were, which the other sex is not a party to. Few men would intuitively know the meaning of a woman snapping a side-curl of her hair with her forefinger, but a friendly female confides that this indicates she is tired of the man she is talking to or associated with, and is ready for a change.

Sometimes it is the gestures rather than the facial expression which reveal the "hidden" thoughts by their inconsistency. A woman who smiles happily when she says she has an "extremely happy" marriage may meanwhile be twisting her wedding ring or tapping her foot impatiently. It is evident that the triad words-expression-gestures offers several variations to be studied and clarified through clinical experience. If all three are consistent, the personality may be termed "well-organized." In less well-organized personalities, words + expression may be inconsistent with gestures, or words + gestures may be inconsistent with expression. In poorly organized personalities, all three may be inconsistent: typically, the Adult ego state may say one thing in words, the Child ego state may say another through facial expressions, and the Parental ego state may convey its sentiments through gestures. Physiologically, each of the triad may be regarded as a final common pathway. In the well-organized personality, the messages from each pathway reinforce each other; in the less well-organized personality, there are inconsistencies between them. The significant point is that in social behavior there are at least three final common pathways, each arising from a separate system or ego state (see Chapter 10), and these systems are often inconsistent with each other. It may be intuitively surmised, and experience bears it out, that in the long run the destiny of the individual will more likely be determined by the systems which control his facial expressions and his gestures, than by the one which puts his sentences together.

Mimicry and gestures are vast and fascinating fields for the group therapist to learn about, and if he learns well there will be few "hidden" feelings (or "real feelings," as they are called nowadays) that will not be revealed to his private gaze.

Listening   There are several kinds of listening. While the therapist is maintaining his visual observation he may at the same time note the grosser aspects of auditory clues, such as coughing, gasping, weeping, laughing, talking, and the content of what is said. If he wants to listen for more subtle indications, he may have to suspend visual observation, lower his head, and sometimes close his eyes as well, to concentrate on the pitch, timbre, rhythm, intonation, and vocabulary of the speakers. Sometimes it is only in this way that he can become aware of the functional aspects of verbalization, whose diagnosis may be largely intuitive: e.g. patients who are primarily talking to themselves rather than to the group, patients who are talking as their parents must have talked, and patients who are talking the way a child of a certain age does.

The careful listener, besides noting inconsistencies such as childlike or dialectic pronunciations by well-educated grown-ups, clear thoughts delivered in a shaky voice, and slips of the tongue contaminating otherwise good delivery, will also observe sooner or later that each of his patients has more than one voice. Under stress or varying circumstances there will be well-marked changes in the timbre, speed, and rhythm of talking, as well as a switch in enunciation and vocabulary. A psychiatric resident had a consistently measured delivery at staff conferences and supervisory interviews. One day he received a telephone call during an interview with the chief. It was an intimate friend, and the resident's manner of talking was quite different from that which he employed professionally. When he hung up, the chief remarked: "I've been waiting almost a year to hear you talking like that to somebody. Now I know you."

Vocabulary is the simplest vocal variable to study without special preparation. In general, there are three types of vocabularies, corresponding to different ego states. 1. Borrowed (Parental) vocabularies are often striking when they are highly mannered. A man who habitually spoke with an Edwardian vocabulary, manner, and syntax readily recognized that this form of speech was borrowed from a respected grandfather and was supposed to have the same effect on the contemporary listeners as his grandfather's talk had on him when he was a little boy. 2. Vocabularies learned as conceptual frameworks and mannerisms for dealing with external reality are classified as Adult. Social scientists and their disciples among PTA members, for example, are notably given to using "this" instead of "that" as an indicative pronoun. Such a tendency, according to the consensus of several therapy groups, implies an over-objectivity and a lack of commitment. "I do this (past action) often," for example, is a kind of apology, an exhibition of "proper" objectivity, even a plea for forgiveness; and at the same time somehow an evasion of full responsibility. "I do that often" has a more authentic ring. The historic "this" is as much of an intellectualism for a social scientist as the use of the historic present tense is for the person given to action. Whether or not such generalizations prove to be valid, they illustrate the kind of thing group therapists can be thinking about. 3. The most dramatic of the Child vocabularies are those motivated by rebelliousness, consisting of expletives and "tough talk." These often alternate, particularly among women, with baby-talk or sugary words of over-compliance. In effect, the therapist who studies his patients carefully will find in each of them at least three different systems of voice, rhetoric, and vocabulary.

Proper listening is manifested by giving the right response, or at least knowing what response would be most gratifying to the speaker. This must be differentiated from the response the speaker has learned to expect. For example, some so-called supportive groups are set up so that a speaker learns to expect as a response what is called in transactional analysis "a marshmallow" or "gumdrop." There may be a continual interplay of outstretched psychological hands as stimuli, and marshmallow throwing as responses. This merely indicates that no one has really listened to anyone else, since the responses become stereotyped and have only a superficial relationship to the content of the stimuli. Anyone who wants people to listen to what he is really saying and to get a really pertinent answer in such a situation is likely to be disappointed.

The therapist should not be beguiled by the currently fashionable talk about nonverbal communication into forgetting the fact that it will take years of study for him to master the subtleties of verbal communication.

BEING LOOKED OVER

Since the patients will be noting everything the therapist does, in an attempt to size him up, he can make it easier for them and himself by behaving in a naturally dignified way instead of trying to hide behind a professional poker face. If he says a few words occasionally during the first hour, that will not seriously impair the patients' ability to distort his image in accordance with their needs. He will do no harm by presenting himself as a reasonably courteous, alert, interested, and enthusiastic person, but behind these spontaneous superficial characteristics a certain reserve should be maintained. His responses, however, should be from his own volition and not forced by pressure from the patients.

His conduct should be guided by aesthetics, responsibility, and commitment, all of which may be novelties to those of his patients who come from unsatisfactory homes; nor will his attention to such criteria impair his standing with those who come from more stable environments.

Aesthetics   It is evident that most clinical psychopathology is unaesthetic. Schizophrenics, manics, and depressives may be physically untidy. Many neurotics are preoccupied with untidy bedroom, bathroom, and kitchen fantasies. Psychopaths and delinquents often live in an untidy atmosphere of county jail cells, broken windows, and bloody sidewalks. Since aesthetic standards, so seldom mentioned in psychotherapy, have a strong appeal for many patients and offer an attractive motivation for recovery, the therapist may set an example by being clean, decently groomed and dressed, and graceful though not pedantic in his manners and speech.

Responsibility   The therapist can make it implicitly clear that he knows at all times to whom he is responsible and for whom he is responsible, and also that he feels a responsibility to and for himself.

Commitment   Most important of all perhaps is commitment. He should set an example to his patients of someone who has a job to do and will let nothing interfere for very long with the progress of his task. This may cause consternation and wonder in a number of his patients who have perhaps never before met anyone who knew what he was doing and went about doing it in a systematic and constructive way regardless of enticements, and who could not be inveigled into abandoning his goal.

The Therapist's Idiosyncracies   Within this matrix, the therapist is bound to exhibit all sorts of idiosyncracies which the patients will be looking for and will think about and frequently exploit. He should, however, never underestimate their ability to appreciate honest effort and estimable characteristics. The therapeutic situation is better if the patient says of the therapist, "He reminds me of my nice grandmother, and he is actually decent, responsible, and committed," than if he says, "He reminds me of my nice grandmother but actually he is a slob."

In general it is more important for the group therapist to know what to do, and to let the patients see that he knows what to do, than to do nothing. For him to act as though group treatment were formal individual psychoanalysis is a pretence. They are different procedures and require different approaches. This topic will be discussed further in Chapter 13.

STRUCTURING THE GROUP

The natural structure of the group should be accepted at face value: that is, the patients are coming to the therapist because he knows more about something than they do. Democracy has many meanings, and the best of them is that of common courtesy. Beyond this, there is no use pretending, as some therapists do, that the therapist and patents are equal in the group—if only for the obvious reason that he is getting paid for being there and they are not, and they expect and are entitled to some services while he does not have a right to expect the same from them.

If he sets up rules, he should remember that for many people in treatment groups, as in other groups, rules are there for the purpose of being circumvented. Explicit rules should be kept at a minimum, since each of them is for one-third of the patients unnecessary, for another third an opportunity for ingratiation, and for the remainder a challenge. On the other hand, without any explicit regulations, the patients will be avidly seeking from the very first hour to find out what is OK and what is not-OK in the society in which they find themselves. He will soon reveal his predilections, in spite of any efforts not to, and a formal statement will only detract from the smooth running of the

group. For the greatest effectiveness, he should indicate in one
way or another that what is OK is whatever furthers the therapeutic program, and what is not-OK is whatever impedes it.

THE THERAPIST'S RESPONSIBILITY TO HIMSELF

In summary, then, during the first three minutes the therapist is
composing himself for a unique experience, for nothing just like
the impending meeting has ever happened before, and nothing
just like it can ever occur again; that is, unless he allows his
groups to fall into utter banality, and it is precisely to prevent
such an outcome that he pays attention to what is discussed in
this chapter. After clearing his mind of extraneous matters, and
reminding himself of some basic principles of the healing arts,
he then tries to penetrate the reality of the situation in which he
finds himself. Finally he mobilizes the capacities he has carefully
cultivated through years of training and experience, and sets
about to exercise them to the utmost, with prudent initiative,
for the maximum benefit of his patients.

In a broad sense, this chapter is the most important in the
book, and a few existential remarks will serve to emphasize that
its implications are even more significant than its explications so
far as the decisive factor is concerned: the therapist's responsibility to himself.

The difficulty that the group therapist runs into if he wishes
to become an authentic individual, arises from the fact that almost anything that can be called a "therapy group" is inherently
beneficial to its members. A respectable percentage of them will
improve regardless of or even in spite of what the "therapist"
does. Under these conditions, the "therapist" who is willing to
accept consensus as a substitute for authenticity can gather with
his colleagues of like mind and exchange "observations" and
"technical procedures."

Therapists who allow themselves to accept such a spurious

situation as their destiny are suffering from the same disability in self-confrontation as the lottery winner. All over the world, able-bodied men are sitting under trees year after year, each of them with an ever-renewed lottery ticket in his pocket, waiting for fortune to smile upon him. When one of them wins, there is a strong tendency for him to feel that it is his skill and intelligence which brought him his windfall, and many of his less lucky neighbors will concur in this opinion. The authentic professional is not content merely to accept such gifts of fortune. He wants to win every time; he is a "compulsive winner." The dilettante is not bothered in the same way as the authentic professional by his losses, that is, by patients leaving, getting worse, or staying in treatment without any visible progress. For the group therapist to be the master of his own destiny requires a commitment which misses no opportunity to learn, uses every legitimate method to win, and permits no rest until every loss has been thoroughly analysed so that no mistake will ever be repeated.

REFERENCES

1. An excellent summary of the anatomy of oral expression can be found in "Labial Lore," *MD* 9:262–9, April 1965.
2. Berne, E. "Concerning the Nature of Communication." *Psychiatric Quart.* 27:185–98, 1953.

4

The Therapist's Responsibility

What happens after the first three minutes is determined less by the therapist's choice of method than by his commitment in regard to his own development, which is immediately reflected in the quality of his approach to his patients. Successive stages in the unfolding of this commitment are manifested by the degree of the therapist's awareness of himself as a being living in a real world. He cannot in all conscience expect his patients to be less vegetative and more alive than he is himself. In ascending order of vitality, he has three therapeutic attitudes to choose from, and these give rise respectively to institutionalized, contractual, or personal group treatment.

GROUP THERAPY AS A SOCIAL INSTITUTION

The therapist who is content to make a comfortable living and stand in well with his colleagues can conduct his group in a manner which has now taken on the status of a social institution. This institutional tendency is found not only in group therapy, but in other forms of psychotherapy as well. Many things which were originally done with daring and creativity are now done for the sake of conformity without critical review of their continued usefulness.

Institutions versus Procedures An institution should be differentiated from a procedure. In giving a specifically indicated intramuscular injection, the conscientious general practitioner goes through certain well-defined steps. First he applies a cleansing antiseptic solution to the skin, then he pauses for the minimum interval required for the antiseptic to take effect, then he thrusts the needle in, then he withdraws the plunger to make sure he has not hit a vessel, then he gives the injection, and finally he puts a piece of cotton over the injection site and perhaps applies gentle massage to the area. Laymen sometimes refer to all this as a ritual, but actually it is not. It is a well-tested procedure, every step of which has a rational justification and necessity, so that in the best interest of the patient none of them can be conscientiously omitted. An institution lacks this consistent element of scientifically defensible rationality. Role-playing takes precedence over effectiveness, stated assumptions are defended against critical examination, unstated assumptions are denied, and organized consensus is used as a weapon against rational inquiry. (Casuistry, however, may be permitted or encouraged by the institutionalized therapist; that is, interpretations may be debated as long as the basic assumptions are not brought into question.)

Institutions may arise from procedures that are outdated but whose elements are perpetuated for personal reasons: fear, pride, prejudice, ignorance, superstition, nostalgia, conformity, dilettantism, time-filling, or external advantage.* Sometimes institutionalization adds to the pleasure and self-esteem of all the parties concerned. There are a number of simple precautions which it is rationally advisable for a woman to take during her

---

* An interesting example is the theory that the African custom of inserting large discs into the upper lip began as a discouragement to slave-raiders, and is now considered decorative — *MD* (Chap. 3, ref. 1), p. 264.

pregnancy. Society, however, sanctions a certain amount of exploitation of the situation beyond the barest obstetrical needs so that pregnancy becomes a social role which can be played jokingly, gallantly, or grimly, and the woman is entitled to make demands which are accepted tenderly, courteously, or grudgingly. Many elements in this role are simply "old fashioned" and may have been "rational" protections in the days when pre-natal development was differently understood.

There are many anthropological examples which illustrate even more cogently the strength of institutional tendencies. In some areas of the Philippines, there is not only an institutionalized way to go about being sick beyond the actual physical disability imposed by the sickness, but also for each different native diagnosis the patient is expected to play a slightly different role.[1] (Cf. Spender.[2]) In some primitive areas where rituals are more highly regarded than procedures, it is often advisable for public health workers giving injections for filariasis or frambesia to present their procedures as rituals by embroidering them in accordance with local institutions, a compromise which the honest worker is forced to make for purposes of expediency. The important point here is that the public health worker is not taken in by his own institutionalization and all debatable clinical questions are decided on scientific rather than institutional grounds.

An Illustrative Anecdote   The following anecdote is slightly distorted for illustrative purposes.

A patrol officer in a remote area of New Guinea asked Dr. Q if he would mind interviewing a local chief, who appeared to be suffering from a psychotic form of depression. Dr. Q went to the man's hut, and after appropriate greetings had been exchanged the following conversation took place.

Dr. Q: "I hear you're not feeling good."
Chief: "You don't look so good yourself yet."

Dr. Q: "I mean I hear you're feeling sad."

Chief: "How are you feeling yourself these days? Are you moving your bowels every day?"

Dr. Q: "Well, you do look sad."

Chief: "You look kind of skinny, too."

Dr. Q: "Are you afraid something bad will happen?"

Chief: "Not much. You must eat more."

Dr. Q: "Well, what I want to say is that I'm a doctor and maybe I can help you if you don't feel good."

Chief: "Oh, a doctor. Wait along here a little time."

The chief thereupon left the hut and returned a few minutes later with a man bearing an armful of enormous yams, which were piled beside Dr. Q.

Dr. Q: "What are those big fellows for?"

Chief: "Suppose you're a doctor, and suppose you help me, then I want to pay you."

Dr. Q: "You can pay me afterward."

Chief: "No, suppose I don't pay now, then I think perhaps I will never pay you. You better take them now. Now are you ready to begin?"

Dr. Q: "Yes. Now we can begin."

At this the chief stretched himself on the floor of the hut and asked: "Where is your mask?"

Dr. Q: "I have no mask."

Chief: "Oh, you've got no mask! Well, if you say you're a doctor and if you have no mask, then you're a humbug doctor."

And with that he got up off the floor, told his servant to gather up the yams, and the two of them walked off.

Patrol Officer (*smiling*): "Well, what's your diagnosis, doctor?"

Dr. Q: "My diagnosis is that if I'm going to be a doctor around here and don't want to be a humbug doctor, then I'd better get a mask."

Roles Actual medicine masks are not used in civilized countries, and in institutionalized group therapy they are replaced by physiological masks and personas. There are two roles in an institutionalized therapy group: therapist and patient. The therapist learns in various ways how to play his role: for example, by reading psychiatric, psychoanalytic, and group therapy journals. The patient also learns how to play his role from various sources, perhaps by reading his medical journals: *Time, Reader's Digest,* etc. Hence the therapist knows what to expect from the patients and the patients know what to expect from him.

Aims The aims of institutionalized group therapy are stated in plausible but ambiguous terms whose interpretation is subject to the idiosyncrasies of the therapist. Operational definitions are avoided if possible because of the implied commitment. Interpretations are preferred to definitions for such words as "support," "sharing," "acceptance," "belonging," and "collective experience," because critical inquiries can then be met by marshaling a consensus of therapists who are in the same nebulous predicament. Essentially, these terms are key words in the slogans upon which the two roles are based. Hence objective inquiries about these concepts are regarded, according to the rules of group dynamics, as attacks on the institution itself. The questioner is treated as an undesirable intruder who must be extruded before the activity of the institution can proceed. One of the favorite terms in this class is "psychoanalytic," which a few group therapists use fairly rigorously, but most would rather not.

Attitude The institutional attitude is one of solemnity or even grimness. A variant is the sugary "marshmallow throwing" which some therapists favor. It is as though both the therapist and patients agreed that recovery would come more quickly if a serious demeanor were preserved, and that any light-heartedness would spoil the effectiveness of the proceedings. This was clearly brought out in reverse when Dr. Q made a joke in a rather sophisticated treatment group. One member remarked: "I don't see why we should come here and pay if you're going to sit there and laugh! Your job is to look serious, and so is ours." Then she added: "You understand it's only my Child that feels that way. My Adult can't see any reason why we won't get better just as fast if we all enjoy ourselves here." The idea that therapy can be enjoyable, and even at times hilarious, threatens the magic which is promised by maintaining a solemn mien. "Everybody" knows that you are not supposed to take institutions lightly and that if you do they will not perform their promised functions. Carefree laughter in therapy groups may be regarded with the same disapproval as it would be in church or in a bank. Dr. Q's patients often talked for a while out on the sidewalk after their meetings. A friend of his once reproached him about this, saying: "You call yourself a psychiatrist, but I passed your office the other day and your patients were all standing there laughing." Among them was a melancholic who had not laughed (she said) for two years before entering the group.

Unstated Assumptions The basic assumption of institutionalized group therapy is that group therapy is good, but it is rarely stated what it is good for. It has never been established in a scientifically acceptable way that group therapy is good in some absolute sense, the way penicillin is good; or even in the relative sense that it is better than other forms of therapy, or than other forms of group activity, or even that it is better than no therapy at all. Another widespread assumption is that selection of patients is good; again, it is not convincingly stated what it is good for, which parties it is good for, or exactly why it is good for them. This question has been discussed previously.

Another unstated assumption is that therapist and patient, which officially on the record are merely temporary roles adopted by equal members of the human race, really refer to two different breeds of people. This leads to extremes of unilaterality. They may even address each other in different dialects, as in some highly formalized courtly societies: one language for therapist to patient, another for patient to therapist. A therapist who spends four years at a clinic is supposed to learn a great deal about psychiatry; a patient who spends four years at the same clinic is not supposed to learn anything about psychiatry, and if he does his knowledge is frowned upon as a mere pretence and as in some way damaging to his progress. Instead of being complimented on his enterprise, he may even be chastised, like a precocious grade school pupil who has had the temerity to read the teacher's guide at the back of his arithmetic book. Patients, like subjects in a psychological experiment, are often assumed to be victims of hebetude, cecity, and other intellectual defects. No alert psychiatrist or psychologist could sit in a specially equipped room for very many hours without realizing that it was bugged and spy-holed; yet patients are oftentimes supposed to be incapable of such insights, which can be conveyed by a single imprudent glance. For their own private reasons, they are content to go along with this assumption and pretend to the investigators and sometimes to themselves that they do not realize what is going on.

Taboos The patient in institutionalized therapy is expected to check his intelligence at the door. It is legitimate for the therapist to make a reasoned analysis of a situation, but a patient who does likewise may be squelched by calling it "intellectualizing." A therapist who does not curb such unseemly behavior may be severely criticized at the next staff conference.

Being "judgmental" is another taboo. It is considered bad form to tell anyone he is untidy or ill-mannnered, or to show respect for craftsmanship, except as a patronizing "supportive" maneuver. Lack of discrimination on the part of the therapist is equated with charity. Initiative on his part is also taboo. It is the institutionalized belief that in spite of his superior knowledge and experience, the patients improve better and more quickly by talking to each other than by listening to him. It is often assumed that they are there primarily or even exclusively to talk to each other, and that that is the chief or even sole function of the group.[3] On these grounds, a therapist who exerts maximum efforts on their behalf is more likely to be criticized than one who exerts minimal efforts.

Stated Assumptions One of the most common stated but unexamined assumptions is that talking is good. Hence the many articles on the "problem" of silence, and the frequent questions from beginners about how to get the patients to talk more. This assumption overlooks the fact that many people receive great benefit from aggregations where silence is the rule, such as Quaker meetings and retreats, where the equally explicit assumption is that talking is bad. Another often stated assumption of institutionalized group therapy is that expressing hostility is good. A naïve student might infer from this that cannibals are necessarily in a state of superior mental health, which they are not; or that Japanese women, who are not supposed to express hostility, are in bad shape compared to American women who have ample opportunity to do so. The assumption that expressing sexual feelings is good is somewhat uncomfortably maintained, because it usually means expressing past sexual feelings or sexual feelings about people not in the group, and not, as in the case of hostility, about people in the group. This assumption is also subject to some criticism, since in Tahiti where sexual freedom is proverbial, at least in the opinion of non-Tahitians, the incidence of psychiatric illnesses does not seem to be notably less than anywhere else.[4,5] The expression of hostility and sexual feelings is thought to be good for the patients, but the therapist is not allowed to reciprocate because it is not part of his role.

A patient who had been referred from institutionalized therapy to a contractual group in another city, interrupted halfway through her first meeting to deliver a dramatic harangue about her hostile and sexual feelings during childhood toward her younger brother. Her outburst was met with notable indifference, whereupon she cried with even more vehemence:

"How can you sit there and talk so calmly? Isn't this a Freudian group? Don't you ever express real feelings?"

"Well," replied one of the more sophisticated members kindly enough, "we tried that, but we like our way better."

Institutional Support Institutionalized group therapy is supported mainly by staff conferences of like-minded colleagues. At these meetings, the object is to present "interesting material," and results are considered irrelevant or are relegated to the status of footnotes. The excuse for such conferences is that they are learning experiences, but anyone who attends them for any length of time soon recognizes that they are essentially rituals. It is taboo, for example, to ask if the patients are getting better, and it is also taboo for a therapist to state that any of his patients are getting better unless he does so apologetically or with qualifications. His standing in the community is even more likely to be jeopardized if he claims that one or more patients got better faster than professional courtesy allows. (They are permitted, however, to do something called "making progress.") In a wider sense, the institution is supported by the more sentimental and commercial sectors of the press and public. Within the therapy group itself, it is supported by the therapist's right to look inscrutable and his privilege of not telling the patients what is going on or what he is trying to do.

Fortunately, there is a countering body of opinion which is skeptical about the value of group therapy, and this keeps the institutionalization from becoming fixed, dominating, and self-perpetuating in the professional community, although it consolidates the therapists who subscribe to the institution.

The Martian Viewpoint Let us suppose that a man from

Mars who was free of earth-bound prejudices sat in as an observer in a number of institutionalized therapy groups. In writing his report, he might say that he sat in a number of rooms, each containing nine people, none of whom was really sure why he was there. Each conducted himself according to certain rules which could be found in the scientific or popular literature. He might recognize that for the most part, certain techniques which were borrowed from individual therapy were used in a makeshift way. He would note the repeated implication that the therapy was person-oriented, but might conclude on his own part that it was actually institution-oriented. He might observe that no matter what individual embroidery each therapist applied, the results of this institutionalized therapy were about the same. He might mention that what happened was different from what he observed at other meetings, such as Boy Scout meetings; but noting the happy faces of the Boy Scouts, and comparing them with the solemn countenances of the patients in the therapy groups, he might wonder why the therapy groups were considered to be therapeutic. He might add as his personal comment that if the people sitting in the room had a clearer idea of why they were there and a more precise conception of what they were trying to do, and if the leader made it clearer to everybody how they were going to do it, the situation might have interesting possibilities.

The Spell of Labels Much of the institutionalization referred to above results from the term "group therapy" itself. The nonmedical therapist particularly may be anxious to be "orthodox," for if he is not he may have to defend himself before more conservative medical colleagues. Hence he is careful always to be aware of "the group," and may be tempted to avoid facing certain issues by taking refuge behind the word "therapy," which does not carry the same implications of well-defined responsibility as the word "treatment." In many localities he is forced into this refuge by legal definitions. He is then consoled to discover that many of his medical colleagues are half-hidden behind the same shadowy screen.

If by some historical accident the subject under discussion had been called something like "joint treatment" instead of "group therapy," much disputation, vagueness, evasiveness, and concern with peripheral issues (such as "The Group") might not have arisen. "Therapy of the Group," for example, is an interesting scientific concept and a legitimate subject for research, but it seems somewhat removed at present from the specific responsibility of the practising clinician, which is to cure each patient who comes to him in the manner best adapted to that patient's individuality, symptoms, and disease. He also has the responsibility of doing that in the most economical and direct manner possible. Since the term "group therapy" cannot be abolished at this late date, it should be relegated to some area outside the clinician's office, so that the clinician can concentrate on his primary function without distractions and free of etymological blandishments. Meanwhile research workers could concentrate on such fundamental and still open questions as the difference between a "group" and a "not-group."

On the other hand, the word "treatment" may be alarming ("threatening") to some patients, including a number who would be willing to participate in something called "group therapy." This in effect signifies a lack of commitment on the patient's part, and that is an attitude the therapist should not cater to, since he then has either to seduce the patient into a serious engagement or else compromise his own commitment. A good policy is not to use any label in clinical work. A surgeon need not tell the patient he needs "an operation" (which is only a label); he can simply tell him what he proposes to do: "You'll have to have your appendix out," or "You should have it removed." A group therapist can similarly use verbs instead of nouns: "I think you should go into a group," instead of "I think you should have group therapy (or group treatment)." [6]

CONTRACTUAL GROUP TREATMENT

Contractual group treatment is a simpler approach which attempts as far as possible to be free of unstated or unwarranted assumptions and institutionalized aims, attitudes, roles, and supports. In order to accomplish this, both therapist and patient start off, insofar as they are able, with the unprejudiced attitude of a man from Mars, and try to evolve out of the actual realities of the situation a contract which is acceptable to both sides.

The Therapeutic Relationship The first question to be settled, perhaps at preliminary individual interviews, is why the therapist and patients are there. This leads to situations which might be shocking to an institutional therapist. For example, if an alcoholic comes for treatment and says "I want to stop drinking," the therapist might ask: "Why?" After listening to what the patient says, he might remark: "Those are not your reasons, those are other people's reasons. Why do *you* want to stop?" If the patient can tolerate such objectivity, he is off to a good start. If he cannot, then both parties know exacly where they stand right from the beginning, and can make their decisions accordingly.

A similar procedure might be followed with "character disorders" and other people who state their complaints in vague or borrowed terminology. If the complaint has something to do with "relationships," the therapist might ask "What do you mean by a relationship?" He will require the patient to give his own definition of such jargon, and if the institutionalized concepts can be reduced to operational terms, he may say: "Well, now I know what you want from me. You want me to help you get rid of your headaches, cure you of beating your wife," etc. If the patient is unable to clarify the situation, the therapist might extend himself so far as to say: "Well, you can't tell me clearly what you want, but my experience is that people who come to psychiatrists should be coming to a psychiatrist, so we'll see if we can find out as we go along what the trouble really is and whether there's something specific I can offer you."

It should already be apparent that this approach requires a certain amount of courage, since it is openly questioning the institution. A resident might have a bad quarter of an hour at a staff conference if he presented the following case history:

"The alcoholic who was assigned to me came into my office and said that he wanted to stop drinking. I asked why, and he said he didn't see any reason why either, and walked out. That, gentlemen, is my case presentation for today."

Since contractual treatment is bilateral rather than unilateral, the next step is for the therapist to say somehing like: "Well, why don't you come a few times and that will give you a chance to look me over and you can see what I have to offer." During the next few visits he can give samples of his wares. At the end of that time he and the patient should be able to have a clear understanding with each other. The patient may feel that what the therapist has to offer is not what he has been looking for, and they can part amicably, both of them having saved perhaps a year or two not spent to the best advantage of either of them. On the other hand, the patient's response may be more favorable; he might feel that what the therapist has to offer is interesting and might help him.

The advantage at this point is that both of them are clear as to how they will know when they are accomplishing something. The patient has by now made a clear statement in operational form of what his difficulties are so that both of them will be able to tell when things are better. In some cases the criterion may be a quantitative one, such as a lowering of diastolic blood pressure or increased earnings by a gambler or salesman; in others it may be the relief of a physical symptom or limitation; in still others, the relief of a psychological symptom such as impotence or a specific phobia; or a change in behavior, such as not beating the children, refraining from taking alcohol or drugs, keeping a job, passing examinations, or finding a respectable girl-friend. Sometimes it is the therapist who sets up the preliminary criteria for improvement; he may, for example, ask the patient to make a commitment to stop simpering, apologizing, or hallucinating.

When Dr. Q decided to start his first marital group, he asked four likely candidates among his patients whether they would be interested. He told them it was an experiment, and that he was not sure what would come of it or exactly what they might hope to accomplish, but that they were welcome to come with their spouses if they wished. These four patients talked it over at home, and all four couples decided to try it in spite of the added expense. By the end of the first meeting, it was quite apparent to everyone present that a great deal was going to be accomplished, and they all knew specifically what they were looking for. It was already evident that each couple had a private unspoken marriage contract upon which the structure of the marriage was based, and that this gave rise to a certain kind of relationship involving certain games which were leading up to a certain payoff. The group situation seemed to offer considerable promise for clarifying these items for each couple. Once this was apparent, Dr. Q made it plain that he considered that his job was to help with this clarification, but that there was no promise implied that their marriages would get "better." Whether they stayed married or got divorced was up to them, but they would at least have better information on which to base their decisions. As it turned out, from this group and subsequent marital groups undertaken with the same contract during the next four years, only one or two of the initially disrupted couples who attended regularly got a divorce. Couples scattered among general groups with the same understanding did equally well. The contract here was directly opposed to the institutions of group therapy. The spouses were never encouraged, and were often actively discouraged, from "offering" each other sharing, togetherness, understanding, support, etc. After adequate samples of such behavior had been observed, that was considered a waste of valuable time which could be more profitably devoted to the contractual work of comprehending the nature of their transactions with each other, and the games and scripts upon which those were based (see Chapter 12). As time went on, they did begin to "understand" each other, in the true sense of the word, so that instead of "supporting" each other and "sharing" with each other in what now seemed to be a kind of *folie à deux,* they felt free to choose between isolation when that was appropriate and co-operation * when that was indicated.

Nosological Differences Specifically, the contract may refer to symptoms characteristic of particular disorders, such as hysterical paralyses, phobias, obsessions, somatic symptoms, fatigue, and palpitation in the neuroses; forgery, excessive drinking, drug addiction, delinquency, and other such game-like behavior in the psychopathies; pessimism, pedantry, sexual impotence, or frigidity in the character disorders; hallucinations, elation, and depression in psychoses. Paranoid conditions are among the few exceptions to the principle of explicit contracts; for there the therapist may have very clear criteria for improvement, but cannot explain these frankly to the patient initially, although he will do so after the patient is properly prepared. The first goal here is not to "cure" the patient, but to arrest the progress of his illness by rendering the archaic thinking behind his delusions dystonic to his Adult ego state.

In special situations such as marital group treatment and family treatment the contract may refer to *specific* changes in the patients' ways of responding to each other.

Amendments The fact that the therapist and patient set up operational criteria for improvement does not mean that the

---

* Co-operation is used here in its bilateral sense, and not in its vulgar sense of "do it my way or else."

ultimate goal is merely the alleviation of symptoms or the attainment of control over social responses. It only means that such changes will be taken as definitive signs of improvement and as gauges of the effectiveness of the treatment. The therapist will always be on the lookout for the determinants underlying the symptoms or responses. This means that the contract will have to be amended from time to time. For example, if the therapist has in mind first the alleviation of symptoms and secondly the investigation of archaic attitudes toward parental figures, he may keep the second part of his plan in reserve until an appropriate time, and then propose it as an amendment to the contract. The principle of contractual treatment, however, requires that unless there are clear contra-indications, as with some paranoids initially, the therapist clarify his own side of the contract as much as possible for the patient, in appropriate stages and in language that the patient can understand at his particular phase of therapeutic development.

The initial contract, therefore, reads from the therapist's side: "You have looked me over and have some idea of what I have to offer and of what we shall be trying to accomplish; if this is satisfactory, we are now ready to proceed." To which the patient can give a variety of answers, each to be considered on its merits. To a more congenial patient he might say: "I'm running a psychiatry store. You're the customer, and now you've seen what I have to offer." This part of the contract, the initial commitment, answers the question "Why are we here?" The patient is there to attain a certain goal which is now well defined, and the therapist is there because he has undertaken the job of helping people attain precisely that sort of goal and knows something about how he as an individual can best do it. At no time is there any implication or statement from him that he is going to behave the way books or magazines or television say he should, nor that he is going to try to approximate a popular model of a therapy group, nor that he is going to be grim or even serious at all times, nor

that he is going to make the patient into a "good, likable fellow"
who has "good relationships," etc. The patient, however, is likely
to infer or assume any or all of these things, and the stage is set
for confronting him with his presumptions sooner or later, to
good advantage; or more likely, for counter-confronting him
when he confronts the therapist with them.

A good example of spontaneous amendment of the therapeutic
contract occurred with a patient who came for treatment because
of obesity, and this was the basis for the original contract. After
about a year, she said one day: "I came here becuse I was fat,
but now I realize I'm here because I'm a faker." From that time,
the therapy was directed toward finding out why she was a
faker.

In the Group   The patient's side of the contract, as far as his
contribution to the group is concerned, is only that he will offer
from time to time for the therapist's consideration samples of
his behavior toward other people. The therapist's side of this
aspect is that whenever he thinks of anything to say that might
be helpful to the patient, he will say it. There is no assumption
on his part, stated or unstated, that group therapy is good in
some vaguely empirical sense. There is only an explicit agreement
that it is worth trying and why it is being tried. Except for the
acknowledged inequalities distinguishing their roles, the patient
is regarded as holding full membership in the human race; he
has a right to look the therapist over, just as the therapist has
a duty to look him over. The therapist has an obligation to learn
from what the patient does, and the patient is expected to learn
from what the therapist says. If the patient feels that he is required to talk, or to express hostility or sexual feelings, that is
again his own presumption; the stated requirement is only that
he give samples of his behavior, whatever that may be. On the
other hand, he may be surprised or even disconcerted, particularly if he has had previous psychotherapy of an institutionalized
type, to discover that the therapist is not there to sit conspicu-

ously unperturbed while he "gathers material," and that he is genuinely pleased if the patient demonstrates genuine improvement. In short, in contractual treatment hardly any demand is made of the patient; rather he is supplied with a license to speak when he feels like it and to say whatever he wants with no exceptions regarding money and other modern taboos which have replaced the older sexual taboos. The therapist is put in the much more difficult position of having to plan his procedure step by step, in the Adolf Meyer tradition, rather than merely hoping for the best in an opportunistic way.

Timing Since the therapeutic contract is usually a long-term one, there need be no hurry in setting it up and ample time can be taken to explore its possibilities both in individual interviews and in the group; then on some auspicious occasion its terms can be agreed upon. In rare cases, however, the contract may have to be set up during the very first interview or the first group session, and then care should be taken to leave plenty of leeway for amendments. Psychoanalysts, who are contractual therapists, but only unilaterally, are divided between these two policies in regard to the "fundamental rule." Some put their patients on the couch immediately, at the first or second interview, with a demand for free association and complete candidness, while others prefer a preliminary period of getting acquainted before placing this unilateral obligation on the patient. The analyst (according to the patients' accounts) does not always state clearly his side of the contract, so that the patients are often left in the dark as to his function. But analytic situations offer the best possible setting for the smooth introduction of a contractual agreement, and two such situations will be used as examples of how it may be done. Using these optimal cases as paradigms, the therapist can adapt his technique to whatever the circumstances demand.

Illustrations Ruth, an intelligent fifteen-year-old girl who had attempted suicide during a love affair, confided some of her family difficulties to Dr. Q in the course of several interviews.

She then said that she couldn't think of anything more to say, whereupon Dr. Q suggested that it might help if she lay on the couch. The patient readily agreed, and it is probable that she had been waiting for such an invitation. She then proceeded with further confidences, some of which were sufficiently startling to put Dr. Q in a difficult position with her parents. She frankly stated that she expected him to intervene, in which case she intended to defy him and continue her peccadillos. This set-up was treated as a five-handed game of "Cops and Robbers" involving three members of her family, Dr. Q, and herself. She was favorably impressed with the game analysis, and this resulted in still further confidences. She then asked whether Dr. Q took notes, and the subsequent exchanges indicated that she was beginning to wonder what his function really was.

A few sessions later she looked out of the window and remarked how beautiful the city looked and how happy she was that day. Dr. Q asked her if she really felt that way and she replied, probably sincerely, that she did. The ensuing silence was broken by Dr. Q who said: "What are you thinking of now?"

Ruth: "Nothing important."

Dr. Q: "You know, I think you might make it as an authentic person."

Ruth: "What kind of person?"

Dr. Q: "I said 'an authentic person.' What I mean is, no jazz."

Ruth: "I'd like that."

Dr. Q: "It won't be easy, and I think you might be lonely afterward."

Ruth: "I'm lonely anyway."

Dr. Q: "Actually, you won't be any more lonely than you are now. Most people have to pick their friends from people who are interested in the same kind of jazz they are, so their selection is pretty small anyway. If you get rid of all the jazz, then you'll have to select your friends from other people who've got rid of the jazz, but there are a few of them around."

Ruth: "That's the kind of friends I want."

Dr. Q: "One problem is your age. Your parents still have complete authority over you, and also people your age have to go along with a certain amount of jazz to get along with the kids at school."

Ruth: "I'd like to try just the same."

Dr. Q: "You'll have to be completely frank and tell me everything. You'll have to leave it up to me to judge what's important and what isn't. There's no hurry, and you won't have to make yourself too uncomfortable about it, but sooner or later within a reasonable time you'll have to come out with everything. Do you want to try it that way?"

Ruth: "Very much."

This conversation took place at her eleventh individual session, one month after she started treatment. The terms of the contract are quite clear: she will within a reasonable time tell him without prejudgment or selection everything that comes to her mind, while he will try to help her fulfill her commitment to become a jazz-free person. The two ambiguities are "reasonable" and "jazz." "Reasonable" was purposely left undefined for technical reasons, to see what she would do with the contract (specifically, to see the effect of her Adult commitment on her Parent and Child components); while from her response to Dr. Q's analysis of her game of "Cops and Robbers," it was likely that they both understood the same thing by the expression "getting rid of the jazz." There was no need at that point for either of them to say aloud that "the jazz" included dramatic suicidal attempts, since it was clear enough to both of them that the contract and her commitment referred to, among other things, the original reason for her coming to Dr. Q.

Bob, the second patient, a thirty-year-old mystery writer, was not quite so receptive to a therapeutic contract at the end of one month of intensive individual therapy. During his twelfth session he said that he had got rid of all the garbage he could think of and didn't know where to go next. When Dr. Q suggested that something might come up if he lay on the couch, Bob replied:

"I knew you would ask me that, but really I don't want to."

Dr. Q thereupon went back to some previous discussions they had had about the possible effects of intensive treatment on Bob's creative work and on his relationship to his motherly wife. He now said that theoretically treatment, if successful, might shift Bob's creative interests and make him more productive and better organized, but that the resulting commodity might not be as salable as his present work, so that there was some risk to his livelihood as well as to the present structure of his marriage, if he continued. Bob went so far as to commit himself to taking these particular risks, but no farther. Hence a clear-cut therapeutic contract had to be postponed, but important groundwork had been laid: Dr. Q had explicitly stated some of the risks he foresaw, and Bob had explicitly committed himself to take certain definitely stated risks if and when he did enter into a contract. After this preparation, they could proceed with the problem of what bothered Bob about lying on the couch. This clarified his symptomatology and made it possible for Dr. Q to state what help he could offer, and at that point the therapy became contractual.

Ratification It is one thing to make a commitment and to begin operations under it, and another to carry it through to its stated goal. As operational ratification proceeds by putting the commitment into practice, either the therapist or the patient may want to make amendments, and these can be frankly discussed. In rare cases, however, the amendment may have to be unilateral on the part of the therapist, which is unfortunate both clinically and existentially. For example, the therapist may have to withdraw part of his commitment if he discovers that a patient previously diagnosed as neurotic turns out to be on the verge of a psychosis. He may not be able to discuss this autocratic modification with the patient until the terminal phases of the therapy when the patient is sufficiently stabilized to appraise in an objective Adult way what happened.

PERSONAL GROUP TREATMENT

Personal treatment adds to the therapeutic contract a unilateral obligation on the therapist's side based on the old ethical attitude that the patient's welfare takes precedence over technique. A delinquent who had visited a friend in difficulties said to Dr. Q: "You know, now I have more doubts than ever about your competence. My friend said 'My psychiatrist is better than yours because he let me go to jail rather than tell me what to do.'"

Justification A personal interest in the patients can always be justified on aesthetic, existential, or Freudian grounds. Delinquency may be frowned upon, as already noted, not for moral or ethical reasons, but because it lacks aesthetic appeal. Slobs may be called to account for similar reasons. Aesthetically, a woman's duty is to look her prettiest; to do this, she is required to keep her skirt pulled down, take baths regularly, and dress harmoniously. In personal therapy, at an appropriate time and after proper preparation, these considerations might be discussed where indicated; the preparation might require a clear distinction between a moral prejudice (on the patient's part) against vanity, and a healthy need (in the therapist's opinion) for aesthetic fulfillment; or between arbitrary middle-class values (derogated by the patient) and the aesthetic imperative (admired by the therapist) which first manifested itself in the caves of Lascaux and Altamira.

Existentially, the therapist should realize that he must have a heavy personal involvement with the human race if he is to keep his membership in it, and that he can do that without becoming imprudently involved with any individual patient. For if he is too impersonal as a psychotherapist, he will be "bankrupt," in the sense that Lillian Ross and Wittgenstein write about, in which the word is almost synonymous with "ludicrous." "By the way," remarks a patient, halfway through a session on the couch, "I murdered my husband last night and hid his body in the closet." "Aha!" says the bankrupt, "Now we have hit something important. What is your free association to closets?" The patient should not be allowed to evade his responsibilities by blaming his condition on circumstances unless they are most extraordinary, such as the accidents of war; nor to sabotage himself out of his own declared commitments.

The Freudian grounds are very similar to the existential ones, and are based on Freud's story about the man with the tired horse: "Since he has undertaken to be a horse, he must pull heavy loads." A man who has undertaken to be a father must support his children; on the other hand, he is not permitted to murder anyone in order to do so, even though he is a psychiatric patient.

Precautions   Such a personal interest, aesthetic and existential, in the patient as a member of the human race (which he has undertaken, or by now should undertake, to be a member of) must be clearly separated from parental injunctions which the therapist may be tempted to impose. The difficulty of making this distinction conscientiously makes personal therapy the most difficult type to carry on effectively, but if the therapist is confident enough and experienced enough to risk it the results are easily apparent and particularly gratifying.

Authenticity versus Spuriousness   The question of authenticity has already been broached. Since this is the only one of man's possessions which cannot be taken away from him without his consent except in the most extraordinary circumstances, and since it is the only lasting legacy a therapist can leave his patients, it is worth discussing further. If the most difficult case is disposed of first, then other cases offer no problem. An actor who uses whatever devices, procedures, and techniques are necessary to give the impression that he is Mark Antony is authentic. An actor who uses any device, procedure, or technique to give the impression that he is a good actor is spurious. Similarly, a therapist who uses whatever techniques are necessary to cure his patients is authentic; one who uses any technique for the purpose of demonstrating that he is a good therapist is spurious. In practice, this distinguishes therapists who are there solely for the benefit of themselves and their patients, from those who are conscious of their colleagues, organizations, publications, and staff conferences.

Since Freud is too complex and superior, and perhaps too peerlessly authentic, to be a model for emulation, a more practical paragon of a therapist is Karl Abraham. In his *Selected Papers* are exhibited all the qualities a good therapist should strive for. He is a keen observer, a thoughtful listener, a tireless collector of data, a curious investigator, a disciplined clinician, a meticulous technician, a conscientious physician, and an independent thinker.[7]

On the patient's side, authenticity means "getting rid of the jazz," as in the case of Ruth mentioned above. In the treatment situation, "the jazz" emerges as attempts to exploit for ulterior advantages what should be a straightforward Adult working contract. The group therapist's job, like the psychoanalyst's, is to frustrate those attempts while maintaining full respect for the authentic person they are designed to protect and conceal like a light hidden under a bushel. The spurious maneuvers constitute the patient's "games," which the therapist, for the benefit of the patient, justifiably regards with an objectivity and sophistication bordering on irony. Only if the patient can attain a similar objectivity can he free his authentic self from these hampering artifacts. The therapist's attitude toward the real person who emerges in the course of successful treatment is quite different from his attitude toward the patient's games.

REFERENCES

1. Frake, C. O. "The Diagnosis of Disease among the Subanun of Mindanao." *American Anthropologist* 63:113–32, 1961.
2. Spender, S. *Learning Laughter.* Harcourt, Brace and Company, New York, 1953.
3. Johnson, J. A. *Group Therapy.* (Chap. 2, ref. 2.)
4. Berne, E. "The Cultural Problem: Psychopathology in Tahiti." *Am. J. Psychiat.* 116:1076–81, 1960.
5. Berne, E. "A Psychiatric Census of the South Pacific." *Am. J. Psychiat.* 117:44–7, 1960.
6. Institutionalized group therapy is not a straw man, but is still widely practised, as the writer knows from personal experience and from reading the literature. For further discussion see Berne, E. "Review: Four Books on Group Therapy." *Am. Jnl. of Orthopsychiatry* 34:584–9, 1964.
7. Abraham, K. *Selected Papers.* Hogarth Press, London, 1948.

5
Methods of Treatment

The situation of the therapist starting with a new group now rests on a sufficiently solid foundation for him to turn his attention to purely clinical considerations. He has settled everything that should have been attended to before the first meeting of the group. He has prepared the scene to the best advantage that circumstances allow. He has spent his first three minutes in the group getting himself into the right frame of mind to proceed most effectively with his therapeutic efforts. And now let us assume that the patients have also been silent during this period, and that this silence is broken by one of the four most common initial moves. Either:

Patient I says: "I read an article on group therapy, and it said we were supposed to do the talking."

Or Patient II says: "What are we supposed to do here?"

Or Patient III says: "I hate to break this silence, it seems almost sacred."

Or Patient IV says: "I'm sorry I was late."

The time has now come for the beginning therapist to select a therapeutic method. He should have, in his preliminary didactic and practical training, become familiar with the most popular approaches, and only a brief résumé will be offered here in order to refresh his memory, before considering the possibilities offered by some of these methods.

RÉSUMÉ OF METHODS

As stated at the beginning, this book discusses only one type of treatment group, assuming that that is the most common type met with in clinical practice: the sedentary social group of adults. This excludes certain specialized forms of treatment without in any way reflecting on their value. Those who wish to practice psychodrama, in which the patients are not confined to their chairs, are referred to the works of Moreno and his pupils which are mentioned in the chapter on the literature of group treatment. The same applies to activity group therapy, in which the patients can structure their time other than by talking. This special technique was developed by Slavson and his pupils. Group therapy with children in most cases is a form of activity group therapy and hence is best done by specialists.

Classification The techniques of treatment which are suitable for sedentary groups of adults were first comprehensively classified by Giles Thomas,[1] following Merrill Moore, in 1943, and his classification still stands as one of the most useful in the descriptive category. He set psychotherapies on a scale with polarities of "analytic" and "repressive-inspirational," ranging from Freudian psychoanalysis at one end to Christian Science at the other. He classifies group therapies similarly, with Schilder at the "analytic" pole and Alcoholics Anonymous at the other. The recent literature is mostly concerned with "psychoanalytic" types of group therapy, under such names as "group-analysis" (Foulkes[2]), "psychoanalytic group psychotherapy" (Mullan and Rosenbaum[3]), and "psychoanalysis in groups" (Wolf and Schwartz[4]).

It is presently possible, however, to classify forms of group treatment in a more precise and systematic way: first, psychologically or structurally, according to the attitude or ego state of the therapist; and secondly, dynamically or technically, according to the focus of his attention.

The Psychological or Structural Classification   Therapy groups may be classified on the basis of the ego state in which the therapist predominantly carries on his work: Parental, Adult, or Child.[5] Groups in which the therapist is predominantly Parental would be placed near the "repressive-inspirational" pole of Thomas's spectrum. Here the therapy centers on exhortations, admonitions, and what is colloquially called "support." With the therapist in an Adult ego state, his interventions consist principally of interpretations, confrontations, and explanations, without Parental declarations, and the therapy lies near the "analytic" pole of the spectrum. The Child ego state of the therapist would find its expression in activity therapy groups, especially with children, which are not included in the present discussion.

The Dynamic or Technical Classification   From another point of view, analytic treatment groups may be classified according to the principal focus of attention as group-analytic, psychoanalytic, and transactional analytic. Group-analytic therapies treat "the group" itself as an entity which transcends in some way not yet clearly defined the psychic sum of its members, and the therapy is centered around phenomena which involve the quasi-independent life of the group as a whole. This holistic approach is implicit in the vocabulary, for example, "basic assumption groups," "collective experience," "contagion," "catalyst," and "common theme." Psychoanalytic group therapies attempt to deal with the unconscious motivations, defenses, fantasies, and resistances of the individual members, often as reflected in the state of the group as a whole, so that there tends to be some overlapping between group-analytic and psychoanalytic techniques. Transactional analysis [5] deals directly with overt transactions and sets of transactions as they occur during the course of the group session. Any holistic conception of the group as more than the sum of its individual members is disregarded almost completely as not relevant to maximal therapeutic progress, although, in case "the group" gets in the way of the treatment program, a thorough knowledge of a more pragmatic type of group dynamics is essential for effective transactional analysis. Since a detailed analysis of transactions and sets of transactions will require clarification of genetic factors, this form of treatment tends to overlap with psychoanalytic group therapy. A fourth type of group technique which is beginning to take form is the existential, and this in turn tends to overlap with the analysis of here-and-now transactions.

In general, each of these forms of treatment tends to favor one or another of the therapeutic attitudes discussed in the previous chapter. Institutionalization is most likely to occur in supportive, group-analytic, and psychoanalytic therapies, partly because of the preference for these approaches among incompletely trained therapists, who accept many things on faith and proceed with many unstated assumptions and many stated ones which are not clearly examined or whose terms are not clearly defined. Transactional analysis and properly conducted psychoanalytic therapy are contractual forms of treatment; existential analysis is more personal.

There is another kind of classification which is of great practical importance, and that refers to the quality of the therapy (or of the therapist). In practice, regardless of the method used, there are "soft" therapies and "hard" therapies. In soft therapies the goals are diffuse and limited, and the technique is opportunistic. In hard therapies the goals are clearly defined and fundamental, and the technique is carefully planned with the aim of reaching those goals by the most direct route possible. A fair analogy would be the difference between interpretive dancing and ballet. The quality which comes through to the observer of a "hard" therapy group may be called crispness. This book is oriented toward hard therapy and crispness.

Under ordinary conditions, in most training centers in this

country, the therapist's choice as he sits in the group will be between supportive (Parental) therapy, or one of the three popular analytic (Adult) therapies: group-analytic, psychoanalytic, or transactional. If he does not care to make a clear choice and prefers to be a kind of broken-field runner, treating group therapy as an improvisation rather than a science, the following discussion will still be of some interest to him. But if group treatment is to have a reliable foundation, it must be demonstrated some day that one method is in general superior to any of the others, and that this superiority rests on a sound theoretical bedrock.

Let us now take each of the four patients mentioned at the beginning of this chapter and subject him to the four major * therapeutic points of view, keeping in mind the specific task to be accomplished: the relief, as rapidly and permanently as possible of his disabilities. The ensuing discussions may at times seem obscure to a beginner, but as he begins to match the descriptions and predictions with increasing clinical experience, they will become more recognizable and intelligible.

THE TYPE I GROUP

"I read an article on group therapy, and it said we were supposed to do the talking."

Supportive Therapy First let us consider the therapist's attitude. The supportive therapist approaches his patients in a Parental ego state (or if he is resentful of them, he may approach them in a Child ego state playing a parental role, very much like a little boy playing doctor). A male supportive therapist might confess to being fatherly; but in some cases he might be mistaken, and his own history, or the observations of an unbiased observer,

---

* Since there are now several hundred group therapists with varying degrees of training and experience in transactional analysis, I take the liberty of including it under this qualification.

might indicate that he was rather being motherly. If he believes in a certain detachment, even in a so-called supportive situation, he may content himself with being merely avuncular rather than paternal; although again, such uncles sometimes appear to an outside observer to be more like aunts. (Interestingly enough, there is no feminine for "avuncular" in English, and "auntular" hardly seems adequate.)

Taking the simplest of these alternatives, the supportive remarks of a "good father" to Patient I might refer either to his laudable interest in group therapy, or to his enterprise in taking the talking initiative. This would immediately indicate to the patients that if they behaved properly they would get approval from the therapist, and they might perhaps conclude that one way to do that would be to talk a lot. With a group of silent catatonics or depressed patients, this might be a worthwhile step in the right direction. Its value for nonpsychotic patients, however, would be questionable, since more and more the content of the proceedings would be determined by the patients' impressions of the therapist's preferences, resulting in a long period of useless talk. Even in that event, however, the therapist might point with pride to the fact that patients who previously talked little were now talking more.

A more sophisticated kind of "supporter" would regard the statement of Patient I as indicating a preference for specific defense mechanisms, including intellectualization as a means of strengthening repression and isolation. This more precise knowledge might be advantageous later in helping to focus supportive interventions on the pertinent defensive system if the patient threatened to give way under stress.

Group-Analytic Therapy Taking Patient I's remarks as indicative of the general condition of the whole group, a group-analytic therapist might consider that at this point the group had a mature structure and constituted a work-group, sharing the common problem of having to talk because of an unspoken demand of the therapist. Patient I's remark might be taken to indicate his willingness, at the manifest level, to resign his own egotistic needs and impulses in favor of the needs of the group in order to maintain his secure position in the group as a whole. It can be seen that there are several promising leads in this over-all view in regard to problems of security, adjustment to the group, and adjustment to the here-and-now problems of reality, in accordance with the ideas of Bion,[6] Ezriel,[7] and Foulkes [2] as discussed further on in Chapter 9. This approach, therefore, might lead in the direction of a better adjustment of the individual in society. The question arises whether the kind of adjustment implied necessarily has the best connotations for the ultimate destiny of the individual patient, and whether it promises to increase materially his range of choices. The writer's observations indicate that this type of therapy seems to have little effect in shaking the individual loose from his underlying needs for unhealthy forms of gratification.

Psychoanalytic Therapy The psychoanalytic group therapist might suspect at this point that Patient I intellectualizes, and that he is heading for either a compliant, a defiant, or an ambivalent relationship to the therapist, the nature of which would be clarified further on in the proceedings. The fact that in his very first statement this patient refers to reading and talking might be of interest to some therapists. The statement itself already constitutes a certain kind of resistance, possibly in two directions: first, the intellectualization previously referred to, and secondly, a falling back on outside authority in order to evade personal issues. During the next year or so the therapist might be able to clarify for the patient some aspects of these preliminary indications; but because of the demands of the other patients, it would be difficult to follow systematically the whole picture. The situation would not be favorable for the kind and quantity of free association required for thorough exploration. The patient would benefit, however, to the extent that exploration and working through could be carried out in the group.

Transactional Analysis Patient I's statement would be classified provisionally in transactional analysis as a "report" of outside activities rather than as a "self-presentation" or "declaration
of position," and as a stimulus to "discussion" rather than to
description or expression of feelings. If the other members followed his lead, there would result a Type I treatment group,
in which they would indulge week after week in the kind of
time-structuring known as pastimes, during which they would
discuss all sorts of extraneous matters (e.g. magazine articles)
whose relationship to their symptoms was no more direct than
an ingrown toenail would be. In one case such a group continued in this kind of a rut for fifteen years, with no significant
clinical changes in any of the patients despite a variety of efforts,
approaches, and techniques introduced by a succession of enthusiastic and hard-working young therapists.* When finally
a therapist trained in transactional analysis was making some
headway in breaking up this routine, he was chided by his
superiors for doing "therapy in the group" instead of "group
therapy" (as they put it). The difficulty was cleared up, in the
therapist's mind at least, as soon as he answered the crucial
question: "Are you there to demonstrate your adherence to a
system of institutionalized rituals, or are you there to use your
technical knowledge to treat patients?"

Type I is the most banal type of treatment group, the type
most frequently reported in the literature, and the type most
frequently heard on tape recordings, as well as the "safest" for
the therapist or "research worker." Often in the course of their
discussions the patients will produce interesting "material"
which the therapist may manipulate according to his conception
of group therapy, to the gratification and edification of the

---

* The members of this "famous" group, at a large metropolitan hospital in
the San Francisco Bay area, became adept at "training" psychiatric residents in group therapy.

patients, but without causing any perceptible dynamic changes nor any consistent change in the type of the group activity. Attendance and withdrawals in such groups are determined by the flexibility of the established members in switching ego states in their discussions. If they insist on maintaining the proceedings at a rational Adult level, anyone who becomes moralistic or Parental is likely to find himself unwelcome and may not return; similarly a patient who injects a playful or Child-like note may be reprimanded for being "immature." If the old members are more flexible, however, they may tolerate a certain amount of switching from one ego state to another, so that new members are more likely to remain.

A Type I group is harmless to patients who are not suffering from a serious progressive disorder, and may serve the purpose of maintaining them at their initial level of functioning with little deterioration except over a long period; and it is always a handy source of "material" for staff conferences and "safe" research projects. If the therapist wishes to accomplish more than that, however, he can save himself and his patients from one to fifteen years of laborious frustration and self-deception by switching the proceedings into some other form of activity just as soon as the patients can tolerate it. Depending on his skill and experience, this will take anywhere from ten minutes to ten weeks. Paradoxically enough, the effectiveness of such switching operations depends more on the therapist's readiness than on that of patients, and his confidence will be heavily influenced by his commitment to a well-planned therapeutic program.

Classical examples of this type of group may occur in obligatory groups such as those set up in prisons, and in hospitals and clinics of the Armed Services. A Type I group may also persist where there are strong secondary gains, as in rehabilitation, relief, and Veterans Administration facilities. In a less difficult form, a similar banality tends to emerge with groups of parents of disturbed children and in marital counseling groups. The characteristic of Type I groups is the persistence of pastimes to the exclusion of more ongoing types of activity. In a group of mothers, for example, the natural pastime is projective Parental "PTA," whose thesis is "what do you do about unsatisfactory children?" They can be allowed to proceed in this way for a week or two, but gradually it must be borne in on them that this kind of discussion, helpful though it may be in yielding household hints, does not make full use of the therapist's education and potentialities, and it might be more appropriate if they became interested in themselves rather than in techniques of raising children. Similarly in a marital group, especially in a "marital counseling" group, the tendency may be to talk about techniques for improving marital relationships, and this journalistic approach (again a variation of "PTA") may go on indefinitely if the therapist does not intervene to offer his wares, which are more productively and honestly designed to deal with psychological realities than with social techniques.

The Type I group, then, will confine itself to pastimes in the form of discussions which are usually at a fairly rational Adult level, unless the therapist pleads with the patients often enough and poignantly enough to engage in some other method of structuring the group time, in which case they may oblige him by switching to Child-like and Parental pastimes under the guise of expressing "real feelings," and these in turn have to be broken into until something more useful is forthcoming.

In the specific case of Patient I's statement, the transactional approach is for the therapist to ask himself, "Why did he say that at this time?" After allowing an interval for a few responses and further transactions, he might then ask Patient I, "What did you expect people to do when you said that?" Whatever the reply, somewhere along the line the therapist would mention (or even "point out") that Patient I had some sort of a provisional theory that the purpose of the group was for people to talk, and he might be asked to discuss or comment upon this theory. In this way it might be indicated to him and to the other listening members that an institutionalized form of therapy following instructions contained in popular magazines was not necessarily what they were there for, nor were any gold stars going to be bestowed on people because they did some talking. This discouraging response from the therapist would, of course, be merely hinted initially, but if the hint were not taken it would be said in clearer and clearer terms. In effect, the therapist undermines as rapidly as prudence permits, the postulate that merely talking about something is going to rid them of their symptoms. The net effect of this would be to transform the Type I group into a Type II group, whose thesis is "What are we supposed to do here?"

The relevant characteristic of a Type I group is its predictability. This means that an experienced observer could, with a fair chance of accuracy, write the notes on next week's meeting before it occurred. Such stereotyped stagnation is not promising therapeutically.

THE TYPE II GROUP

"What are we supposed to do here?"

Supportive Therapy The "good father" response to this question is to tell the patients what to do and then allow them to receive encouragement and approval for doing it. In transactional language this is called "stroking." Again, with psychotics this may be very effective as a preliminary measure, but in the case of neurotics it may only be encouraging an unprogressive compliance.

In a more sophisticated way, the support might be directed toward strengthening specific defenses. The question may indicate a tendency to reaction formation by compliance, or in the scheme of Anna Freud,[8] it may be a preparation for projection, introjection, or reversal, with preliminary inhibition.

Group-Analytic Therapy The basic assumption (in Bion's sense) behind this question might be interpreted in various ways. It might signify the beginning of a fight-or-flight group in which the patients are fleeing from taking the initiative because that might threaten the survival of the group. Its dependency significance, however, might be the predominant one. If Patient II had asked, instead of "we," "What am I supposed to do here?" this might invoke the basic assumption of pairing in his relationship with the therapist, a measure for preserving the group so that (in Bion's words) "the members can sink themselves in the group without needing to develop." In Ezriel's system, the original question might be taken as a move toward the "required relationship," and might lead to the emergence of a "common problem" which was "shared" by several members. In Foulkes's approach, Patient II is signifying his willingness to suspend his individual desires in favor of the group authority in order that he can feel secure in the group.

Again, these interpretations might have the effect of getting the patient to examine his behavior in groups as a problem in adjustment, but do not show much promise of going beyond that if a strictly group-analytic program is followed.

Psychoanalytic Therapy It is possible from the patient's use of "we" rather than "I" that there was some sort of early alliance in his family with ambivalent compliance or rebellion against the parental authority. Passivity and dependency, as those words are used loosely nowadays, come immediately to the fore in his question. This query may contain anal implications, indicating an unwillingness to give up voluntarily (retention), or promising a pseudocompliant manifestation of obstinacy (gas), or a hostile compliance in which he lets loose beyond the expected limits (enema compliance). There may also be some phallic or oral fears evident in his request for instructions, so that he will be sure not to go beyond the limits which might bring on punishment or oral calamity. Some of the transference, resistance, and defense implications of these factors can be inferred as further information is forthcoming.

With this approach a reconstructive sector analysis might be possible insofar as Patient II would permit it. His use of the group in the service of his resistances would be interesting and instructive to observe, but it would be difficult to counteract effectively because of the manifold opportunities presented and the tendency of the other patients to co-operate unwittingly or enthusiastically.

Transactional Analysis   If the other members follow the lead of Patient II, this promises to be a Type II therapy group in which the patients will play a compliant game of "Psychiatry," meanwhile carrying on all sorts of other games on the outside behind the therapist's back. They may learn a lot from the therapist and be able to use what they learn insofar as they choose to. They may become very "good" patients inside the group, and particularly helpful with new patients, introducing them to the terminology and rules of the particular variety of "Psychiatry" played in that group. In the hands of some therapists, the members of Type II groups may become obligingly free in expressing hostility, sexual feelings, and "real feelings." The license and approval they get in the group, and their natural competitiveness, may encourage them to continue this behavior outside the group, sometimes with unfortunate consequences to their marriages, social lives, and daily labors. Ordinary people whom they meet in everyday life, and who are accustomed to more tact in the expression of emotional reactions, may find the less judicious members of this type of group disconcerting to cope with.

Type I groups composed of patients who are professional colleagues, especially psychologists ("It says in the journals we are supposed to express Real Feelings here"), and Type II groups where laymen are enjoined to be uninhibited and are stroked when they succeed, may both end up playing a variant of the game of "Psychiatry" known as "Greenhouse." Here feelings are exhibited as though they were rare tropical flowers. In cases where inhibitions are used to attract attention, the switch to expression may be beneficial, but it is not a good policy to break down the doors indiscriminately. In other cases the impulses that the inhibitions are designed to deal with may in the long run prove more powerful than the therapist expected — and he must always think of the long run because it is more important than the short run. The results of imprudent group license may not become apparent to him until the dénouement of some extra-mural operation (which the patient has neglected to mention in the group) is brought dramatically to the therapist's attention when it may be too late to do anything about it.

People who are already too free with their emotions, psycho-paths, and dishonest people will enjoy a Type II group more than a Type I group because they can exploit it better. By com-plying with the therapist in the group, after he has indicated what they are supposed to do, they earn additional freedom on the outside. Impulsive marriages, suicide attempts, and grandiose or spiteful investments of large, family-crippling sums of money may result. Quieter developments may also occur. One patient played an intelligent and insightful game of transactional "Psychiatry," and was very helpful to new patients and to old ones who could not understand their behavior clearly. He re-fused to be budged from this game over a long period despite the concerted efforts of the other members and the therapist. One day the therapist said in an everyday, nontherapeutic tone of voice: "By the way, how are you?" The patient said: "I think I'm getting arthritis." It then became clear that while he sat in the group semester after semester improving in all sorts of ways, some of them important, he was quietly ossifying his basic prob-lems in calcium.

The transactional analyst, in order to prevent such outcomes, will at the earliest appropriate moment ask Patient II to explain his question. This request may embarrass or confuse the patient. If he is not glib, he may blush, splutter, or stammer. It will soon become evident that he had not one theory, as in the case of Patient I, but two or three theories about the technique of group therapy. He wanted the therapist to express a preference in order to comply initially and later to undermine the situation. Once this project has been brought to light and headed off, the transactional analyst can tell Patient II and the others what they are actually supposed to do; namely, what the contract is and what technique he proposes to use in order to fulfill it.

A Type II group can be switched away from institutional compliance more easily than a Type I group, so that with Type II the therapist may very quickly be in a position to put his planned therapeutic program into effect. His chief problem at that point will be whether to lay down as part of the therapeutic contract that the patients will not make any major decisions without first discussing them with the group. This provision has the advantage that any patient who breaches it can be confronted with having broken his commitment. On the other hand, it offers a tempting challenge for an exercise of ingenuity which many patients cannot resist: how to breach it without being found out, or in such a way that the therapist's confrontation can be confounded. In principle it is desirable for the patients to make such a commitment. The chief error to be avoided is to let the patient conclude that the therapist has a Parental need to see that the agreement is kept. It must be made clear that it is an Adult decision of the patient and not a Parental injunction of the therapist which is at stake. This is a delicate distinction to make because of the eagerness with which patients of the type under discussion will seize an opportunity to feel themselves rejected. They want him to "care personally," but this is a luxury neither he nor they can afford. If they can "get to him" by breaking a commitment, they will be tempted to do so. If they cannot get to him, they may feel frustrated because he is not "more involved." Thus his concern for their welfare becomes a factor which at this stage must be handled with the utmost subtlety. In particular he must differentiate carefully between his attitude toward the patients' games, which is what they present initially in treatment, and his feelings for the real people behind those façades.

For example, if Patient II's secret project is suicide, he may want assurance that people would be shocked if he did it. If he thought the other members or the therapist would react with "Isn't it awful!" or "I told you so!" that might make it worthwhile. But if they indicate that they are not going to say either of those things, then they may be performing a life-saving function for that patient. But their objectivity may upset him until he perceives that it is a manifestation of something more profound than the perfunctory threnody he was willing to settle for.*

One suicidal patient of this type, who was continually wondering in a bewildered way what he was supposed to do long after the others had settled down to self-examination, turned the family savings over to a high-pressure stock broker he had been negotiating with. He announced this to the group after the fact, when it was too late to do anything about it. After a brief discussion, it was evident to him as well as to everyone else in the group that he was actually gambling with his life. He was not very clear as to the conditions of his financial investment, but if by chance it turned out well in spite of his unbusinesslike approach, then he would be relieved of his depression for a while; if, as seemed more likely, he lost his money, then he would have a "legitimate" excuse for another suicide attempt. His final declaration was, "Okay, then, I promise I won't commit suicide if I lose the money." This, of course, confirmed the group's diagnosis of the ulterior motive for the investment. It simultane-

---

* For a different approach in this connection, see Miller, E. R., and D. A. Shaskan, "Group Management of a Disgruntled, Suicidal Patient." *Int. J. Group Psychother.* 13:216–18, 1963.

ously implied that he would continue his quest for a "legitimate" excuse for suicide and was determined to outwit the others in this connection. All this was turned to good advantage by shifting the focus from his specific excuses for his suicide attempts to the basic motivations for this deadly game. The net of maneuver in which the patient was entangled and in which he sought to entangle those about him, including the members of the group, was cut away with Alexandrian directness, laying bare the act of suicide itself as the final knot which lay between himself and freedom. The strands of this knot could now be traced down to their anchorage in the archaic roots of his depression without distraction from extraneous convolutions.

One purpose of this anecdote is to emphasize that it was the members of the group who detected the two hidden implications in the patient's statement: the confession of intent and the intransigence of goal, which the patient was trying to hide from himself and from them. But, in spite of himself, he had absorbed so much insight, which he had previously denied having, that he could not help joining in the affectionate laughter with which this sophisticated group greeted his ambiguous renunciation.

Briefly, then, statements of the psychological form "What are we supposed to do here?" are invitations to the therapist to set up a game of "Psychiatry" so that the patients can compliantly elaborate their self-presentations under the rules he sets up. The members of such a group tend to specialize in tentative presentations and careful descriptions of feelings which occurred in the course of games played outside the group. Just as a Type I group is an ideal medium for supportive therapy, a Type II group offers many opportunities for a group-analytic therapist. Indeed, it was a question of similar form which led Bion to his insights into group psychology. While the patients are playing "Psychiatry" as a pastime in the group, they are engaged in games of a much more sinister nature on the outside, whose results they present, often with dramatic understatement, as disruptive operations to the proceedings. If the therapist breaks up an impending Type II group, or one which has been switched from Type I to Type II, by asking Patient II the reason for his question, the members may feel so discomfitted that they will be afraid to speak for a while. In that case, the group may become a Type III group.

THE TYPE III GROUP

"I hate to break this silence, it seems almost sacred."

Supportive Therapy   The supportive operation of this opening would perhaps be some reassurance that it was all right to talk, or the more precious form "Well, see, you did break it and it didn't hurt." The latter, however, might indicate to the patients that the therapist is more interested in his own embroidery than he is in them. Once more, with psychotic patients where mere talking might indicate some loosening of the psychosis, this might be a worthwhile intervention. But with neurotics it might give the impression that the therapist is overly sentimental and easily taken in; in which case, after getting what private gratifications they could from the group, at times complying with the therapist, at other times toying with him, they would leave. Then they would either go to someone more tough-minded, or else, confirmed in their position that life is made up of inanities, they would continue their neurotic behavior in ways perhaps more subtle and subdued but occasionally more baneful.

The more sophisticated approach would support and strengthen the specific defenses implied by the hesitation: gentle regression, inhibition by reaction formation, or possibly introjection of a certain kind of awesome parental figure.

Group-Analytic Therapy   This might be taken as a classical opening remark in a dependent group, on the basic assumption that there is an external object, namely the therapist, which will provide security for the immature organism. It might signify, in Ezriel's thinking, the relationship which the patient has to avoid in external reality but dares to undertake in the group. It might very easily lead to some discussion of a common problem such as the problem of starting conversations or of breaking silences; tending gradually into a discussion of social difficulties in general, with the patients "sharing" each other's experiences. With the realization that their difficulties were not unique, their social relationships might improve to some extent. Once more the clash between the individual and the group which Foulkes speaks of is demonstrated here in that this patient feels uneasy because he wants to say something when the group apparently wants to keep silent. In Bion's thinking, perhaps, this situation would result in the sickest member of the group, typically a paranoid, doing most of the talking and becoming a so-called sub-leader. There is also an underlying implication that the leader is possessed of magical powers. Since this is always present in the patients' minds at some level, the Type III opening helps to bring to the surface right at the start something that in any case would have to be dealt with sooner or later.

Actually, this implication of magic is one of the few "group phenomena" of which it can be said with some certainty that it is not an artifact introduced by the individual leader. The belief in the leader's magical powers actually does seem to be present, at least initially, in the mind of each member, and in that sense is shared by all the members and is part of the group mentality, the group assumptions, the group culture, or whatever term the investigator prefers to use in this connection. It can therefore be legitimately handled by demonstrating its universality, which may help the patients overcome the temptation to be unduly influenced by it, and induce them to approach the therapy in a more rational way.

Experience seems to show, however, that in spite of its universality, it is more effective to deal with this misconception on an individual basis, preferably at the time each patient signifies his readiness to go into the problems which it implies. Hence with a Type III opening, it may be said again that the group-analytic approach may be of some value, but it is not necessarily of maximal value. Although it may lead in various directions which are more or less productive, it is nevertheless only indirectly related to the patients' symptomatology. Especially in the initial phases, it is difficult to establish convincingly for them that their belief in the magical powers of the therapist and their religious attitude toward the group are directly related to their specific symptoms.

Psychoanalytic Therapy   This statement may be attacked at almost any psychodynamic level. As a resistance, it may be regarded as implying a certain amount of projection, as though to say: "It is not my fault I am not talking, it is the people around me who make me feel that it would be discourteous." As a defense, it implies a regression to a state of awe in which one is so absorbed or engulfed by the environment that one's own feelings become irrelevant. Transference implications are also visible, since the therapist seems to be put in the position of a holy man or a magician. Modally, the statement might indicate a conflict between expulsive and retentive tendencies. Zonally, there are hints of all three types of libidinal fixations. The awe itself may derive from the "oceanic" feelings of an early oral stage. There are anal echoes of shouting obscenities in church and all that underlies such impulses. The phallic element emerges in a possible primal scene suggestion.

For certain neurotic patients of a classical type, such considerations might be of immediate therapeutic value, and the openings for psychoanalytic work in the group might be sufficient for a partial resolution of some underlying conflicts. But again the lack of opportunity for sustained free association and working through presents difficulties.

Transactional Analysis   This is an opening statement which could lead into a Type III therapy group process, with the favored game of "Gee You're Wonderful, Professor" ("But You'll Never Budge Me"). Such a group offers an ideal medium for transference cures, and there is no doubt that as long as the patients keep attending they will feel better and have fewer bad periods; many of their symptoms will remain latent as long as the external stress does not rise above a certain level. It is here that Bion's observations and the transactional aspects most closely approximate each other. This group is rather openly working on a basic assumption which, as already noted, reads: "An external object exists which will provide security for the immature organism." In Bion's thinking, this kind of group is based on something like a religious system in which independent thought is stifled, heresy is righteously hunted, the leader is criticized because he is not a magician who can be worshipped, and a rational approach on his part is rejected.

It is true that if the therapist is not transactionally sophisticated the group may tend in the directions Bion mentions, but very few therapists, even unsophisticated ones, would allow it to progress to the actual state he describes. Even the most skillful worker, however, will eventually have to face an assumption which is an irreducible minimum, and which can be expressed in transactional terms by the statement that the therapist is a magician who has the patients' cure locked away in his desk drawer; they would not be surprised to learn that he could have cured them the very first week, but he withholds the cure for reasons which are not too clear but are based partly at least on the fact that he is either mean, punitive, or stingy. Nevertheless, there is a lot of good in him, and it seems likely to each member that if he complies with the therapist's desires, finds out as much as he can about what the therapist wants and conducts himself accordingly in the group, the therapist will eventually bring out the long awaited cure and present it to the patient.

In transactional language, this is called "Waiting for Santa Claus." The attendance in such a group is likely to be spotty because the proceedings are largely irrelevant, being mostly acts of compliance. The tendency initially is for the members to come for a few weeks, but when they judge that the cure will not be forthcoming in the near future, attendance begins to drop off. One or two of the more persevering members continue to come regularly. Others begin to have occasional absences which become more and more frequent. Still others withdraw for periods of several weeks and then revisit the group for a week or two to observe the therapist and see if he is any closer to unlocking the magic desk drawer. If the bestowal of the cure still does not appear to be imminent, they will again absent themselves for some weeks, and return hopefully once more.

These cycles go on throughout the year, resulting in a gross attendance of perhaps 60 to 70 per cent, made up of a sort of random selection of patients at each meeting, except for the one or two who believe that faithful attendance is one of the magical conditions they must fulfill; these will get to the sessions no matter what external difficulties they have to overcome. Such patients appear week after week, sometimes year after year, much to the gratification of the naïve therapist. Then suddenly they withdraw and are never heard from again, leaving the therapist the option of either feeling slightly bitter about their ingratitude, or more constructively, wondering how he let himself be taken in. The patients with cyclical attendance are less indulgent toward the therapist and are likely to drift sooner than the others if he does not produce what they are waiting for.

This kind of group is a trap for the narcissistic Child-like therapist who plays "Patsy" for the patients in the game of "Gee You're Wonderful, Professor," and also for the thoughtful benevolent Parent therapist who responds with "I'm Only Trying To Help You." The Child therapist they seduce by continually showing amazement at his skill, insight, perceptiveness, forcefulness, powers of observation, intelligence, beauty, and virtue; the Parental therapist is beguiled by their sustained reports of improvement until he begins to believe that he really is helping them. They will oblige him either way, by either admiration or improvement, in order to soften him up so as to get their cures more quickly; but when they become convinced eventually that he is not going to do his part, they will take revenge — and in a sense they are justified.

They will even comply with his specific approach: allow themselves to be "supported," produce and share "common group problems," demonstrate transference reactions and sibling rivalry, or analyse transactions with academic gusto. These operations may have a very real basis, but the therapist is apt to interpret them at a more cogent level than is justified; actually, they are semi-ritualistic acts of compliance arising from a very archaic level of the personality. The patients readily manifest pseudo-Adult functioning, while their real ego state is a child-like one.

The remedy, therefore, is as quickly as possible to get things to an Adult level by confronting the patients with rational, transactional interpretations, and by carefully exposing the apotropaic (magical) elements in their underlying fantasies and setting them aside for handling later when the group is well advanced. It is of little use to try to deal with these elements without first establishing a firm, stable, well-defined Adult ego state. Considerable preparatory work is usually necessary before the patients will have an adequately functioning instrument available for becoming really objective about their initial attitudes. The effectiveness of this approach is demonstrated by the fact that as soon as it is instituted the attendance pattern begins to change. In one case [9] a Type III group which had had the typical attendance pattern for about a year or so, with a gross attendance of about 70 per cent, was transformed under supervision into a productive transactional analysis group with an attendance of about 95 per cent during the ensuing year.

Transactionally, then, the proceedings of a Type III group tend to resemble superficially those of a Type II group, centering around self-presentations and descriptions of feelings. In Type III, however, the self-presentations are less tentative and inhibited, and the descriptions are less careful, at times verging on direct expressions of emotion rather than being mere editorial comment. A more decisive difference is that the members of a Type II group, including the therapist, confine themselves largely to playing a rather bland game of "Psychiatry" which is little more than a pastime, while a Type III group is enlivened by the vigorous patient game of "Gee You're Wonderful, Professor," to which the therapist may respond with either "I Knew It All Along" or "I'm Only Trying To Help You." In the latter case the patients follow through with "Hah! See If You Can Help Me." The active exhibition of this game gives the Type III group a common feature with a Type IV group, in which games are played with more abandon.

THE TYPE IV GROUP

"I'm sorry I was late."

Supportive Therapy   Supportive therapy for this opening is an error for any but the most experienced therapists. If the patient is merely expressing his regrets as a matter of courtesy — for example, if he is a lawyer who could not get away from the courthouse — then he will need no forgiveness. In most cases, however, the therapist who replies supportively "That's all right!" will be seriously handicapped in his further dealings with the patient. The patient is setting up a game of "Schlemiel" (disrupting the proceedings and then asking for forgiveness) and as soon as the therapist offers the desired forgiveness he has played into the patient's hands. It will be difficult for the patient to attain confidence in a therapist whom he can manipulate with his very first move. Furthermore, the patient has now transacted the most significant business he has planned for that group meeting, and anything else he does during the rest of the session is largely irrelevant, unless the therapist is playing "Kick Me" and offers him an unexpected opportunity which he cannot resist.

A very experienced therapist, however, may offer forgiveness with full awareness that the patient will want to interpret this as falling for his game. He will say "That's all right!" in such an ambiguous way as to sow the first seed of doubt in the patient's mind as to whether the therapist is completely gullible. The therapist's courtesy is irreproachable, but the patient may nevertheless sense from this, his very first transaction in the group, that this new person who confronts him offers more of a challenge than most of the other people he is accustomed to dealing with.

Group-Analytic Therapy   This is evidently part of a fight-or-flight operation, since the patient is avoiding work by coming late. He is also avoiding all the kinds of relationships described by Ezriel, including the "required" one. His lateness might become a "common problem" for the group, if the therapist allowed or encouraged that to happen. At a more sophisticated level, his apologetic attitude might become the "common problem." From Foulkes's point of view, it might be said that the patient has imposed his individual needs on the group authority by taking it upon himself to be late.

Psychoanalytic Therapy   Being late is one of the most overt forms of resistance, since it simply avoids the analytic situation. The apology in such cases, especially if the patient simpers, is prognostic of the patient's relationship to the therapist. The aggression is passive anal, but more active aggression may soon make itself felt. Beneath this is an oral disappointment and a severing of unstable primal object relations. The passive withdrawal or sulkiness masks oral as well as anal sadism which was early inhibited. A breathless arrival may possibly turn out to indicate some sexual significance to hurrying, and perhaps implies premature ejaculation. The quest for forgiveness, which is often overlooked in discussions of this kind of resistance, is fundamentally a derivative of oral sadism, perhaps a reaction formation, but is more accessibly referred to the anal regression. The relationship between constipation, laxatives, and enemas in the patient's developmental history may sometimes help to clarify some of the details of his difficulties with people, such as doing things at the last minute. This investigation of toilet attitudes cannot always be carried on satisfactorily in the group. It may be even more difficult for the underlying oral problems to be elucidated and worked through by free association under such conditions.

Transactional Analysis Actually, this is the best opening to work with, since the patient who comes late is wasting no time in setting up his games; and the therapist, if he is alert, may move ahead very quickly in this group, eliminating the pastime phase in a matter of minutes and starting almost immediately with game analysis. The patient who is sorry he is late, particularly if he is a breathless arrival, will undoubtedly apologize again for something sooner or later, and perhaps may offer multiple apologies every time he speaks: apologetic gestures, simpering, qualifications of what he says, and ambiguous placating offers such as "Correct me if I'm wrong" or "I don't mean to interrupt, but . . ." He will undoubtedly succeed in eliciting magnanimousness from some of the other patients, so that right from the beginning the transactional analyst can make use of the proper function of the group, which is to demonstrate the complex involvements which people are likely to get into if they are not fully aware of what is happening to them. In this case, he has something to say not only to the agent who apologizes, but also to the respondents who are seduced into false magnanimity.

There are several possible approaches to Patient IV. One is to wait until he has apologized repeatedly, point out that he is apologizing, and later demonstrate that almost every time he talks he is apologizing in several different ways that he may not even be aware of, especially when he is engaged in self-presentation. Alternatively, the lateness itself can be made the focus of attention; it has usually been a recurrent problem for him, and such a discussion can bring out many interesting and important factors in his background which are of more than academic or archaeological interest since they are related to something that has already taken place in the group. Such an immediate practical incursion into the patient's problems may be a cogent example for the other members.

The direct transactional approach would be to ask Patient IV, "What response do you expect when you say that?" The irrationality of his breathless arrival, which gets him there at best only a few seconds earlier, and its function as a propitiatory operation, may be broached if it is thought that he can maintain his Adult objectivity in the face of such a confrontation. If the patient defends it as a gesture of courtesy, the enterprising but judicious therapist would consider mentioning that an even more acceptable courtesy would be to arrive on time. The patient will either seize the opportunity to be hurt or humiliated by this dry retort, or will try to defend himself further. If he continues to defend himself, the therapist has made a mistake in timing, and is wasting his efforts. But if the procedure is successful, and the patient has no reply, he has already passed beyond the initial phase of his therapy. The opening moves of his game have been completed (to his disadvantage), and the therapist can now proceed to other matters while waiting minutes, hours, or weeks to observe how the patient goes about retaliating.

It should be noted that the therapist's position, if he has performed properly, is impeccable. All he has done is decline to play into the patient's hands, while carrying out his stated duty of objective appraisal. He is not playing a game with the patient, he is just more or less firmly refusing to play the patient's game, which is a variant of "Schlemiel." If the patient chooses to be humiliated rather than edified at this point, that is his own decision, and the therapist is prepared to deal with the consequences. The chief errors to be avoided are imprudence in moving too quickly with a patient who cannot tolerate it, prissiness or self-righteousness because the therapist is being more objective than the patient, or pleasure from regarding the situation as a personal victory. If everybody, including the therapist and Patient IV, ends up relaxed, interested, curious, and perhaps a little amused, then the situation has no doubt been handled properly. If the interest and curiosity are maintained until the next meeting, with everybody wondering whether Patient IV will arrive then early, on time, or late again, a good start has been made. If he stays away, then the therapist will have to review the situation in his mind and try to find where his judgment failed. An overly cautious therapist, however, runs as many risks as an overly cautious surgeon. If he waits too long, occasionally something may burst.

During the proceedings described above, the skillful therapist will leave plenty of opportunities for other patients to join pertinently in the discussion, so that when Patient IV has had enough for one day, so to speak, and the therapist is ready to move on, he will have workable indications as to where to move next.

SUMMARY OF GROUP TYPES

Type I The proceedings in a Type I group consist of reports and discussions of events. These can continue indefinitely as pastimes. With schizophrenics who play such pastimes as "Isn't It Awful?" and "Why Do They Do This To Me," such a group offers many opportunities for supportive therapy.

Type II The Type II group is apt to develop into a game of "Psychiatry" in which the patients superficially comply with the therapist's wishes but from time to time have aggressive, re-bellious, or provocative episodes. Thus they present themselves as "good children" and may from time to time describe their feelings, especially in relation to external events, but these presentations and descriptions may prove unreliable. The proceedings offer good material for group-analytic therapy.

Type III The Type III group is likely to be filled with declarations and expressions of feeling. The patients play "Gee You're Wonderful," and the therapist typically replies with "I'm Only Trying To Help You." This group is more actively engaged in internal games than the other two. Because of the frequency of archaic reactions, there are many opportunities for psychodynamic interpretations.

Type IV The Type IV group starts off with expressions of feeling and can be kept on that level by an alert therapist. These expressions, however, constitute moves in the multiform games which arise in this type of group, and the authenticity of the feelings is always open to question in the therapist's mind. These questions form the basis for appropriately timed interventions.

"REAL" VERSUS "AUTHENTIC" FEELINGS

In all these groups the therapist intuitively searches for authenticity. Most therapists can distinguish between authentic tears and those which are shed for dramatic purposes, although skillful actors and actresses may create difficulties of interpretation even with such gross expressions of emotion. With more subtle manifestations, almost all therapists are likely to misjudge occasionally, sometimes in one direction, sometimes in the other, depending upon whether they are overly critical, or overly indulgent, or naïve.

Guilt feelings are almost always lacking in authenticity, and represent social conditioning which the patient as an autonomous person would be unwilling to accept. Such feelings may be very "real," but the distinction to be made here is that between "real" feelings and "authentic" feelings. Guilt about his own misdeeds is rarely authentic, because the patient may continue the misdeeds and feel "really" guilty each time. This tendency is most dramatically illustrated in clinical practice in the self-castigation of the alcoholic hangover, which does not stop the patient from drinking the next time. Authentic guilt feelings about his own behavior will lead the patient to make an Adult decision rather than a compliant Child's resolution, in order to avoid the unpleasant guilt feelings. If he repeats the offence and again has the guilt feelings, it may be surmised that the guilt feelings give him some perverse sexual satisfaction. The only clearly authentic guilt is guilt not for oneself but for others: the guilt of belonging to a race which is capable of some of the things other people are doing.

TERMINATING THE FIRST MEETING

The correct termination for a meeting of a supportive therapy group is the neutral "Let's see what you have to say next time." For all other groups, the correct termination, which makes the therapist's position clearer, is "Let's see what happens next time."

LATER PHASES

As an illustration of what may occur at a later phase of therapy, the following typical transaction may be considered:

Patient IV: "I feel guilty when I play the piano."

Patient III: "I feel guilty too, when I drink."

Supportive Therapy   The supportive maneuver here would be to discuss playing the piano as a harmless occupation and to try to induce Patient IV to forgive herself so that she can get the enjoyment and benefits of her music. Even in a supportive group the therapist would probably ask her to elucidate further and then offer encouragement or absolution at appropriate points. The case of Patient III is more difficult since it is not considered good form for a therapist to give absolution or encouragement for troublesome drinking. The tendency here would be to try to get the patient away from drinking and encourage other activities, lending approval when the patient succeeds in diverting her interest.

Group-Analytic Therapy On the surface this appears to be a working group, although some might consider it a dependency group in that the patients are asking for forgiveness. There is also a tendency to pairing between the two patients. This might threaten to become intimate and hence be apprehended as possibly calamitous in Ezriel's system. Certainly they are sharing a common problem and are willing to submit their individual idiosyncracies to the judgment of the group.

Psychoanalytic Therapy There are two common approaches to Patient IV. One deals with her confessions of guilt, which might be related to self-destructive tendencies. The other interjects the sexual significance of piano playing. The second is not likely to be especially meaningful to her in her present situation. Patient III invites inquiry into certain tendencies common in "alcoholics": oral self-indulgence followed by guilt; underlying depression which leads to self-indulgence; and self-destructive or rebellious tendencies.

Transactional Analysis The transactional question is why Patient IV interjects this confession. Patient III, however, is a more obvious candidate for confrontation since she is obviously playing a game of "Me Too" and is very likely the one the other patients feel most protective toward and least competitive with. Analysis of that game at this particular time might well lead naturally into a discussion of its function as making herself appear harmless in order to receive the protection of the group, and this might soon bring up the question of what she does to them after they have played into her hands.

This short example, together with the others given above, should suffice to illustrate, at least, how these four commonly used approaches might be applied in various typical situations.* Since the supportive, group-analytic, and psychoanalytic therapies each have their own literature, further information about them can be obtained from the sources mentioned in Chapter 9. The transactional approach will be discussed in detail later in this book.

COMPARISON OF METHODS

The well-trained group therapist will be familiar with all four of the common approaches and may vary his technique according to circumstances, but he will generally end up strongly favoring one or the other. Ideally, his preference will be based on carefully evaluated personal experience after conscientiously using each method for a period of two or three years, supplemented by listening to tapes taken by other therapists, attending seminars, sitting in as observer with friendly or even with hostile colleagues, and reading the literature. The writer's position, after following such a curriculum, is as follows:

Supportive Therapy Supportive therapy can easily become institutionalized. This encourages the therapist to conceal his own idiosyncracies behind a Parental attitude which is usually well received both by his patients and by his colleagues at staff conferences. It is of only limited value to the patients, since as soon as the support is removed they may easily fall apart again. Thus the results tend to be minimal rather than maximal for the therapist's learning and development and for the patients' stability.

A patient who complained of depression and fear of social

---

* These illustrations are based on the writer's personal observations. Others may interpret them differently if they have sufficient clinical material relating to the specific examples chosen.

activities, and who had also been frigid during twenty years of marriage but felt too undeserving even to complain about that, received individual "supportive therapy" (what she later called her "weekly transfusion") for a period of two years, during which her spirits improved and she ventured out occasionally. She terminated this treatment when she moved to another city, and much to her consternation, within two months she was back where she had started. She went to another therapist who introduced her into a treatment group. For several weeks she strove to reconstitute the "supportive" situation by trying to set up a game of mutual "marshmallow throwing." The group reacted in a tough way to her honeyed invitations for support, until one day she said, "You know, for the first time I feel I can really get better — if I keep coming here." After a long struggle, she began to improve "from below." She became as tough as the others, and as skeptical as they were of new patients who naïvely tried to use "supportive" operations to ingratiate themselves with the group and to conceal their archaic fears and rages.

Group-Analytic Therapy Group-analytic therapy assists the patient in "adjusting" to his social environment, and this may have an important influence on his destiny. Such an adjustment, however, is often accomplished at the expense of his own autonomous development; but even that may be an advantage in cases where the autonomous development is going in a pathological direction. In its pure form, this type of therapy makes the patient aware of some of his fears and unhealthy compliances, but does little to cure him of his symptoms or to resolve underlying conflicts. Experience shows that group-analytic therapy, like supportive therapy, can be carried on for years with the same patients without much self-sustaining change in their personalities. Some group-analytic therapists specifically repudiate any attempt "to uncover deep-seated conflicts and problems." [10]

People who make a hobby or profession of being patients, so

as to "belong" to a clinic or to ensure continued disability payments, find this type of treatment securely innocuous. It gives them a "feeling of belonging" to "the group." As long as the therapist talks about "the group," and not about them personally they may continue to come for years. One patient was "fired" from such a group by a new therapist when the patient stubbornly objected to the introduction of a more vigorous approach. Whereupon another patient remarked, "Isn't it a shame to do that to him after all he's done for the clinic for so many years."

Psychoanalytic Therapy   Some competent experienced therapists describe convincing results with psychoanalytic group therapy,[3] or "psychoanalysis in groups."[4] Others are not so convincing,[11] or the results seem to be based on something other than "psychoanalysis."[12] But there is not sufficient evidence in the literature to justify equating any kind of group therapy with orthodox individual psychoanalysis in which the patient is seen four to six times per week for periods of two to six years or more.[13] Some of the technical reasons which discourage such a comparison have been discussed previously. Such an equation would require a much more rigorous overhauling of psychoanalytic theory than has yet been attempted, and is only tenable if psychoanalysis is defined much more loosely than the orthodox schools presently encourage. Group therapy, however, has been used by orthodox analysts, both on its own merits,[14] and as an adjunct to individual psychoanalytic therapy in overcoming special types of resistance in specified areas.[15]

The few senior analysts who have become interested in group therapy make only modest assessments of what they can accomplish in this way. Such conscientious reports are helpful in overcoming the not unjustifiable skepticism which many responsible clinicians feel toward this form of treatment. Part of the skepticism is due to the fact that "psychoanalytic group therapy" is attractive to many workers with incomplete psychoanalytic training, ranging from serious students to dilettantes. In any case, it can be fairly said that the application of psychoanalytic principles to group therapy is in some measure a makeshift procedure, since it is based on a technique designed for individual treatment.

Transactional Analysis Transactional analysis is an approach derived directly from the treatment group, with indigenous concepts and indigenous techniques. It is designed to produce quicker and more stable results for a greater variety of patients. It is easier to learn than psychoanalysis, given the same conscientious commitment. The beginner can start to apply its principles after only a few weeks of training, although as in the case of any other technique, it may take some years to attain expertness, and that can hardly be done without a period of competent supervision.

Comparison between various forms of psychotherapy is always open to serious criticisms. One principle which should not be neglected, however, is that only people who have an intimate acquaintance with a technical instrument are competent to pass judgment upon it. A transactional analyst who had not had formal education in psychoanalysis would not consider himself competent to judge the latter, and psychoanalysts should be expected to show the same courtesy toward transactional analysis. Among the many judges of the effectiveness of various types of group treatment are the patients themselves. Those who have been subjected to more than one type of approach have no hesitation in expressing their confidence in transactional analysis. Many of them prefer it, and if they have to move, are reluctant to continue group treatment where transactional analysis will not be available. Using a more objective criterion, it has already been noted that attendance records in transactional groups, as compared with other types of treatment groups, are quite encouraging.

There is no doubt that a knowledge of psychodynamics and group dynamics is necessary in order to carry on effective group

treatment. They form the essential background, but the therapeutic operations themselves can deal more directly with the
indigenous material of the group proceedings, which take the
form of transactions. There is a vast literature on psychodynamics, but an approach to group dynamics which is of practical
use to a group therapist is difficult to come by; and by the end
of the first meeting, the therapist may already be confronted
with problems which require some knowledge of that subject.
The next chapter, therefore, will be devoted to the dynamics
of psychotherapy groups.

REFERENCES

1. Thomas, G. W. "Group Psychotherapy: A Review of the Recent
   Literature." *Psychosom. Med.* 5:166–80, 1943.
2. Foulkes, S. H. *Therapeutic Group Analysis.* International Universities Press, New York, 1964.
3. Mullan, H., and M. Rosenbaum. *Group Psychotherapy.* (Chap.
   1, ref. 1.)
4. Wolf, A., and E. K. Schwartz. *Psychoanalysis in Groups.* (Chap.
   1, ref. 2.)
5. Berne, E. *Transactional Analysis in Psychotherapy.* Grove Press,
   New York, 1961.
6. Bion, W. R. *Experiences in Groups.* Basic Books, New York, 1961.
7. Ezriel, H. "A Psycho-Analytic Approach to Group Treatment."
   Brit. J. Med. Psychol. 23:59–74, 1950. "Some Principles of
   a Psycho-Analytic Method of Group Treatment." *Proc. First
   World Cong. Psychiatry*, Paris, 1950, 5:239–48, 1952.
8. Freud, A. *The Ego and the Mechanisms of Defence.* Hogarth
   Press, London, 1948.
9. Berne, E. *The Structure and Dynamics of Organizations and
   Groups.* (Chap. 2, ref. 4), pp. 191–5, "An Ailing Psychotherapy Group."
10. Johnson, J. A. *Group Therapy.* (Chap. 2, ref. 2.)
11. Kadis, A. L., J. D. Krasner, C. Winick, and S. H. Foulkes. *A
    Practicum of Group Psychotherapy.* Harper & Row, New York
    and London, 1963.

12. Slavson, S. R. *Analytic Group Psychotherapy*. Columbia University Press, New York, 1950.
13. Berne, E. " 'Psychoanalytic' versus 'Dynamic' Group Therapy." *Int. J. Group Psychother.* 10:98–103, 1960.
14. Ackerman, N. *The Psychodynamics of Family Life*. Basic Books, New York, 1958.
15. Jackson, J., and M. Grotjahn. "The Treatment of Oral Defenses by Combined Individual and Group Psychotherapy." *Int. J. Group Psychother.* 8:373–82, 1958.

6

Group Dynamics

A sound knowledge of group dynamics is as important to a group therapist as a knowledge of physiology is to a physician. The two classical concepts that are currently stressed in this area, provocative though they are, are not sufficient equipment for a scientific therapist: the principle of identification with the leader, first outlined by Freud [1]; and its corollary, the therapy group regarded in the transference sense as a kind of "family." The identification concept, even in its competent and detailed elaboration by Scheidlinger,[2] does not serve to explain adequately many aspects of the relationship between the therapist and his patients; in fact, since one desirable effect of therapy is to release the patient from the bonds of such an identification when it exists, it is also necessary to understand what happens in a group when the members are not identifying with the leader. As to the concept of the group as a "family," this is often applied in a naïve and uncritical way, which offers only a rudimentary approximation to the clarification of the actual clinical occurrences.

With this conventional equipment alone, the therapist will be confronted repeatedly with situations for which he is unarmed and theoretically unprepared. It is therefore necessary for him to acquire a more comprehensive, consistent, and pragmatic approach to group dynamics if he wishes to deal effectively with all the vicissitudes that will arise in his daily work. Such an approach, which has proven its practical value, is offered below. The terminology is taken from the writer's book *The Structure and Dynamics of Organizations and Groups*,[3] and what is offered here is a summary applied specifically to small therapy groups of not more than ten members.

In some institutions, therapists are confronted with the necessity of dealing with larger groups running from ten to two hundred members. At present there is no theory competent to determine the rational handling of such congeries, since in effect the members become divided into two classes, performers and audience. In order to approach such situations with any degree of precision, it would be necessary to have a reasonably rigorous theory of audiences, and that is not yet available. Hence the conduct of such larger groups is mostly an empirical art and will remain so pending further theoretical developments. In the meantime, as a stopgap, some of the principles given below can be profitably extrapolated to larger groups, albeit with some loss of confidence.

In order that the analysis of group situations in the following scheme be practical and realistic, it is necessary that for each aspect an appropriate diagram be drawn giving the actual details as found in the situation being studied.

THE SEATING DIAGRAM

Every presentation or discussion of a problem in group therapy or group dynamics should be accompanied by a seating diagram such as that shown in Figure 1. A simple gauge of its value is the number of times the members of the audience will glance at such a diagram during the course of the discussion if it is drawn

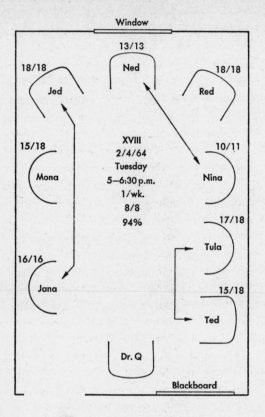

Window

13/13
Ned

18/18
Jed

18/18
Red

XVIII
2/4/64
Tuesday
5–6:30 p.m.
1/wk.
8/8
94%

15/18
Mona

10/11
Nina

17/18
Tula

16/16
Jana

15/18
Ted

Dr. Q

Blackboard

Fig. 1. A seating diagram. A diagram like this is drawn on the black-board whenever a treatment group is discussed

on the blackboard — and the discussant should make sure beforehand that a blackboard is available. Nothing leads to straying thoughts and unproductive comments as much as trying to keep track of John, Jane, Tom, Mary, Dick, Debbie, Harry, and Holly (or Mr. A, Mr. B, Mrs. C, Mr. D, etc.) without such a visual aid. A long pointer should be used, particularly if a tape-recording is being presented, and the presenter should point to the speaker (including himself) *every* time the speaker changes. A seating diagram answers automatically dozens of questions which would otherwise take up valuable time if they had to be answered orally. It also eliminates questions arising from sheer confusion in trying to keep track of who is who without visual aid. A common example is trying to remember who the spouses are in a marital group. This can be indicated definitively by simple arrows on a seating diagram, with no strain on anyone's memory or attention.

The central feature of the diagram, the seating arrangement itself, answers many questions of group-dynamic or clinical interest: the relative positions of men and women, and of spouses (if any); it tells who sits near the therapist or near the door, and who far away from either or both, and who sits opposite in the therapist's direct line of vision; who likes an isolated seat; and, if a table is used, who prefers to sit away from it. Many other examples will occur in special situations from time to time. Various informative items can be appended next to each seat: age, diagnosis, length of time in the group, or whatever else may be pertinent.

The information in the center of the diagram is equally useful. It shows the serial number of the group meeting in Roman numerals, the date, the day of the week, the hour and length of the meeting, the number of meetings per week, and the number of members present compared to the total membership (as a fraction). The percentage refers to the total aggregate attendance over the life of the group compared to the total possible attendance during that period. This shows how attractive the group is to the members and, in effect, measures the group cohesion. If it is over 90 per cent the attraction (cohesion) of the group is superior, and the audience should pay close attention to the presentation to find out how the therapist succeeded in maintaining such a high degree of cohesion; if it is under 70 per cent, there is something wrong and the therapist should not rest content until he finds out where he is in error. All these numbers and figures together constitute the schedule of the group, which should be included with every seating diagram.

The significance of most of the items in the seating diagram and schedule, at least as they apply to treatment groups, has been considered in previous chapters, and will not be further discussed.

THE GROUP AUTHORITY

The Authority Principle   The authority principle in its simplest form is as follows: each member of an organizational hierarchy feels constrained to comply with the wishes of those above him. This compliance in practice takes the form of playing the organizational game. At the Adult level the therapist attempts to meet the formally stated terms of his therapeutic contract in its administrative and professional aspects. At another level, however, he is careful to preserve certain unstated but recognized conditions. Experience has shown, for example, that in a public agency which plays "I'm Only Trying To Help You" the worker is expected to discharge a small proportion of his patients as improved, but if he goes beyond the permissible minimum he will be challenged, and sometimes fired. This phenomenon is familiar in industry, where in certain situations workers who exceed their quotas are looked upon with disfavor; there the restriction is overtly stated, however, and may even be part of the written contract, while in social agencies its covert influence may be indignantly repudiated. It is evident, however, that a worker in such an organization who is too efficient threatens to disturb the administrative and budgetary plans of the agency, and must be slowed down on some pretext or other. Usually the brakes are applied at the level of the staff conference, where the zealous worker may be told that he is discharging patients or clients too quickly because they have "only intellectual insight" or because "their basic problems are still unsolved" — even when the stated purpose of the agency may only be to find jobs for its clients, which has nothing to do with insight or "basic problems."

More commonly, there may be a strong tendency to stick to conservative methods of treatment in order to avoid unusual occurrences that would require special reports, since these are equally upsetting, although in a different way, to superiors. None of these restrictions, perhaps, would be explicit, but they would have some implicit influence on the therapist's behavior, particularly in times of stress during the course of the therapy.

In effect, the therapist imputes to his superiors a set of unstated expectations and restrictions which he feels obliged to adhere to. He might not be conscious of these most of the time, but under certain emergency situations they might come vividly to mind. If for example a patient in such an agency should climb up on the window sill several stories above the street and threaten suicide, the therapist would become acutely aware of some of the possible consequences if the patient were to jump: the report to his superiors, the report of the superiors to the agency head, the agency head's report to state or national headquarters, and so on. It might even occur to him that the incident could become a political issue reaching into the highest echelons of government under pressure from influences he is familiar with in his daily work: taxpayers' associations and veterans' organizations, for example. If he rebels frequently against these stated or unstated constraints, he may be labeled a "psychopath," "paranoid," or "troublemaker" — the last, perhaps, justifiably.

In drawing an authority diagram, such as those shown in Figures 2A and 2B, the chain should be taken right up to the highest echelon. In a state agency, that would be the governor. If the agency receives federal funds, the chain ends with the President. This may seem like carrying matters to an extreme, but it is not as pedantic as it looks at first sight. Most patients and clients in government-supported agencies know that they have the privilege of writing letters of complaint to the highest headquarters, and some of them do. The experienced therapist is well aware of this possibility, and naturally prefers to avoid it. Thus, whether he likes it or not, or whether he faces the fact squarely or not, every therapist in a public agency is potentially limited to some degree by ill-defined restrictions based on organizational factors. Since these restrictions do not apply to therapists in private practice to any appreciable extent, there is a qualitative distinction between group therapy in a public agency and that in private practice which every organizational therapist had better face rather than attempt to ignore.

In order to understand these influences as thoroughly as possible, it is necessary to investigate four different aspects of the organizational authority: the personal, the organizational, the historical, and the cultural.

The Personal Authority The therapist's feeling of freedom and his willingness to take risks depend to some extent on the personalities of his superiors. An administrator with little interest in psychodynamics might take an intransigent view of an untoward incident, and his staff might feel apprehensive about any departure from the most conservative, or even stereotyped, forms of group therapy. A supervisor with a more sympathetic attitude toward therapeutic problems might encourage his staff in new ventures and make them feel that he would stand behind any sincere attempt to improve their proficiency. Hence the therapist's estimate of his personal standing in the hierarchy and his assessment of the expectations of his superiors are strong influences in determining the boldness and freedom of his therapeutic approach. In both cases he should recognize that his superiors are vulnerable to the press and to the budgetary authorities, but his approach to his patients will be different if he is restricted by fear of the administration than if he is motivated by consideration for it.

These influences are set up and discussed in the personal aspect of the authority diagram, which answers the question "Whom do you have to deal with?" In this connection, the authority principle may be stated in its more extended form as follows: each individual in an organizational hierarchy imputes a special set of expectations to each person above him, and these imputations form parameters on all of the therapist's transactions with his clients and patients. The stress imposed by these influences is directly proportional to the intensity of the immediate transactional situation. The more the therapist is aware of this principle, the more ready he is to deal with it when it becomes of practical importance. Not all therapists will be equally affected by these considerations, however, and some may disregard the personal element.

The Organization Chart At the extremes, there are two types of therapists in the organizational sense, the "political" and the "procedural." The political therapist will give strong weight to the personalities of those above him insofar as they impinge on his professional activities. The procedural therapist will do what he thinks is right and justify himself according to the rules without regard to the personalities of his superiors. Each therapist should try to decide on a basis of past behavior to which side he leans. The political therapist should familiarize himself with the personal aspect of the group authority, while the procedural therapist should pay special attention to the formal

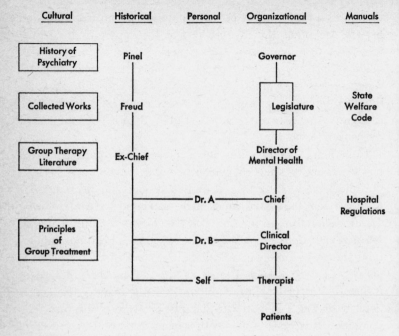

Cultural	Historical	Personal	Organizational	Manuals
History of Psychiatry	Pinel		Governor	
Collected Works	Freud		Legislature	State Welfare Code
Group Therapy Literature	Ex-Chief		Director of Mental Health	
		Dr. A——Chief		Hospital Regulations
Principles of Group Treatment		Dr. B——Clinical Director		
		Self——Therapist		
			Patients	

Fig. 2A. A formal authority diagram of a treatment group

organization chart in order to have a clear idea of his "official" position in the hierarchy and his organizational relationships with the other members. Then if acute difficulties arise in the course of therapy, each will be prepared beforehand to answer for the consequences in one way or the other. This will diminish his "organizational anxiety" and enable him to deal better with the matter at hand.

The Historical Aspect Precedent, of course, is always important when stress arises in social situations. A therapist's knowledge of his predecessors may serve as a useful guide for his own behavior; on the other hand, it indicates what kinds of difficulties he may run into if he wishes to introduce a technical innovation.

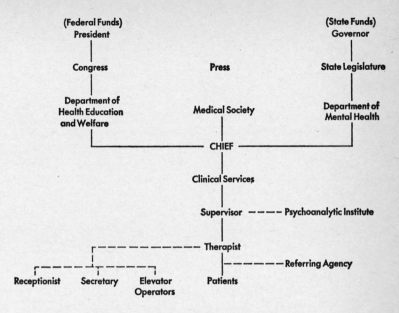

Fig. 2B. An informal authority diagram

The staff of a clinic founded by a psychodramatist may take a different view of an attempt to introduce gestalt therapy than the staff of one founded by an orthodox analyst. A traditionally experimental clinic will take a different view of LSD than a traditionally conservative one will take.

The Cultural Aspect The written word is the first appeal of the procedural therapist and the backstop for the political therapist. The cultural aspect of the authority diagram lists the canonical works that guide the activities of the organization. Professionally, these may be the works of Sigmund Freud; or perhaps those of one of his dissidents or opponents. Administratively, they may include the welfare code of the state, where the aims of the organization may be explicitly stated in legal terms. At the local level, there may be a manual for the guidance of clinic or agency personnel. The therapist should make sure that he is familiar with the contents of all these canonical writings.

THE GROUP STRUCTURE

Small therapy groups usually have a simple structure, consisting of an external boundary that separates the members of the group from the rest of the population, and a single major internal boundary that separates the therapist from the patients.

Complex Leadership   There may, however, be a minor structure within the leadership, including a co-therapist or assistant therapist. As noted previously, it is often difficult to state clearly the purpose of having more than one therapist, and experience shows that in most cases it is a handicap. This can easily be tested by starting the group with two therapists and continuing afterward with one. The reasons usually given for co-therapy are of an institutional nature and remain unconvincing to contractual therapists. Teaching, however, may be a legitimate reason for having an assistant therapist.

The Structural Diagram   The structural diagram of a simple treatment group is shown in Figure 3. This structure has a defect not occurring in more highly organized groups. It does not distinguish between the leader and his executive arm, the group apparatus; a distinction which is of paramount dynamic importance, and which must be clearly grasped. When functioning as a therapist, the therapist is an activity leader. When he is performing other duties, such as answering the telephone, opening and closing the door, arranging the furniture, announcing the time of the next meeting, and keeping internal order, he is functioning as his own group apparatus. It is essential that in his own mind he separate these two functions, which are as different as those of a judge and a bailiff in a courtroom. In more highly organized groups, the leader has a staff to do the work of the apparatus. When he is dealing with pressures from

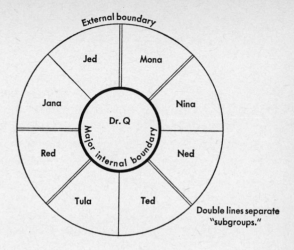

Fig. 3. Structural diagram of a treatment group

outside the therapy chamber, the therapist is the external apparatus of his group; when he is keeping order among his patients, he is the internal apparatus. Only when he is engaged in transactions directly related to the therapeutic work is he a leader. If these distinctions are not clear in his own mind the patients may become confused as to his function and the therapeutic situation may be fogged.

This is most clearly brought out in certain types of public agencies and in correctional work, where the leader works not only as a therapist, but also as a delegate of the group apparatus of the organization as a whole. A social worker may control the funds allotted to the patients in her group; there are agencies where a therapist to needy mothers has the task of rehabilitation combined with the duty of conducting "night raids" if someone suspects that a client is not really eligible for benefits; in correctional work, the parole or probation officer may carry handcuffs and have the authority to imprison members of his therapy groups

who transgress the conditions of their liberty. Where such punitive functions are combined with those of therapist, it is particularly important for the therapist to clarify his two roles to himself
and his clients. Sometimes the roles are so irreconcilable that
the situation cannot be resolved and therapy proceeds at best in
a tentative, limping, opaque style, with therapist and patients
always on trial with each other.

Briefly, the difficulty lies in the fact that the therapist can be
provoked at any juncture into swinging from his Adult professional role into his Parental punitive one. Even if his actual ego
state is Adult throughout, he is almost inevitably perceived as
Parental when he shifts. The best he can do is appeal to the
Adult aspect of his clients by clarifying his dilemma, and to do
this effectively may require considerable courage in facing it
squarely himself. A parole officer, for example, is after all not
only a therapist but also an informer, and any attempt to gloss
this over with euphemistic terminology will sit better with himself and his superiors than it will with the hard-boiled men who
face him.

Even the private practitioner has to resolve certain conflicts
in this area. Is his job as a cashier and bookkeeper to be relegated
to his police function, or is it to be treated transactionally as part
of the group process?

A special aspect of the structural diagram becomes significant
in marital or family therapy, where in effect there are minor
boundaries in the membership region (Figure 4). In a marital
group, each couple functions as a separate entity in situations
of stress, so that the therapist is then dealing with four sub-
groups rather than with eight individuals. Similarly in a family
group, the parents may function as a subgroup forming a united
front against the children, who in turn function as another subgroup. The therapist should carefully distinguish in such situations when the members are acting as individuals, in which
case he is dealing with a simple group, and when they are split

into conflicting or allied subgroups, in which case he is dealing with a compound or complex group.

THE GROUP DYNAMICS

The External Group Process   The dynamics diagram considers the forces acting on the major group structure, that is, the external boundary and the major internal boundry. In the external group process (comprising transactions between the group and the external environment), external pressures are met by the group cohesion. Usually this aspect of the process is latent during most of the life of a therapy group, and plays little part in the proceedings. If the external environment becomes turbulent, however, the group must begin to mobilize to prevent disruption. If an agency is in a state of change or upheaval, both therapist and patients may recognize that at any moment external pressures may terminate the existence of the group. This creates special situations which are interesting to study. For the most part, however, external pressures can be ignored in the ordinary course of therapy.* It should be noted that external pressure may be either positive or negative. An executive order terminating group therapy in the agency and a party of people talking loudly outside the door while waiting to use the meeting room, both constitute positive external pressure; a holdup in the applications of new patients while there are vacancies in the group constitutes negative external pressure.

The Major Internal Group Process   The action in the group centers on the major internal group process at the major internal boundary, comprising transactions between the members and the therapist. Here the group cohesion, represented by the leadership, meets agitation from the membership, as shown in Figure 4. The patients exhibit their individual proclivi-

* In the Southern states, the current governmental demand for integration constitutes an external pressure which may override all the other dynamic forces in the group.

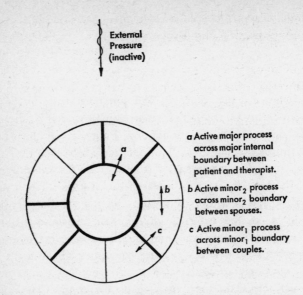

Fig. 4. A dynamics diagram of a mixed marital group

ties in action for or against the therapist. This may be regarded in transactional terms as between the Child in each patient and the Parent or Adult of the therapist; in psychoanalytic terms, as an interplay of transference, therapeutic maneuvers, and countertransference.

The Minor Internal Group Process Transactions which pit individual proclivities of patients for or against each other constitute the minor internal group process. In a more formal sense, the membership may be conceived of as divided into regions, with the boundaries labeled $Minor_1$. The $Minor_1$ process then consists of transactions across these boundaries. If each region is occupied by only one individual, then no further classification is necessary. If some or all regions are occupied by sub-groups such as married couples, however, then those $Minor_1$ regions have internal boundaries labeled $Minor_2$. In that case transactions involving one couple with another constitute the Minor$_1$ process, and transactions between spouses comprise the Minor$_2$ process.

It is of some interest and profit to sort the proceedings of a group meeting into those which are part of the major internal process (direct or indirect transactions between the therapist and the patients); and those in the minor group process (transactions between patients which do not involve the therapist); and where indicated, the minor process should be broken down into Minor$_1$ and Minor$_2$. This offers a useful and fairly rigorous framework for discussing such problems as how much the therapist should talk, and what happens when spouses do or do not sit near each other.

The relationship between the various aspects of the group process is expressed in the principle that the external, the major internal, and the minor internal group processes are to some extent mutually exclusive, so that energy employed in one aspect is taken from the reservoir available for the other aspects. The complete equation would read: External + Major + Minor + Group Activity = K (group cohesion at a given moment).

THE GROUP IMAGO

The organizational structure (formal role relationships) of a small therapy group is simple, consisting of two roles, therapist and patient, typically with one slot for therapist and eight slots for patients. The individual structure (the roster of people present) can be directly observed, since the entire personnel are assembled in one room. The private structure, that is, the group as seen through the eyes of each member, is found in the group imago of the member. This private structure is the most decisive structural aspect for the outcome of the individual's therapy.

Differentiation The variables in the group imago are both

qualitative and quantitative. The qualitative aspects concern the transactional, functional, and libidinal roles which the other members fill for the subject, and the nature of the slots activated by and for them in his imago. These qualities are historically determined, and their investigation is a matter of careful and systematic analysis of the psychodynamics of his transactional stimuli and responses. There are four general types of slots found in the imago of every member of a group, as illustrated in Figure 5, each type having certain cathectic peculiarities. The leadership slot will be invested with the same libidinal characteristics that would be involved in the transference if the patient were formally psychoanalysed; thus the leadership slot is a "transference" slot. The self-slot may be characterized psychodynamically as a narcissistic slot. Differentiated slots correspond psychodynamically to "extra-analytic transferences." Undifferentiated slots form a reservoir for further differentiation.

The basic quantitative variable is differentiation, inferred from behavior and confirmed by free association, introspection, and dreams. Sometimes dreams indicate a greater degree of differentiation than is otherwise manifest; in such cases, differentiation of certain group members is referred to as "latent" or "repressed." A group may be under-differentiated, fully differentiated, or over-differentiated in the imago of a given subject. Under-differentiation may occur when there are more members than there are differentiated slots in a patient's group imago. If, as in Figure 5, there are five differentiated slots: the leadership slot, the self-slot, and three membership slots; then the other four members may be relegated to the undifferentiated slot, where they are colloquially known in transactional terms as "these other good people," "the rest of you," or "these other jerks." The slots now occupied by Dr. Q, Red, Mona, and Jana, may already have been activated in Jed's group imago at the time he entered the group (his provisional group imago), and may be cathected

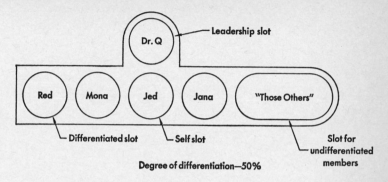

Fig. 5. A group imago

according to early experiences, say with his father, a brother, his mother and a sister.

Such an imago can become fully differentiated in two ways. The four "others" may be distributed between the four slots already activated, so that Jed behaves toward three or four of the women as though they were mothers or sisters, and toward three or four of the men as though they were fathers or brothers. The imago is then homomorphically differentiated. Or Jed may activate new slots as time passes; son and daughter slots, teacher, nursemaid, and grandparent slots, etc., depending on his early family history and his present attitudes. This is heteromorphic differentiation; the previously undifferentiated members are put into newly activated slots.

Now let us suppose that the patient whose imago is fully differentiated heteromorphically, so that he has nine active slots (including the self-slot), is transferred to a new group with only four members. He then has the option of either shutting down four slots (usually the least significant ones) or of assigning some or all of the members of the new group to more than one slot. In the latter case, the new group will be over-differentiated in his imago. This will be manifested by his behaving transactionally in different ways at different times toward the same member; he may shift from treating her like a mother to treating her like a sister and back again, which she and the other members of the group, including the therapist, may find incomprehensible and disconcerting if they do not understand the principle involved.

ANALYSIS OF TRANSACTIONS

The analysis of single transactions may constitute a definite phase of group therapy, in which case it is advisable to draw transactional diagrams such as that shown in Figure 6. The detection and rectification of crossed transactions is of particular importance, and in the major process they constitute transference and countertransference actions * and reactions. The principle at stake here is one of the rules of communication. If a crossed transaction occurs, communication will be broken off unless and until the crossing is rectified; conversely, if communication is broken off, it can be resumed when the crossed transaction is found and rectified. This will be discussed more fully in Chapter 10.

* The passive tendency of much conventional psychotherapy is illustrated by the implication at many conferences and in much of the literature that the patient's sole right is to "react." A patient who reacts is usually diagnosed neurotic or psychotic, and that is OK. A patient who acts, instead of reacting, may be called a psychopath or sociopath, and that is not-OK. In transactional analysis, the patient is considered without prejudice equally as an agent and as a respondent. He acts when he offers a transactional stimulus, and he reacts, or responds, when he offers a transactional response. The conventional statements are "The patient's reaction was . . ." and "My reaction was . . ." Conventional therapists are sometimes startled at transactional conferences to hear: "The patient acted," or "I acted." The notion of a therapist acting (rather than merely intervening) is disconcerting to some people, and the notion of a patient acting instead of reacting is threatening or reprehensible. The commonest fallacy is a failure to distinguish Adult "action" from archaic "acting out."

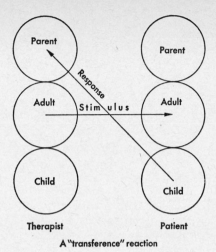

Fig. 6. A transactional diagram: crossed transaction type I

SUMMARY

In summary, then, for a group therapist to consider himself competent he should have some background in group dynamics and in particular should be familiar through practice and experience with the use and significance of the six basic diagrams mentioned above. He should always have sufficient information about his group to be prepared to draw any of these diagrams when occasion arises or when it would be helpful in understanding what is going on in therapy. The advantages of such diagrams, and the principles they represent, are listed below.

1. The seating diagram offers the considerable pedagogical advantages of a visual aid. It discourages hypothetical questions and emphasizes the uniqueness of each situation in the here and now.

2. The authority diagram uncovers covert influences on the operations of the therapist which he might prefer to ignore. The authority principle states that the therapist tends to be in-

fluenced by expectations which he imputes to those above him in the hierarchy.

3. The structural diagram emphasizes the advantages of structural simplicity if the therapist wishes to maintain a continuous grasp of the significance of the proceedings. The principle here is to make a clear distinction between disparate functions.

4. The dynamics diagram helps the therapist sort out the proceedings in a meaningful way. The principle is that the external, the major internal, and the minor internal group processes are to some extent mutually exclusive, and that energy employed in one aspect is taken from the reservoir available for other aspects.

5. The group imagos are constructed from perceptions of "real" personalities. They serve to clarify the more cogent relationships underlying the institutionalized and banal transactions and self-presentations which are common in therapy groups. The principle at stake is that of differentiation.

6. Transactional diagrams help to clarify problems of communication. The principles at stake are the rules of communication.

REFERENCES

1. Freud, S. *Group Psychology and the Analysis of the Ego.* Hogarth Press, London, 1940.
2. Scheidlinger, S. *Psychoanalysis and Group Behavior.* W. W. Norton & Company, New York, 1952.
3. Berne, E. *The Structure and Dynamics of Organizations and Groups.* (Chap. 2, ref. 4.)

7
Teaching

In practice, teachers of group therapy can be divided into three rough categories, conveniently called demonstrators, consultants, and supervisors.

Demonstrators Some people whose interests and training are not primarily medical (usually psychologists and social workers) acquire experience in group therapy through choice or assignment. In the course of time, some of them become teachers. If such a person is especially adept at dealing with people in groups, he may be able to offer instructive and even elegant demonstrations in therapeutic technique. This competence rests on his personal talents and a sound knowledge of psychotherapy and clinical science, together with whatever he brings into the curriculum from his own specialty. In order to qualify as a teacher, he should continue in active practice as long as he is teaching, and familiarize himself thoroughly with new developments in the field. (These two basic standards have not always been met.) Unfortunately, no matter how talented he may be, a nonmedical teacher is not administratively qualified to take full responsibility for patients, and therefore cannot function professionally as a supervisor. This administrative disability, which

159

sometimes causes resentment in competitive situations, is recognized by applying the historically honorable term "demonstrator" to this type of teacher.

Consultants People with exceptional skill in individual therapy, psychoanalysis, social psychology, or other pertinent fields, are sometimes used as consultants in group treatment, even though they may not have had group therapy experience. To render the best possible services, such consultants have to familiarize themselves by reading and observation with the principles of modern group dynamics and group treatment, and to keep up with developments in those fields. Within a matrix of such understanding, psychoanalytic consultants, including those who are less experienced in many-person transactions than in individual psychodynamics, can contribute to the deeper understanding of specific situations, and show how to use the group to the best advantage for the resolution of special types of individual conflicts. In these respects they function as consultants in the true clinical sense of the word.

Supervisors For over-all supervision, however, neither didactic knowledge, a talent for therapeutic technique, nor a clear understanding of specific aspects and situations is sufficient, nor indeed is a combination of all three. The supervisor not only has to know many fields, but also has to know how it feels to take responsibility for everything. His basic training should include medical and surgical diagnosis, pharmacology, clinical psychiatry, individual psychodynamics, and group dynamics. He should have had several years of experience in applying this knowledge in the rough and tumble of sustained group therapy in an environment which required him to take the responsibility for what happened.

To take some representative examples, he must be competent diagnostically to pick up the atypical manifestations or transactions which distinguish the thyrotoxicoses and gastric ulcers from the anxiety neuroses, the meningiomas and porphyrinurias from the hysterics, the paretics from the schizophrenics, and the pituitary tumors from the "eating problems." If patients are taking drugs, of whatever kind and for whatever reasons, he must be competent pharmocologically to evaluate both the somatic and the psychological effects as they influence the course of recovery — whether they retard it, as in the case of alcohol and narcotics (and sometimes thyroid and cortisone), or promote it, as in the case of sedatives and tranquillizers. As a clinical psychiatrist, he must know not only how to commit a psychotic to a hospital, but also how to avoid committing him. In individual psychodynamics, he must know not only how to elicit anal material and hostility, but also how and when to stop its flow. And as a group dynamicist, he must know not only when it is better to keep quiet than to speak, but even more important, when it is better to speak clearly and firmly than to keep quiet. He must know all these fields because it is his first duty to keep his students from making irretrievable errors (*primum non nocere*), and his second duty to help them attain the maximum therapeutic result with the minimum expenditure of time and wasted effort.

The technical virtuosity of the superior demonstrator, the specialized knowledge of the consultant, and the over-all competence of the supervisor each finds its place in the training program for group therapists. On the other hand, those who elect to become teachers of group therapy should be aware of their own assets and limitations. Demonstrators should be prepared to defer on occasion to medical knowledge, consultants to the wider experience of supervisors, and supervisors to the specialized knowledge of demonstrators and consultants.

The Curriculum The basic curriculum may be designed around a three-year residency program or its equivalent, conveniently divided as follows:

First Year: Theoretical (Didactic Lectures and Journal Club)
Second Year: Clinical (Clinical Presentations and Observation)
Third Year: Practical (Supervised Leadership)

Since formal training in group treatment is still in its infancy, the pedagogical principles are by no means thoroughly tested. The following somewhat idealized syllabus is designed as a basis for further study and development. Each item has been tested several times in practice. Similar curricula have been outlined by other writers.[1,2]

DIDACTIC LECTURES

The first semester should be devoted to two sets of about eight lectures. These are best given weekly until the syllabus is completed, after which the subject can be dropped for the remainder of the semester. That is better than trying to spread it over the whole semester by meeting every two weeks, since in that case continuity and sustained interest are sacrificed. It is also advisable to have each set given by a single lecturer.

Basic Principles The object at this stage is the inculcation of sound basic principles. There are certain attitudes which should be drummed into students if they are to become professionals rather than dilettantes. Eclectic presentation of "a variety of viewpoints" (which is often merely a polite way of evading the issues) can come later. The first requirement is a solid position from which to evaluate other viewpoints, and that position must be a biological and operational one. As in any branch of medicine, the student must first learn to look at what there is to see before he attempts to compare the values of various approaches. The surgical resident learns such homely arts as sterile technique and urinalysis, and the basic principles of ionic balance, before he is ready to decide how much of the stomach to cut out. A French colleague illustrated the situation succinctly when asked what he learned in the army as a specialist in tropical medicine. Instead of discussing the relative values of different anti-malarials, or the distinctions between obscure fungal skin rashes, he replied: "I learn what you 'ave to learn: 'ow to look at [feces]."

Size of Classes The preferred size of audience is eight to twenty people. With fewer than eight the lectures tend to become diffused into colloquies; with more than twenty it is difficult for the lecturer to become familiar with the idiosyncracies of each person taking the course. Such familiarity is necessary in order to assess the talents and potentialities of individual students and begin to consider how to deal with personal characteristics which might impede learning or therapeutic effectiveness.

It is not easy for the student to get a useful grasp of basic material from lectures alone, and he should be given a very brief reading list: one which he is likely to cope with in the allotted time. The instructor should make free use of the blackboard, and if he gives the course repeatedly he may want to construct other visual aids. Each point should be adequately illustrated by clinical material, offered sometimes before and sometimes after the point is made. The fresher and more recent the examples, the more spontaneously will they be presented and the more they will impress the audience; they should be simple, concise, convincing, and shorn of irrelevancies.

Initial Lectures The first series of lectures should be concerned with the observation of how people act in groups, in the simplest terms. These are matters which can be approached on a purely behavioral level: which muscles the patient moved, which words he said, and how he said them; which muscles his respondent moved, which words he said, and how he said them. The next step concerns how to draw inferences from such observations, how to verify them, and how to use them predictively. Each lecture should be about a specific topic.

The introductory course can then proceed logically to clinical problems. After the preliminary foundations, a general framework for the classification of social behavior is given, along with its application to the common psychiatric categories. Then follows an outline of general group dynamics which the student may find useful not only as a group therapist, but also as an organizational or industrial consultant. The course is completed with one or two lectures concerning the application of all these principles to therapy groups. It should be noted that none of this is restrictive. The resident is still free to think about and use everything that he knows concerning clinical psychiatry, psychotherapy, and psychodynamics; what he is mainly being taught is to emphasize initially observation above speculation, individual behavior above diagnostic categories, and people in action above the concept of "the group." Experience through the years indicates that all this can be concisely, intelligibly, and usefully encompassed within the framework of transactional analysis.[3]

It has already been stressed that this introductory series is presented in lecture, rather than seminar, form. The instructor, if he is properly prepared, will have a large amount of well-organized information to impart. This will leave little time for tangential discussions, which will have to be politely and firmly abbreviated by suggesting that they are more appropriate for the journal club. A few minutes may be left at the end of the hour for answering pertinent questions. Two-hour sessions, if they can be arranged, leave more time for introducing cogent clinical illustrations. The mere act, on the lecturer's part, of distinguishing between "relevancy" and "irrelevancy" in the field of group therapy will have a salutary effect on the future careers of his students.

Subsequent Lectures The second set of lectures in the first semester should deal with the professional approach to group therapy. The first lecture might deal with group therapy as a social institution and the distinction of that form from group treatment as a contractual therapeutic instrument that sacrifices institutional compliance in favor of clinical effectiveness. Briefly stated, this means that the therapist's task is not to conform to a sociological model of "a therapy group," but to perform as rapidly as possible whatever operations are necessary to cure each patient of his ailments, since that is what he is (or should be) expected to do. Otherwise the term "therapist" is a misnomer, as any medical dictionary will corroborate. This leads directly into the next topic, which is setting up the various aspects of the organizational contract and the contract with the patient. The third lecture can deal with specific types of contracts and the difficulties they create. Many of these difficulties arise because the "therapist" is expected to function simultaneously as an arm of the internal apparatus of the mother group. In correctional work, for example, as mentioned previously, he has the duties of an informer and the authority of a policeman, and unless he can keep these distinct from his role as a clinician, his therapeutic effectiveness will be seriously impaired.

Group Dynamics This again leads naturally into the next topic, which merits two or three lectures, and that is the therapy of ailing groups. A group therapist, if he is worth his salt, will in time become something of an expert in practical group dynamics and will have something to contribute to the field of social psychiatry. He may be qualified to act as a consultant to industry, nursing schools, social agencies, hospitals, and other organizations, and he should be prepared for this from the beginning. It is instructive (but unfortunately not always diplomatically feasible) to spend one lecture analysing the very organization in which the teaching is taking place.

When this minimum of basic preparation has been completed, there may be time for one or two additional lectures. These may be profitably spent by the lecturer riding his own hobbies, so that the students may have the benefit of his specialized knowledge of whatever fields his fancy has wandered in.

The didactic lectures will offer the instructor a medium for demonstrating the correct procedures for conducting firmly structured groups with the greatest effectiveness, and he should make good use of this opportunity.

The second semester may be devoted to weekly meetings of a journal club, where special topics may be covered. Here the students will have their chance to express themselves, and the teacher will have his opportunity to become better acquainted with them as individuals.

The objects of the journal club are twofold: to acquaint the student with different schools of group therapy and with the application of group therapy to special categories of patients, and to emphasize that the body is important.

Syllabus A comprehensive syllabus should cover the following "schools" and methods as applied to group therapy: psychoanalytic, psychodramatic, didactic, gestalt therapy, existential analysis, transactional analysis, occupational therapy, activity therapy, industrial therapy, and therapeutic community. The English writers should be discussed: Bion (Chap. 5, ref. 6), Foulkes (Chap. 5, ref. 2), Ezriel (Chap. 9, ref. 11), and Maxwell Jones (Chap. 9, ref. 13). Trigant Burrow (Chap. 9, ref. 2) should not be neglected. It is necessary to know Gierke (Chap. 2, ref. 4) for group dynamics, and anyone not familiar with his work can be considered a "primitive" in this field. Aristotle's *Politics* and Plato's *Republic* are instructive collateral reading, sufficiently thought-provoking to warrant a session on each. In regard to special categories of patients, different age groups should be covered—childhood, adolescence, and old age—then marital groups and family group therapy. The student should be familiar with the literature on alcoholics, drug addicts, psychotics, prisoners, and parolees. Beyond that, there are any number of specialized topics: the blind, the obese, and the stutterer are examples.

Somatic Topics It is of the greatest importance, however, to reserve time for certain "somatic" topics which are pertinent to group treatment. This is gratifying to residents newly graduated from medical school, and is essential if there are nonmedical personnel among the students. Prime subjects are the work of Spitz (Chap. 12, ref. 1) concerning emotional deprivation in infants; experiments on the handling and nonhandling of newborn animals, and the effects on the adrenal glands; Penfield and Jasper (Chap. 12, ref. 8) on the "re-experiencing" area in the tempero-parietal region; the reticular activating system; sensory deprivation; the physiology of the electroencephalogram; the pharmacology of tranquillizers; and the psychological after-effects of electro-shock therapy. Elementary brain physiology, the anatomy of the sympathetic nervous system, and psychological changes accompanying endocrine disorders are also worth-while topics to review. A session on the facial muscles will help the students become better observers.

Some of the conventional subjects included in courses for group therapists may be dealt with at the journal club: e.g. the history of group therapy, the selection of patients, and the "phases" of group therapy. The syllabus given above is perhaps too inclusive for most journal clubs and in practice represents a basis for selection rather than a requirement. A less ambitious minimal collateral groundwork should include (1) psychodynamic (psychoanalytic) group therapy, (2) psychodrama, (3) marital and family therapy, (4) the therapeutic community, (5) Bion, (6) Penfield and Spitz, (7) Gierke; and perhaps (8) a session on the alcoholic.

At the journal club, the instructor will have an opportunity to demonstrate to his students that the most aggressive or talkative member is not necessarily the one who makes the most cogent

contributions to the group activity. He will not, of course, say
this out loud, and will resist any temptation or request to turn
the journal club into a "process group," but his behavior will
make clear that he knows what he is doing at every juncture,
and that he is a strong enough leader to make sure that the
business at hand is accomplished regardless of complications
that may arise.

THE CLINICAL SEMINAR

In his second year the student will be confronted with actual
clinical situations presented *in extenso* and will have an opportunity to demonstrate his own way of approaching clinical
problems. Since a typical clinical seminar involves the presentation of an entire group meeting, often with background material
as well, one hour is hardly adequate, and it is almost mandatory
to schedule such a conference for an hour and a half at least.
Indeed, the chief problem of the teacher here is to bring some
sort of order into the situation which will keep the audience
from going off in all directions.

Specificity It is therefore suggested, first, that every clinical
presentation start with a specific question to be answered. This
focuses the discussion and prevents the wandering and daisy-
picking which is apt to afflict such meetings. It serves to direct
the audience's attention during the presentation toward particular aspects of the complex and unwieldy network of transactions:
not the aspects that strike the fancy of each individual, but those
that bear on the stated problem. Under these conditions, the
bright guesser and speculator can have his say and make his
contribution without distracting the audience from the main line
of thought.

The Seating Diagram Secondly, the seating diagram and
schedule should be drawn on the blackboard, since as already
noted, they answer innumerable questions visually and save a

great deal of time. If a tape is being presented, the presenter should use a pointer to indicate on the diagram the agent and respondent of each transaction, eliminating distracting verbal questions or calls.

Analysis of Single Transactions An interesting and instructive way to conduct a clinical seminar is to present a tape and analyse the proceedings one transaction at a time: one stimulus and one response. The members of the seminar then make whatever deductions and predictions they can about the agent and the respondent: e.g. what the parents of those involved said to them when they were children, and what vicissitudes they have undergone since; or in a transactional group, what game is being initiated and what the outcome is likely to be. The next transaction is then played and similarly discussed. Under these conditions an experienced transactional analyst may be able to predict not only the general trend of the next few minutes, but almost word for word what many of the members are going to say.

Properly conducted, this is not a guessing game. It sharpens the clinical perception of the participants, discourages idle speculation, and encourages clinical relevancy, since their predictions are subject to immediate testing as the tape unrolls. This gets around a basic defect of many clinical conferences. In the usual case, someone says, "Let's hear more about it sometime." Then the matter is either dropped for a variety of reasons, or if the same patient or group is presented a second time, such a long interval has elapsed that no one is held accountable for what he said at the original presentation. By using the single transaction method, everyone must take responsibility for his predictions on the spot, so that dilettantism is curbed. This approach also impresses on the students the possibility and desirability of planning ahead for therapeutic technique on the basis of predictive and deductive probability.

Whole Tapes Another method is to present the whole tape

before any discussion takes place. This may work if the taped session lasts less than an hour, but if it lasts longer than that this plan should not be attempted, since there will be too much information for productive digestion in the remaining time. In most cases, presentation of more than thirty minutes of tape has proved unprofitable. A seminar that ends only in intellectual colic is hardly worthwhile. The solution is a verbal account by the therapist.

The presentation of a long segment of tape may be used to illustrate a specific point or raise a particular question. To succeed, this device requires firm leadership. Otherwise, such a partial presentation is likely to elicit only a lot of time-consuming questions about what went on before and after the segment, with the presenter awkwardly stammering apologies and qualifications. The teacher who allows his seminar group to get into such a soggy condition is offering a poor example to his students. At this stage, when they are actively preparing to undertake leadership of their own groups, he should be demonstrating crispness, efficiency, and mastery of the proceedings.

If a complete meeting is presented, either verbally or on tape, time becomes precious. It is best to concentrate on the proceedings rather than to spend a large fraction of the allotted period going over the clinical histories of the patients. If specific questions about the past seem relevant to the actual proceedings at a given moment, the presenter may be interrupted to clarify concisely the historical point in question. Solemnity is not necessarily an indication of superior talents or personal qualities, and an occasional laugh or joke when it is legitimate may loosen up the thinking processes. When the presentation is finished, the discussion can proceed.

There are two main systems of discussion, which may be called for convenience the European and the American. In the European system, the leader asks the junior member of the seminar to comment, and works up the hierarchy, he himself giving his opinion last. This diminishes the tendency to refrain from speaking because one differs from those who are more experienced; here one can only contradict one's juniors. In the American system, each one speaks when the spirit moves him, which often results in the less aggressive and junior people remaining silent. In a scientific situation, this is not necessarily the most enlightening procedure. The American system gives equal rights, but the European system provides equal possibilities. In any case, it is probably a mistake for the leader to give his opinion or analysis first, since this will almost unavoidably cause the most timid students to refrain from voicing theirs. He may, however, initially indicate what he thinks are the most productive lines for the discussion to follow, which actually makes it easier for the more reserved members to express themselves.

Invited Speakers The clinical presentations of the staff may be interspersed with lectures and demonstrations by specialists in allied fields, just as in the case of the journal club. The chief personal duty of the leader of the clinical seminar is to set an example of competent leadership, and this includes his pedagogical obligation, which is to see that the meetings are interesting and provocative as well as instructive.

THE CONTINUOUS CASE SEMINAR

The continuous case seminar is designed primarily for third-year residents or students who have had a thorough didactic and journal indoctrination in their first year and have attended a clinical seminar in their second year. It can be held every two weeks with one therapist presenting during the first semester and another during the second semester; or instead, if the seminar meets weekly, two therapists can present, each on alternate weeks. The chief duty of the leader of a continuous case seminar is that he should retain a good grasp of all that has happened since the seminar began. It is preferable to start with fresh groups, so that the development can be followed from the beginning. They should also be as "clean" as possible; that is, no co-therapists, no "research" gimmicks, and a minimum of patient selection. The absence of distractions, and the variety of patients, will offer the students the best opportunity for concentrating on the main issue, which is the treatment of psychiatric disabilities by the application of the most effective techniques at each moment.

The temptation is strong to present a group with a co-therapist at such a seminar, on the assumption that the co-therapist will check the observations of the therapist so that the presentation will be more "accurate." Besides the previously stated objection to a group having a co-therapist (that with such an added complication it is almost impossible to understand with any confidence what is going on), there is the additional difficulty that in a seminar the interruptions of one therapist by the other may become distracting, so that the listener is kept in a state of apprehension that he will not be permitted to carry on a concentrated train of thought. The goal in this seminar is clarity and simplicity of demonstration, and nothing should be allowed to interfere with that.

Recordings versus Verbal Presentations   Once more it is necessary to take up the question of tape recording versus verbal presentation. It is probably best to base the seminar on verbal presentation, since then the whole proceedings of each group meeting can be run through and retained in memory better. Occasionally, however, about every fourth or fifth session, a tape recording should be presented so that the students can become more closely acquainted with the patients and can check their own observations against those of the therapist. The single-transaction method described in the previous section is useful in this connection. There should be a clear understanding that the comments on each transaction should be relevant enough so that they can be related to what follows on the tape. After the students have made their observations, it is incumbent on the teacher to give his predictions. These statements can then be checked against the next ten or fifteen minutes of the recording. If the teacher is competent, his predictions should be more accurate than those of the students, and he will thus demonstrate to them that knowledge, experience, and thoughtfulness are of value in group treatment, so that they can look forward to relying less and less on speculation, guesswork, and opportunism. In this way he also introduces the students to the concept of therapeutic planning and demonstrates its practicality. If they see that the therapist, under the teacher's supervison, is able to carry out a prepared ongoing therapeutic program, this will further emphasize the fact that group treatment can be scientific in the predictive and variable-controlling sense.

The single-transaction method offers a challenge which not everyone has the courage to meet initially. It is different from the institutionalized speculations that take up the time of many psychiatric staff conferences. Besides its rational value, it has the existential force of holding experts accountable for what they say, providing no refuges in ambiguity or in forgetting. A tape recording presents a sample of the vocal behavior of each patient. From such samples in one mode, a listener interested in his own personal development can learn not only to infer what the patient did in other modes, such as gesture, and to predict what he is going to do next, but also to infer what he did in the past and what was done to him in the past.

OBSERVATION

When the student or trainee is adequately prepared pedagogically, he may be permitted to sit in on the meetings of a treatment group conducted by a competent demonstrator or supervisor. Some groups can tolerate without discomfort two observers in addition to the therapist, providing there are five or more members, and even periodic changes of observers need not necessarily disconcert them. The student should sit in the same group for at least three to six months, and a year is preferable. It should be clear to everyone present that the observer is just that, and nothing more. It should be explained to the patients that he is a student who wants to learn how to do group therapy and that he is a reputable professional person. The group's permission should be asked on introducing the first observer and on changing observers.

Preparing the Group In anticipating observers, a pedantic preliminary "preparation" and analysis serves mainly to confuse the patients and stimulate an infinite regress of fantasies. The simplest and most effective procedure is to have the observer, at his initial meeting, wait outside while the therapist goes in and asks the group if they mind having an observer. If they have questions or fantasies, or the therapist wants to know their fantasies, he can spend as much time as he cares to dealing with these matters on the spot. If their consent is unanimous, the therapist, as soon as he is satisfied, fetches the observer, introduces him to the group, and offers him an inconspicuous seat. If the patients ask the newcomer questions, he should answer politely and as concisely as possible. If they care to discuss their fantasies further, this can be permitted, but such a discussion may degenerate into a pastime only remotely related to the therapeutic goals—except in certain cases of paranoia, where a patient's fantasies about the observer may be directly relevant to his condition.

If one or more patients object to the introduction of an observer, the student can be so informed and leave. Since none of the patients has seen him, he can hardly take this personally; or if because of previous circumstances the objection is on personal grounds, it will give him something to think about advantageously. If after an accepted observer has sat in the group for some time one or more patients feel that his presence is undesirable or is impairing the effectiveness of the treatment, this will have to be discussed and the observer may have to discontinue. One group, for example, felt uneasy because the observer was a clergyman, and raised their doubts after a few months at a meeting which he was unable to attend. It was agreed to try it without him for six weeks to see whether their objections were valid and whether they really "did better" without him. The therapist then informed him that the group felt inhibited by the presence of an observer and wanted to try it without one for six weeks. At the end of that time, the therapist had the unpleasant duty of telling his respected friend that his withdrawal would have to be permanent. Only by keeping in mind that a therapist must always master his personal feelings in favor of the welfare of his patients, was he able to perform this task with proper firmness.

The Observer's Departure When an observer's time is up or for some other reason he has to discontinue, that may be announced about the middle of the last meeting at which he will be present. This will give the patients time to express any urgent feelings which they may have about the matter. Actually, for the most part their interest in the observer and his departure is determined by the therapist's attitude. If he makes a point of such things as "separation anxiety" the patients will oblige him and there will be a great deal of talk about separation anxiety; but there is no convincing evidence that such talk will benefit any except those in whom the departure arouses a definitely pathological reaction. If the therapist takes the impending departure as a matter of course and one patient insists on going into his feelings in detail, he may be asked why he finds the situation more distressing than the other patients seem to. It may be that he has read that he is supposed to feel bad, or in some other therapy group he was told that he was supposed to feel bad on such occasions.

Only rarely is the departure of an observer directly relevant to a patient's symptomatology; it will be a significantly traumatic event only for very disturbed individuals. For most, there may be some simple natural regret at losing a familiar figure; in that case a dignified reserve may be preferable to and more elevating than an exhibition of mawkish feelings. In short, if the therapist encourages his patients to feel deprived, they will often comply; but if they are expected to do a man's or woman's job of taking command of their own feelings and behavior, then they are just as likely to comply in that direction. Thus the therapist must learn to distinguish in such situations between genuine regret, spurious game-playing, and significant psychopathology. The first is admirable, the second wasteful, and the third pathogenic, and each should be treated appropriately.

Functions of the Observer   The observer may perform minimum services in the group without abrogating his role. He may function as a group apparatus to answer the telephone or the door or to take attendance. In post-group discussions he may occasionally point out something that the therapist has missed. If this happens often, however, then the therapist is at fault and is not observing his group carefully enough. This is important because if the student observer gets the impression that the therapist is slovenly, he may not rise above that level himself. If on the contrary he is impressed with the therapist's sharpness, that sets a good example for his own future career. In this connection as in others, the competent supervisor will always be master of the situation as far as is humanly possible.

One-Time Observers   The question of the one-time or two-time observer may come up on special occasions. An infrequent one-time observer may not be too disconcerting, but if this situation arises too often the patients may decide that they are being used as guinea pigs, and accordingly spend their time either putting on a good show or revolting against the therapist instead of getting better.

Concealed Observation The therapist should remember that basically all neuroses and character disorders, and possibly all psychoses as well, result from dishonesty on someone's part. This automatically answers the problem of the concealed one-way window or microphone. The patients may compliantly pretend not to know about them or not to mind them, but if they go to another therapist later they may express themselves quite differently about it. They may have spent their whole time in the group putting on a show for the first therapist, acting as though they did not know what was going on and laughing up their sleeves at him. A therapist who is dishonest with his patients cannot fairly expect them to acquire the ruthlessly honest attitude which is necessary for recovery. If any bugs are used, the patients should be fully informed about them and about who is going to be at the other end and why they are being used. They should be employed as sparingly as possible. If they are used habitually, the situation may have to be regarded as research or teaching rather than therapy. The patients may "adjust" to microphones or concealed windows, but the cost remains to be determined. If they co-operate, their co-operation and investment of time should be appreciatively recognized by the therapist.

An Illustrative Anecdote Dr. Q was requested by some colleagues in Utah to take a tape recording of one of his group sessions and send it to them. He asked permission of the members, and set up his machine. Then they began to ask questions, which he felt obligated to answer. They took a slightly cynical but good-natured attitude after the reasons were clarified to their satisfaction. The following week one member asked him, "Well, how did we go over in Utah?" The implication was that they had spent the previous meeting putting on a show, and were now ready to settle down to business again.

INDIVIDUAL SUPERVISION

Most profitable to the beginning therapist is individual supervision, in which he and the supervisor can concentrate without distraction on the proceedings of the group. Sometimes it is interesting if the same material is used later at the continuous case seminar; the therapist then gets the benefit of discussion from both the supervisor and the other students. Such a combination, of course, eliminates certain suggested features of the continuous case seminar, such as prediction on the part of the supervisor, since he has already heard the proceedings before the seminar; but it will soon become evident that the supervisor's foreknowledge and the therapist's awareness concerning the material offer compensations when it is presented for the second time.

Phases in Learning A student who has been through the didactic lectures, the journal club, the clinical seminar, and the continuous case seminar has a good academic background for beginning the systematic study of applied group technique. If he has done previous group therapy under less rigorous supervision, that will have served to introduce him to the difficulties he is likely to meet and which his individual supervision will teach him to "handle." If he has not yet had practical experience in conducting his own group, his supervisor should bear in mind what the student may not realize until he has been confronted with it: that there are three phases in applied learning. The first is to learn the theory and principles of group dynamics and group treatment, after which the student may be able to listen intelligently to discussions of clinical material and perhaps contribute some useful comments of his own. The second phase is watching the application of the theory by others at the continuous group seminar and during his experience as an observer. The third phase is when he himself tries to apply what he has learned and to take responsibility for what he does.

Each of these advances (from theory to observation, and from observation to practice) holds its own surprises and perhaps consternations. An apt analogy is the intelligent Papuan bush man whose teacher gave him a book about motor cars, so that he learned a great deal about such vehicles without ever having seen one. When eventually a Patrol Officer appeared with a Land Rover and gave the native his first ride, he was fascinated by the actual hardware and the application of the things he had been reading about. An even more poignant experience was in store for him, however, when he moved to Port Moresby and first took the wheel of a motor car himself. During such transitions the supervisor has a particularly good opportunity to make observations about the student therapist's strengths and weaknesses. The neophyte's early comments about clinical material, and his early interventions in his own group, will reveal as much about his commitment as about his insight. Most weaknesses in moving from one phase to another arise more from ambivalence than from lack of talent, as subsequent developments often show.

PERSONAL GROUP THERAPY

The Group-Process Group   The so-called group-dynamics or group-process group or workshop may be edifying for group dynamicists, but is not directly relevant to the job of a group therapist; in his case, it may do more harm than good by beguiling him into dilettantism. A group therapist who wants personal group experience should go into a situation where he is treated strictly as a patient, and not as anything else. The problem here is the same as with the "didactic analysis." A didactic analysis is not a half-hearted analysis, nor a sampling of the analytic wares, nor an "interesting experience"; it has to be the real thing if it is to be of real value to the candidate in his subsequent professional work. From the teacher's point of view, the first rule for any kind of effective psychotherapy with colleagues is to treat them first as patients and only secondarily, if at all, as colleagues. An intelligent colleague will usually understand this himself, and will be the first one to request such a set-up when he enters treatment. If he is willing to or wants to settle for less, the teaching therapist will save himself time, energy, and often future embarrassment by postponing treatment or sending the colleague elsewhere.

The Student and Psychoanalysis   The student's entrance into a therapy group as a patient can be concurrent with his didactic work or await its completion, but he should preferably not attend seminars or lectures plus a therapy group conducted by the same leader. A complicated situation arises with students who are in or are contemplating psychoanalysis. It is not usually considered advantageous to undertake psychoanalytic group therapy concurrently with individual psychoanalysis. The writer's experience is that not many orthodox analysts are in favor of such a combination. On the other hand, transactional group therapy tends to confuse people who are concurrently in psychoanalysis because they are subject to two different approaches as well as two different therapists at the same time, and they tend to compartmentalize; this does not help either the group therapist or the psychoanalyst. A student who is contemplating psychoanalysis is apt to feel that the individual analysis takes precedence over group therapy for both personal and organizational reasons, and hence is likely to terminate his group therapy soon after his analysis begins; or, with some analysts, as soon as it begins.

Prospective analysands should therefore postpone their analyses until they have obtained the maximum therapeutic benefit from group therapy. Active analysands should perhaps postpone group therapy until their analyses are completed. Each of these cases, of course, presents technical difficulties for whoever is the first therapist. Of the two, the second situation is probably preferable, that is, to complete psychoanalysis before undertaking group therapy. A sound recommendation and solution to this difficult problem will not emerge until several collections of cases have been thrashed out at analytic and group-therapy scientific meetings, and a combined study of this type is not yet practical. At present, the only statement that can be made is that it is helpful for a group therapist to have had personal experience as a patient in a therapy group. But even that is only a pious assumption, since in fact it has never been critically evaluated, and so still remains part of the lore of institutionalized group therapy.

WORKSHOPS

In practice, these are of three kinds of workshops: half-day, all-day, and two-day. From another point of view, they can be divided into "let's-get-acquainted" or "coffee break" workshops, and work workshops. "Coffee break" workshops are pleasant social events at which the speaker has only to say a few things that the audience wants to hear, and let them say a few things they want to say; such events present no problem to the adaptable leader.

At a work workshop, the coffee breaks are before the meeting begins at 9:00 or 9:30 a.m., and after it ends at 4 or 4:30 p.m., with an hour or an hour and a half for lunch. The speaker may concede ten-minute breaks at 10:50 and 2:50, but they may not be necessary if he has enough to say to keep his audience interested. Work workshops are only for people who really want to learn, and for instructors who really want to teach. For the rest of this discussion, we will be referring only to work workshops.

Whatever the total length of the workshop, it can be conveniently divided into half-day segments, each designed to last about two and a half hours. The following is a good plan for a one-day session.

(1) In the morning, the speaker speaks for an hour or an hour and a half on a well-defined topic; the remaining time is spent answering questions. (2) The speaker returns from lunch earlier than most of the audience and sits in on a local therapy group, if one is available, at the institution where he is speaking. The audience re-assembles; the local therapist gives his version of what happened in the group meeting, and after that the speaker gives his. The speaker then demonstrates how the morning topic specifically applies to the local problems. The last hour is again spent in answering questions.

There is no need for the local people to have their free discussion while the speaker is there; they can do that some other time. As long as he is there they should make maximum use of his presence and what he has to offer. For a half-day session, either activity (1) or an adaptation of (2) may be planned. For a two-day session, the second day may follow a similar program; either another topic, or a more advanced version of the same topic is taken. For example, a transactional analyst might offer transactional therapeutic theory and technique the first day, and transactional group dynamics or advanced game analysis the second day. If the speaker has written something about the topics selected, he should tell his sponsors or send them reprints so that interested members of the audience can obtain some preliminary familiarity with his ideas. If he has not written anything himself, he might recommend one, or at most two, good sources in the literature on his topic for preparatory reading. If he recommends more than that, his workshop may turn into a "coffee break" workshop as the discussion wanders off in too many directions, causing his audience to become restless. The speaker will put himself on his mettle to improve his skill if he takes the position that premature audience restlessness is due to his own deficiencies rather than theirs.

The Alternating Workshop An interesting variation is the alternating workshop. This requires a staff of well-trained group leaders in addition to the principal speaker. The speaker talks for an hour or so, after which the audience breaks up into small groups to discuss and experiment with the new ideas. It is the firm duty of the educated group leaders to keep the discussions focused on relevant territory. Such dual sessions can be held three times a day: morning, afternoon, and evening. The participants will not get tired if the speaker has enough new ideas to keep them interested in such an intensive program, and if the group leaders are ruthless enough to protect them from the usual menaces of small groups.* This system has been found very effective in teaching transactional analysis in short workshops, where a large number of novel ideas have to be absorbed in a brief time. The necessary review conferences between the speaker and his staff can be held in the open so that any of the participants who wish to do so may listen in. This gives the staff a chance to demonstrate their planning. Instead of telling Alice in Wonderland stories of what happened at the last set of group meetings, they make it clear that the chief interest of the immediate past is to help them make immediate plans for the immediate future. Rather than impotently ruminating and speculating about something that happened at this morning's meeting, each leader must answer the decisive question: "What are you going to do about it at this afternoon's meeting?"

* Common types are the "free discussion demander" ("I talk for forty minutes, two others can talk for ten minutes each, and the rest of you keep quiet"); the late-comer ("Give me a ten-minute résumé of what happened in the last five minutes; anything less and I'll pout"); the astrologer ("Do you believe in extrasensory perception, Doctor?"); the rambler ("When I was practising in Bulgaria . . ."); the "wooden legger" ("I've got a cast on my leg, so you've got to listen"); and the name-dropper.

REFERENCES

1. Kadis and others. (Chap. 5, ref. 11.)
2. Mullan and Rosenbaum. (Chap. 1, ref. 1.)
3. An outline suitable for such an introductory course, conveniently set up for classroom use, can be obtained from the International Transactional Analysis Association, P.O. Box 5747, Carmel, California. The ITAA will also supply tape recordings of a four-lecture condensed introductory course as given at the Annual Summer Conference on Transactional Analysis.

8
Research and Writing

In his commemorative address "Experience and Experiment in Biology," [1] Paul Weiss epitomizes some current trends in the philosophy of science. His remarks, along with those of other seasoned and thoughtful writers on methodology, are immediately relevant to the pursuit of research in group therapy. Weiss stresses the value of experience as a background against which to evaluate experiments, and as an essential for getting the most out of experimentation. The following statements (included here with Dr. Weiss's permission) seem especially cogent; the present writer's glosses are added in parentheses.

"Experimentation used to be deliberate, not improvised; planned to reduce confusion, not just to add profusion; it was meant to be relevant and incisive, not just trifling and redundant." (This is reminiscent of Singer's remark [2] that "Dissection in the fourteenth century did no more and was asked to do no more than verify Avicenna — whom nobody doubted." The same might be said of group therapy in relation to Freud in our own century).

"In the tradition of those past centuries, designing an experiment has been like training a gun at a target, rather than like spattering buckshot all around at random in the hope that something somewhere might be hit.

"The mere fact that something has not been done or tried before is not sufficient reason for doing or trying it. It takes originality to conceive innovations of true significance or of relevance to the solution of a problem or to the assessment of a theory." (In group treatment, this can be taken to mean testing a significant assumption, e.g. "Talking is good," rather than testing the less important consequences of an assumption which itself remains unexamined, e.g. "It was good they talked this way rather than that way").

"We see bewildered youngsters composing research projects like abstract paintings: picking some colorful and fashionable words from recent literature, and then reshuffling and recombining them into another conglomerate, yielding a stew of data, both undigested and indigestible.

"The experimental discipline has rightly eradicated faith in any *a priori* truth . . . but let us guard the young generation against seduction by the opposite extreme, no less pernicious: undisciplined experiments, unguided by ideas."

(It is doubtful that computers will replace people, but they will certainly soon replace people who are trained only to do things that computers can do better).

An Illustrative Example   Dr. Q recommended to a patient that she transfer to another therapist because she was not making satisfactory progress in the group. The other members immediately went to work to persuade her to stay and to try to be more objective about her games so that she could give up some of them long enough to listen to what people were trying to tell her. When Dr. Q. related these proceedings at a meeting of young therapists, they immediately went to work on a *post facto* explanation of why it had happened so: the other members felt threatened by separation anxiety, by the patient's lack of progress, and so on, concluding that the group's reaction was almost inevitable. Dr. Q then mentioned that he had made the same recommendation to another patient in another group the previous week, but on that occasion the other members concurred with his suggestion, and the patient left the group to go elsewhere. No doubt both outcomes were "explainable," but one incident was valueless without the other in any sense approximating a scientific approach. The only way to make such "explanations" tenable is to ask, not "How would you prove it?" but rather "How would you disprove it?," and then proceed to try to disprove it.* In the example cited, each case could be "explained" separately, but unfortunately (or in a better sense, fortunately) taken together, each one "disproved" the explanation offered for the other. Only by considering such contrary outcomes can group theory become more than an exchange of letters between deferential colleagues.

RESEARCH DESIGN

When a group therapist decides to undertake a research project, he should evaluate it with the sophistication to be expected of an experienced clinician. He should ask himself what complex motivations underly his interest in that particular problem. These motivations are most conveniently considered from a structural point of view. What does his Adult really hope to learn? What will his Parent be doing in the situation? Why is his Child interested in the problem, how will his Child tend to exploit the project, and what will his Child be doing with the data? This enquiry puts the research in rational perspective. If it appears that the archaic motivations predominate over the neopsychic ones, then the whole project may be questioned and the experimental design may have to be radically changed or abandoned. In one case involving "group dynamics," the degree of deception verged on the sadistic, and was apparent to almost

* See J. R. Platt, "Strong Inference," *Science* 146:347–53, 16 October 1964.

everyone but the experimenter; but he fought vigorously for his academic "freedom" and pushed the project through, eventually causing considerable uproar in the scientific and political community. The question at issue was not the validity or value of the results, but whether they warranted the degree of exploitation of the subjects. A less determined person might have preferred to let someone else take the initiative in such a dubious project, where the quantitative relationship between the archaic (Child) and the rational (Adult) motivations was brought into question by numerous competent commentators.

In another analogous situation, a young group therapist, by some odd personal criteria of selection which did not violate, but were not contained in, his stated requirements, ended up with a therapy group consisting of attractive young women with a common marital problem. A question arose here not because of the interesting uniformity of the group, but because the therapist did not anticipate his final population (viz. personal attractiveness and sexual frustration were not among his stated criteria). Here the Adult commitment was research on female anxiety, the Parent was doing undeclared and biased research on unsatisfactory husbands, and the Child was secretly fascinated by peripheral aspects; hence the effectiveness of the project was probably impaired. In this case the supervisor suggested a review of the therapist's motivations, with beneficial results in his work.

Since archaic (Child) and borrowed (Parent) attitudes nearly always influence experimental design, at least in dealing with human subjects in the social sciences, their mere presence does not indicate revision as long as the rational (Adult) aspects dominate the others. In that case, the Child and Parent will not impair the value of the research, but will give it a special flavor. Thus in studying the effects of alcohol, a teetotaler with a strong Parent might design a different experiment than an alcoholic with an active Child, but if rational (Adult) considerations took charge of these underlying tendencies, rather than the other way round, both designs might be quite sound. Nevertheless, it would be advisable to have a neutral party do the preliminary motivation analysis. In some cases it would be almost impossible to find such a neutral party. This applies particularly in studies of "juvenile delinquency." Anyone who has listened to a large number of staff conferences dealing with cases in that area may come away with the conviction that both sides are equally rational, but that there is a "selective rationality" depending upon whether the discussant is on the side of the victim or of the aggressor, and that there is a further division of feeling as to who is the victim and who is the aggressor.

An Illustrative Case   A 15-year-old boy attacked an 8-year-old girl, who had to be hospitalized. When this case was brought up at a staff conference, the discussants split into three groups, all equally rational: (1) the "squares," who saw society as the victim to be protected from the aggressive boy; (2) the "bad" people, who wanted to punish the boy; and (3) the "good" people who wanted to keep the boy from becoming the victim of an angry aggressive society by "curing" him. They all agreed pleasantly enough to the traditional suggestion from a visitor that their divergent views might be tested by "research," and that more of that was needed. They were taken aback, however, when the visitor added that he meant research on discussions, not on juvenile delinquency. One discussant said hopefully: "Oh, you mean a survey of attitudes?" The visitor said firmly no, not a survey, but a real effort to find out how so many people could sound equally rational when they were expressing contrary opinions. The conference broke up with considerable uneasiness. Juvenile delinquency is a subject about which people are particularly apt to become angry if the institutionalized polysyllabic safeguards against emotional expression are removed from the discussion.

From the above examples, it should be apparent that while

covert influences may not necessarily impair the experimental design, they are likely to show up in interpreting the data. Thus it would be desirable for every experiment on alcohol to be interpreted by a teetotaler, a "neutral" person, and an alcoholic, and for all three interpretations to be published simultaneously. There is a sufficient supply of well-trained scientists in each category to make this feasible, if the suggestion could be taken seriously.

There is some need for additional information concerning the influence on social action of tape recordings and observers. Indeed, in many cases the stated hypotheses upon which experiments are based are less significant than what is revealed about the behavior of human beings under intrusive observation. If a patient is talking, say, about his troubles with his wife, in his mind the social contract (politeness) calls for the therapist to listen to what he is saying. If the therapist responds, "While you were talking, you were blushing," he has broken this contract by observing the patient instead of listening to him. The patient's reaction to the intrusion is often more clinically significant than the content of what he was saying. A continuous intrusion by a tape recorder is more subtle, and it is difficult to assess its effects on various types of people under different circumstances.*

These illustrations emphasize that an important duty of a researcher to himself, and of a supervisor to his students, is to see that talents, resources, time, and energy are used in the most productive manner, and that they are not indentured to canons of "research" which are themselves insufficiently examined. Experimental study of the canons in many cases may be more urgently needed than experiments undertaken according to the canonical rules. It would seem just as important to study tapes of conferences of observers as to listen to tapes of the

* For some interesting experimental observations in this regard, see E. A. Haggard, J. R. Hiken, and K. S. Isaacs, "Some Effects of Recording and Filming on the Psychotherapeutic Process," *Psychiatry* 28:169–91, 1965.

groups they have observed. Such an infinite regress might yield decisive equations for progress. The study of data-interpreters is one of the most urgent problems in the social sciences at present, but it is difficult to find investigators who are not themselves working within the same canons.

For example, the simplest experiment in group dynamics and social psychology (one which has been performed many times in various forms at the San Francisco Transactional Analysis Seminars [3]) is concerned with the question "What happens when two people are in the same room?" The conventional way of setting up such an experiment, according to consultants, is to consider various methods of observation and recording for the accurate gathering of "material" or "data" which could be analyzed, and then varying the conditions imposed upon the people who were "put" in the room. The seminar approach, however, is different. Either no conditions at all, or else a standard set of conditions are imposed on the participants, and what is varied is the method of observation. This was done under the later validated assumption that the state of being observed is itself the most important parameter in such situations, and that this overrides other (reasonable) conditions. The emergent factor, usually overlooked, was the effect on the observer himself of the act of observation, and the derivative effect that his reactions had on the subjects of the experiment. In this respect, the personality of the experimenter himself, no matter how "objectively" he dealt with the situation and gave his instructions, was the most relevant influence on the reactions of the subjects. Once this is stated, it is "obvious" to an experienced clinician; but researchers are not always meticulous in considering that factor, perhaps in the hope that such a very difficult variable will not have to be dealt with.

The game element associated with some social and psychological research is revealed by the following empirical observation. Commonly, the role of the investigator is seriously and specifically examined only when the scientific community is unwilling to accept the results of his investigations. If he says what they want to hear, they will ask him the color of his eyes only *pro forma*. But if he is a Freud or a Kinsey or a Rhine, they will demand a complete ophthalmoscopic report.

This illustration leads directly into the next set of problems confronting the resarcher in group therapy.

RESEARCH VERSUS TREATMENT

Experience shows that it is possible for patients who are being observed or who are part of a research project to obtain therapeutic benefit in the group situation, but further studies are necessary to assess properly the deleterious or beneficial effects of such manipulations. The overriding consideration is probably not the research design, but the very fact that the patients are being used as experimental "subjects." In this regard, there are at least three significant polarities to consider: (1) Pure treatment groups versus experimental groups of whatever kind. (2) Patients participating in fully explained experiments versus those participating in research which has not been fully explained. (3) Observed "control" groups versus observed "experimental" groups in the usual sense.

In game language, the patients are all playing different games, and usually they are not very constructive games or the players would not be patients. The therapist has two options: either to make the patients game-free or to teach them new games. The moment he consents to experiments, he is teaching them a new game which offers them a new role as experimental or research subjects. This may be more constructive than their previous games but it cannot usually be considered an optimal therapeutic goal. That goal must be freedom from games, or in practice, freedom to choose at any given moment what games they will play. Requiring them to play the role of experimental subjects infringes on this freedom more than just being "patients" does. Furthermore, the therapist in an experimental group undertakes a role other than that of therapist; this puts him under the same disability (previously discussed) as a probation officer who has to play the role of policeman in his groups as well as that of therapist. The effect of such a disability can be demonstrated if a disinterested therapist takes over a probationary group for one or two meetings; the difference in the proceedings with a "police" therapist and with a disinterested "nonpolice" therapist soon becomes apparent. Analogous observations can be made if an "experimenter" therapist in a research group is replaced for one or two meetings by a "nonexperimenter" therapist. These inherent paradoxes can be resolved, but it requires sound clinical experience and determination as well as intelligence to resolve them.

Similar paradoxes emerge, as already noted, if the therapist wants to make "statistics" about his therapeutic results.[4] In the example cited (p. 39), the patients considered the idea to be of dubious value, and in fact quaint, but willingly gave him permission to use them as "objects" in this limited and well-clarified sense, since in other respects he treated them as people. It has long been suspected in clinical psychiatry that a therapist who starts out with the idea of making statistics will obtain different results from one who does not initially have that in mind. This problem arises almost every time a new form of treatment becomes popular, from insulin to the latest tranquilizer.

In group treatment, it is best to maintain the position previously emphasized: that a group is either a pure treatment group or an impure treatment group, and in the latter case the therapeutic results may be diluted. The patients should understand that clearly if they are invited to participate in a research project. Thus forewarned, they may be able to deal effectively with the complications.

Such questions, then, as how and when tests are to be administered, and by whom, can only be validly answered after the canonical principles underlying research in group treatment have themselves been subjected to careful experimental evaluation. In some cases it appears that the more elaborate the research project, the more lifeless and uncreative the proceedings of the group, a paradoxical and self-defeating relationship. Neither the Chi-square nor the circumlocution has so far been a satisfactory measure of what is occurring in such situations.

Perhaps all this has been best summarized from a practical point of view by Orne, who states "it may be fruitful to view the psychological experiment as a very special form of social interaction." [5]

WRITING PAPERS

The clinician should regard the reputable publication of an article as an honor to himself, and should be willing to make himself worthy of it. His obligations are the same as those of all writers. The first is integrity, whether it be scientific or artistic, and the second is craftsmanship. Craftsmanship here is almost synonymous with literacy. If his teachers have sent him forth semi-literate he should make good the deficiency by assiduous study of grammar, syntax, rhetoric, and style, either on his own or at night school. Even with these elements, composition is still a difficult art to master, and he should not consider it an imposition if he is required by his teacher, supervisor, or personal standards to rewrite an article six or seven times before the result is satisfactory.

An apprenticeship in writing should be part of the training of every aspiring young clinical scientist. The supervisor will perform a service to his students by maintaining ruthlessly high literary standards, so that in the end they are forced to express themselves gracefully. He can do that by making meticulous notes on the margins of successive drafts which the student submits to him. He should keep in mind that Joseph Conrad, one of the great masters of the English language, was also a qualified sea-captain, a profession at least as exacting as that of group therapist; yet he found time to develop this mastery — even though he did not learn English until he was grown and already knew several languages. If the institutional staff does not include someone qualified to act in an editorial capacity, a clinician proficient in that field should be found somewhere and invited to join. In a few cases, in spite of the most conscientious application, the difficulties will appear insuperable. People who cannot cultivate an ear for writing should rely on outside assistance, which will most likely be found in the English department of the adult education system.

It is helpful to read the articles in *Science* regularly, and compare them occasionally with the articles in psychotherapy journals. The differences are brought out sharply by Federn in his article "The Neurotic Style." [6] The article writer can save himself a good deal of worry by eliminating the troublesome parasites which afflict many publications in the field of psychotherapy: the first and last pages. Almost every reader, for example, knows initially that the therapy of X is important for the reasons A, B, and C, and is aware finally that further research is indicated, without being told so by the writer in more than two sentences. As a beginning, "important," "complexity," and "interwoven" should be eliminated from all first pages, and "perspective," "deepen," and "broaden" from all last pages. Federn makes it clear that important complexities are interwoven with the need of some authors to apologize for not yet having deepened and broadened our perspectives.

WRITING BOOKS

Even more distressing than the illiterate article is the illiterate and inadequate book. In every city and village in America there are aspiring young writers who would consider it a privilege to participate in the editing of a book. In almost every high school and college there is a student who is an outstanding grammarian and who would be flattered to have this talent employed for such an important undertaking. Some of these young people are conversant with the minutest rules of syntax and can turn out manuscripts that are impeccable in this respect. Furthermore, the reactions of an intelligent English student may be more valuable than those of a more sophisticated critic in the pre-publication phases of book-writing. Thus any clinician who is not confident of his writing proficiency can obtain competent assistance at little expense. The book writer should remember, however, that a certain proportion of American teachers and students are themselves illiterate, and should make certain that he is employing a genuine scholar.

A book is always more useful when it has adequate indexes. It is helpful, for example, if a clinical work has not only a sub-ject index, but also a case or patient index, and certainly an author index, or at least a combination of all three. Purchasers in the professions often use the author index as an aid in judging new books. Psychotherapists, for instance, are more apt to buy a book labeled "Psychoanalytic" if it contains numerous refer-ences to Freud. Certain types of people prefer books that lean heavily on Jung. Some avoid books whose author index indicates that they promise merely to rehash the canonical ideas of a few academically established authorities, and some buy only books of that kind. Hence the inclusion of an author index is only fair to the discriminating purchaser or library reader. A glossary is always useful to neophyte readers, and also serves to orient the more sophisticated reader to the author's specific viewpoints. A semantic note indicating what the author means by such copu-las as "is," "means," and "represents," may serve to clear the air between the writer and the scholarly reader; to take a familiar example, what is such a reader going to do with a statement like "'The red riding-hood of 'Little Red Riding Hood' *represents* menstruation"? To whom — you, me, him, "them," or her?

A final note as to bibliographies and style. The bibliography in alphabetical order may be prestigious, but it is almost useless. If it is in numerical order, it is easier to locate in the text the contribution of any author cited. As to style, this should be kept uniform throughout a single work. By using and adhering to a style manual (such as that put out by the American Medical Association [7]), the writer will give the impression of carefulness and consideration for the reader.

REFERENCES

1. Weiss, P. "Experiences and Experiment in Biology." *Science* 136:468–71, 11 May 1962.
2. Singer, C. *A Short History of Anatomy from the Greeks to Harvey.* Dover Publications, New York, 1957.
3. Steiner, C. "No Exit Revisited." *Transactional Analysis Bulletin* 1:36, 1962.
4. Berne, E. *Transactional Analysis in Psychotherapy.* (Chap 5, ref. 5.)
5. Orne, M. T. "On the Social Psychology of the Psychological Experiment." *Amer. Psychologist* 17:776–83, 1962.
6. Federn, P. "The Neurotic Style." *Psychiat. Quart.* 31:681–9, 1957.
7. *Style Book and Editorial Manual.* American Medical Association, Chicago, 1965.

9

The Literature of Group Treatment

In order for the student to consider himself literate in his chosen field, he should have some over-all familiarity with the literature on both group treatment and group dynamics, and there are certain items that he would do well to read in their entirety. He should bear in mind that the modern writings are not necessarily superior to the older ones, which are often more stimulating and informative and better written than many of the new. The following selected references will give him an adequate foundation for intelligent thinking and discussion.

GROUP TREATMENT

A summary of the significant literature on group treatment up to 1945 is contained in the symposium published in that year under the editorship of J. L. Moreno.[1] Both the book and the bibliography are somewhat overloaded in favor of the editor, with some corresponding neglect of other contemporaries, but it is nevertheless the best survey available up to that time. The student should look through this book and read the items that are obviously of more than specialized or passing interest and that form part of the real groundwork of the subject. There are also two papers of this epoch which he should have read. One is Trigant Burrow's 1928 paper [2] "The Basis of Group Analysis," which may be taken as the germinal paper of group treatment as we know it today, although there is no doubt that others contributed substantially from many different aspects. The other is Giles Thomas's 1943 paper,[3] in which he reviews and classifies the methods of group therapy commonly in use up to that time. Thomas's paper stresses many of the writers who are neglected or only mentioned in passing in Moreno's symposium, and hence balances the other.

The literature of the late 'forties is well covered in the bibliography on group psychotherapy published by the American Group Psychotherapy Association in 1950,[5] and its supplement published in 1954.[6] A careful perusal of these titles will familiarize the student with the main trends during that period, and he can pick out whichever items strike him as important for his reading list.

The third bibliographical period runs from 1951, when the *International Journal of Group Psychotherapy* [4] began publication, to 1960. This is best covered by leafing through the *International Journal* from Volume I on, or consulting the annual index of that journal and picking out for special study whichever titles stimulate the student's interest. Because this literature is almost entirely empirical, there are no objective criteria for recommending one article over another. The few theoretical articles included are not recommended because for the most part they are speculative, and hence not easy to evaluate. There are also many articles on the subject of group therapy scattered throughout other periodicals during this decade, as well as a few books, and in most cases these can be located from the bibliographies of articles in the *International Journal*. The other journal principally devoted to this field goes under the simple title *Group Psychotherapy*.[7] There is little cross-fertilization between these two journals, however, and references from one to the other are conspicuously sparse. The conscientious student, therefore, should inspect the files of both. The texts of Slavson [8] and of Bach [9] belong to this period.

Special mention should be made of what might loosely (and without prejudice) be called "the English school." The student is advised to read the easily accessible publications of Bion,[10] Ezriel,[11] Foulkes,[12] and their colleagues. The work of Maxwell Jones [13] on the therapeutic community can also be included here.

Since 1960, there have been three noteworthy developments. The first is the surge of interest in family therapy. Some of the outstanding writers in this area (besides others to be found in the *International Journal* and the *American Journal of Orthopsychiatry*),[14] are Ackerman,[15] Bell,[16] Grotjahn,[17] and Satir.[18] In addition, there is a new journal, *Family Process*,[19] which will keep the student up-to-date in this rapidly expanding field. The second new development is the growth of transactional analysis. The two basic works on this approach are both by the present writer: *Transactional Analysis in Psychotherapy*,[20] and *Games People Play*.[21] The recently founded *Transactional Analysis Bulletin* [22] is compactly written, and, as of the present writing, the student should be able to read through the whole file in one or two evenings; this will enable him to keep up with what is happening in transactional analysis. The third phenomenon of recent years is the emergence of a "new generation" of psychoanalytic group therapists, and there are three books that may be consulted for the recent developments in this specialized field: Rosenbaum and Berger's symposium of sixty-four writers,[23] Mullan and Rosenbaum's text,[24] and Wolf and Schwartz's monograph on "Psychoanalysis in Groups." [25]

GROUP DYNAMICS

The student should remember that proportionately, there were just as many intelligent people in the world in the old days as there are now. Many of them were relatively isolated as thinkers, and had the additional advantage of being unhampered by the demands of methodological and material technology and the need for academic and journalistic compliance. Hence they could concentrate to a considerable extent on pure clarity of thought. (This possibility still exists nowadays, but there is a greater variety of pressures, banalities, and distractions to avoid.) Many of the classical philosophers gave a great deal of attention to the problems of group dynamics, although not under that name. The intellectual contributions of the three centuries from 1500 to 1800 were most ably and authoritatively surveyed by Otto Gierke almost a hundred years ago, and the most relevant parts of Gierke have been summarized in a very palatable way by Ernest Barker of Cambridge under the title *Natural Law and the Theory of Society*.[26] It is ostensibly a legal treatise, but actually it is probably the best extant work in the broad field of group dynamics. Indeed, the very title is thought provoking: that what we call "group dynamics" was called "natural law" by the most accomplished individuals among our ancestors in social philosophy. The student should read, study, and ponder at least the translator's introduction, and as much of the text as he is able to assimilate.

An over-all view of the nineteenth and early twentieth centuries can usually be found in any good sociology textbook, such as that of Hinkle and Hinkle.[27] The psychoanalytic approach to group dynamics dates from this period, and is found in Freud's monograph *Group Psychology and the Analysis of the Ego*.[28] There he refers to Le Bon,[29] McDougall,[30] and Trotter,[31] who may be consulted as able exponents of the naturalistic approach to group dynamics. Freud's views are examined critically and carried forward in their relationships to later writings in Scheidelinger's book *Psychoanalysis and Group Behavior*, subtitled *A Study in Freudian Group Psychology*, a subject which every clinician will want to become familiar with.[32] The student, however, should not be beguiled into neglecting what is new in the field since Freud published his book in 1922. Unfortunately he will find that some of his weaker colleagues have been snatched from good companions by the Scylla of social psychology ("Nothing worth while was written before 1923"), while others have been drowned by the Charybdis of "orthodoxy" ("Nothing worth while was written after 1922").*

The emergence of group dynamics as an experimental discipline came into full flower following World War II. There are two symposia which will give the student a wide sampling of this approach: one by Cartwright and Zander,[33] the other by Hare, Borgatta, and Bales.[34] Not all of these papers will be impressive or interesting to the clinical worker, but there are sure to be some in each of these books that he will find interesting and instructive. Most recent is the transactional approach to group dynamics (as distinguished from the "interactional" approach). This is directly derived from the therapy chamber rather than the laboratory, and hence it is most pertinent for the group therapist. It has already been summarized, insofar as it applies to therapy groups, in Chapter 6, and will be found *in extenso* in the writer's book *The Structure and Dynamics of Organizations and Groups*.[35]

SPECIAL TOPICS

Besides the basic items given above, the following suggestions are offered for people who wish to pursue special topics.

PSYCHODRAMA

Dr. Moreno (in a private communication) recommends as a suitable introduction to this subject his article in the *American Handbook of Psychiatry*.[36] This includes an authoritative bibliography.

---

* About Scylla, the less said the better. Charybdis stole the oxen of Hercules, and was turned into a whirlpool.

GESTALT THERAPY

This interesting development, still in a highly experimental stage, is outlined by Perls and his associates.[37] It should probably not be attempted except under the guidance of an experienced senior psychiatrist.

EXISTENTIAL THERAPY

This is still highly individualized. A good introduction to the subject is found in Rollo May's small handbook.[38]

SOCIAL PSYCHOLOGY

For an over-all view of the social psychologist's approach to social dynamics, Krech and Crutchfield,[39] or J. F. Brown[40] may be consulted.

OMISSIONS

No doubt each reader will think of some work or topic which he would like to have seen included in this chapter. Nevertheless, anyone who has read or is acquainted with all the works cited here can consider himself reasonably, or even exceptionally, well grounded in the literature of the subject.

REFERENCES

1. Moreno, J. L. (ed.). *Group Psychotherapy: A Symposium.* Beacon House, Beacon, N.Y., 1945.
2. Burrow, T. "The Basis of Group-Analysis." *Brit. Jnl. Med. Psychol.* 8:198–206, 1928.
3. Thomas, G. W. "Group Psychotherapv: A Review of the Recent Literature." *Psychosom. Med.* 5:166–80, 1943.
4. *International Journal of Group Psychotherapy.* Vols. I–XVI ff. International Universities Press, 227 West 13th Street, New York, N.Y. 10011.
5. & 6. *Bibliography on Group Psychotherapy.* American Group

Psychotherapy Association, 227 West 13th Street, New York, N.Y. 10011. Vol. I, 1950. Vol. II, 1954.

7. *Group Psychotherapy.* Beacon House, Inc., Beacon, N.Y.

8. Slavson, S. R. *Analytic Group Psychotherapy.* (Chap. 5, ref. 12.)

9. Bach, G. *Intensive Group Psychotherapy.* Ronald Press Company, New York, 1954.

10. Bion, W. R. *Experiences in Groups.* (Chap. 5, ref. 6.)

11. Ezriel, H. "Notes on Psychoanalytic Group Therapy: Interpretation and Research." *Psychiatry* 15:119–26, 1952.

12. Foulkes, S. H. *Therapeutic Group Analysis.* (Chap. 5, ref. 2.)

13. Jones, M. S. *The Therapeutic Community.* Basic Books, New York, 1953.

14. *American Journal of Orthopsychiatry.* American Orthopsychiatric Association, 1790 Broadway, New York, N.Y. 10019.

15. Ackerman, N. W. *The Psychodynamics of Family Life.* Basic Books, New York, 1958.

16. Bell, J. E. *Family Group Therapy.* Public Health Monograph #64. U.S. Public Health Service, Washington, 1961.

17. Grotjahn, M. *Psychoanalysis and the Family Neurosis.* W. W. Norton & Company, New York, 1960.

18. Satir, V. *Conjoint Family Therapy.* Science & Behavior Books, Palo Alto, Calif., 1964.

19. *Family Process.* Vol. I, 1962. 428 E. Preston Street, Baltimore, Md.

20. Berne, E. *Transactional Analysis in Psychotherapy.* (Chap. 5, ref. 5.)

21. Berne, E. *Games People Play.* Grove Press, New York, 1964.

22. *Transactional Analysis Bulletin.* Vol. I–V, 1962–. Box 5747, Carmel, California.

23. Rosenbaum, M., and M. Berger (eds.). *Group Psychotherapy and Group Function.* Basic Books, New York, 1963.

24. Mullan, H., and M. Rosenbaum. *Group Psychotherapy.* (Chap. 1, ref. 1.)

25. Wolf, A., and E. K. Schwartz. *Psychoanalysis in Groups.* (Chap. 1, ref. 2.)

26. Gierke, O. *Natural Law and the Theory of Society.* (Chap. 2, ref. 5.)

27. Hinkle, R. C., and G. J. Hinkle. *The Development of Modern Sociology.* Random House, New York, 1954.

28. Freud, S. *Group Psychology and the Analysis of the Ego.* Hogarth Press, London, 1940.
29. Le Bon, G. *The Crowd.* Ernest Benn, London, 1952.
30. McDougall, W. *The Group Mind.* G. P. Putnam's Sons, New York, 1920.
31. Trotter, W. *Instincts of the Herd in Peace and War.* The Macmillan Company, New York, 1916.
32. Scheidlinger, S. *Psychoanalysis and Group Behavior.* W. W. Norton & Company, New York, 1952.
33. Cartwright, D., and A. Zander. *Group Dynamics, Research and Theory.* Row, Peterson & Company, Evanston, Ill., 1953.
34. Hare, P., E. Borgatta, and R. Bales (eds.). *Small Groups.* Alfred A. Knopf, New York, 1955.
35. Berne, E. *The Structure and Dynamics of Organizations and Groups.* (Chap. 2, ref. 4.)
36. Moreno, J. L. "Psychodrama." *American Handbook of Psychiatry.* Basic Books, New York, 1959, Vol. II, 1375–96.
37. Perls, F., R. F. Hefferline, and P. Goodman. *Gestalt Therapy.* Dell Publishing Company, New York, 1965.
38. May, R. (ed.). *Existential Psychology.* Random House, New York, 1961.
39. Krech, D., and R. S. Crutchfield. *Theory and Problems of Social Psychology.* McGraw-Hill Book Company, New York, 1948.
40. Brown, J. F. *Psychology and the Social Order.* McGraw-Hill Book Company, New York, 1936.

II
Transactional Analysis

10
General Principles

The Therapist's Duties Group treatment, as the term is intended here, is contractual rather than institutionalized. After a patient presents himself for treatment, the therapist in some way or other at an appropriate time clarifies what he might be able to do to ameliorate the patient's condition. If and when the patient accepts the stated or implied offer, in whatever form it is made, the treatment can proceed according to the therapist's plan.

Group treatment is proposed only after careful consideration, with reasoned clinical judgment, of all the possible approaches available in the psychiatric community. This is different from what is commonly thought of as the "selection" of patients for group therapy. Here it is not a question of the patient being "selected" or "rejected," but of a clinical prescription. No patient is rejected for group treatment; he may, however, be selected for some other form of active, ongoing treatment. The difference is not semantic, but prescriptive. Shock treatment, psychoanalysis, and group treatment may be thought of, initially at least, as mutually exclusive, so that one or another is prescribed, according to the indications, with or without adjuvant drugs. If

group treatment is not considered the best prescription, the
patient may have to be referred elsewhere — for shock treatment
or psychoanalysis, for example. In no case is the patient permitted to prescibe group treatment for himself, but his inclina-
tions may be given some weight in the therapeutic decision,
which may well determine his whole future and that of his
family also. The entire past training and experience of the
therapist are brought to bear on the choice of treatment to ensure that the patient will receive the maximum benefit by the
method selected. The therapist's prescription tests his clinical
judgment just as the selection of a medication tests the quality
of a physician as much as his diagnostic skill does.

Assuming the justifiable election of group treatment, the
groundwork has been laid during the preliminary diagnostic
period. When the therapist thinks (not "feels") that the preparation has been adequate, the patient is introduced into a treatment group. If the patient is reluctant, the therapist has to
consider carefully whether to exert pressure in a given case, or
whether to allow time for additional preparation in order to
implement his decision to the best advantage.

Once the therapeutic goals have been clarified, it is the therapist's duty to attain them with the greatest economy of time,
money, effort, and discomfort, using his best judgment in applying all the therapeutic techniques at his disposal. These include
physical, chemical, and psychological methods, alone or in combination. Group treatment may be the preferred prescription
for a given case at a given time, with some other forms of therapy excluded, but as treatment proceeds the therapist may
change his mind. What we are concerned with here is the optimal application of psychological methods, but these methods are
still subject to comparison with other approaches. For example,
Winkelman prescribed large doses of chlorpromazine for ambulatory patients, sustained for as long as ten years, and states
that "half of the schizophrenics had a lasting remission," and

more than three-quarters of them were "markedly improved," while two-thirds of his psychoneurotic patients were "significantly improved." [1] If group therapy is to justify its existence, it should be able to meet such challenges, by assembling equally good or better clinical reports which can be subjected to critical scrutiny. This puts it squarely up to the group therapist to demonstrate that he gets even more decisive improvement in at least 70 per cent of his patients.

Psychoanalytic Therapy In many cases, it is clear that the most appropriate treatment is formal orthodox psychoanalysis. Since that is not available for a variety of reasons to the majority of psychiatric patients, a modified version, psychoanalytic psychotherapy, is more commonly employed. As already noted, that form of treatment is not specifically adapted to the group situation. The continued insistence on applying it there has not yielded either theoretical development, technical advances, or maximum clinical results (e.g. decisive improvement in at least 70 per cent of patients).

It should be borne in mind, furthermore, that even in cases where psychoanalysis is "theoretically" the best approach, in practice it is not always the most desirable. Psychotherapy is too often a race between constructive reorientations and destructive tendencies, and psychoanalysis, by its very virtue of meticulousness, is a slow process; hence it may win the battles, only to lose the war. What the group therapist should strive for is to win the war first, and fight the battles later.

Criteria for a Therapeutic Method There are several important criteria for a practical approach to group treatment. Such an approach should be available to as many therapists as possible, and effective for as many types of patients as possible; it should be as basic as possible; it should be indigenous rather than borrowed; and it should meet the standards for a rational, ongoing therapy:

1. Many psychotherapists have not had psychoanalytic train-

ing, and such people should be able to find their places in the therapeutic community so that their talents can be applied to the best advantage.

2. There is no convincing reason to abandon Freud's dictum of thirty years ago: "You know already that the field in which analytical therapy can be applied is that of the transference-neuroses, phobias, hysterias, obsessional neurosis, and besides these such abnormalities of character as have been developed instead of these diseases. Everything other than these, such as narcissistic or psychotic conditions, is more or less unsuitable." [2] It would be advantageous to have a more general form of treatment that would be suitable for wider application.

3. The most desirable approach to group treatment would in addition offer a hard foundation upon which psychoanalytic therapy and other forms of therapy could build as indicated by the needs of individual patients and the skills of individual therapists. In this way it would be useful both to its own trained practitioners, and to those with specialized knowledge of other therapeutic approaches.

4. The factors that differentiate group treatment from individual treatment and the advantages offered by a group setting should be recognized in some form of treatment which is indigenous to the therapy group, rather than floating group therapy in the juice squeezed out by organized intellectual pressure from individual therapeutic methods. Such an indigenous method should not interfere at the later stages with the carrying out of specific therapeutic maneuvers based on other approaches.

Transactional analysis meets these criteria for an improved method of group treatment. It requires less training of the therapist than psychoanalysis; it is effective for the large majority of psychiatric patients of all types; it opens the way for the application of specialized treatments; and it evolved indigenously from the group-therapy chamber.

5. In order for the therapist to carry out his therapeutic

contract, he must have a sound knowledge of the therapeutic approaches available and use his judgment to select the one most suitable in the group for the largest number of patients. He must then have some concept of the specific goals of psychotherapy, and he must be able to plan his operations so as to accomplish those goals in a systematic way.

Taking as the most general statement that psychiatric patients are confused, the goal of psychotherapy then becomes to resolve that confusion in a well-planned way by a series of analytic and synthetic operations. Again in the most general descriptive form, these operations will consist of decontamination, recathexis, clarification, and reorientation. Decontamination means that where the patient's reactions, feelings, or viewpoints are adulterated or distorted, the situation will be rectified by a process analogous to that of anatomical dissection. Recathexis means that the effective emphasis the patient puts on various aspects of his experience will be changed. Clarification means that the patient himself will have some understanding of what is going on so that he can maintain the new condition in a stable form and, hopefully, extrapolate the previous processes without the help of the therapist into new situations that he will encounter after the treatment is terminated. Reorientation means that as a result of all this, the patient's behavior, responses, and aspirations will be changed to be what some reasonable consensus would regard as more constructive.

Transactional analysis, besides meeting the general criteria for usefulness stated above, has the following specific advantages as a psychotherapeutic method:

1. It supplies a framework, structural analysis (that is, the separation of discrete ego states), within which decontamination can take place. It makes a statement about what is contaminated and what is contaminating, namely, that one named ego state is contaminating another.

2. Structural analysis also supplies a framework for the ap-

plication of recathexis; that is, it states the systems involved so that the therapist can determine in which direction the cathexis should be encouraged to flow.

3. Transactional analysis, because of its clear-cut statements rooted in easily accessible material, because of its operational nature, and because of the small size of its specialized vocabulary (consisting in practice of only five words: Parent, Adult, Child, game, and script), offers an easily learned framework for clarification.

4. Again because of its operational nature, it provides an immediate and easily verifiable check on the patient's degree of reorientation.

All this may be summarized pragmatically by saying that from the contractual viewpoint, because of its general applicability and rapid effectiveness, transactional analysis provides the therapist with an instrument for accomplishing his contract with great economy, and one which does not interfere with later operations based on specialized knowledge or designed for particular conditions or particular patients.

Because of (or in spite of) its immediate cogency, the therapeutic results of transactional analysis compare favorably in stability with those of any other approach. Every therapist has "lucky" cases now and then, where patients make remarkable progress with unexpected rapidity. The conscientious student may find that transactional analysis increases such therapeutic "luck" by a considerable factor. In the same way, some mining prospectors have an occasional stroke of luck, while some specially trained mining engineers seem to have "luck" more consistently.

GENERAL CHARACTERISTICS OF
TRANSACTIONAL ANALYSIS

A transactional analyst makes a point of keeping the patient informed of what is happening to him as he goes along, thus often earning his gratitude as well as his improvement. This runs counter to the institutionalized dogma that the patient is not supposed to know what is happening to him, and will get better to more advantage if he is kept in the dark. Thus far, no untoward effects have been noticed from patients having a clear understanding of what is going on in the therapeutic situation, of exactly how far they have progressed, and of how much still remains to be done. The specialized vocabulary of five words can often be taught in a sound way in two or three sessions, with clinical demonstrations from the immediate proceedings of the group.

Since most patients are eager to learn, their alternatives lie between a small vocabulary of well-assimilated operational and experiential terminology which they have personally verified at the clinical level under planned guidance, or a larger vocabulary of ill-digested concepts which they have acquired adventitiously or surreptitiously. The "danger of intellectualization" is another fear which has been institutionally exaggerated, so that the word "intellectualization" is often used carelessly as an epithet which derogates not only the specific defence, but also the patient's useful application of his intelligence to the solution of his problems. In practice, there is little difficulty in making the distinction by those who give it their unbiased attention, so that not only the therapist, but the patients as well can soon learn to recognize the difference between intellectualization and using intelligence.*

After the patients begin to feel more comfortable in a transactional therapy group and affective expression becomes more vigorous, the therapist must learn, as in all forms of therapy, to distinguish between melodrama, institutionally encouraged acting-out, and authentic expressions of feeling; nor must he suc-

* As Anna Freud says, "The intellectual work performed by the ego during the latency-period and in adult life is incomparably more solid, more reliable and, above all, much more closely connected with action [than the infant's intellectual activity in sexual investigation]" — *The Ego and the Mechanisms of Defence*. Hogarth Press, London, 1948, p. 180.

cumb to a popular misconception of psychoanalytic treatment, which is sometimes thought of by outsiders as a continual storm of affective expression. Transactional analysis, like psychoanalysis, clears the way to expression of genuine affect rather than encouraging mere abreaction or dramatic incidents based on spurious motivation, which often serve mainly as a relief of boredom in patient and therapist. "Affectivization" of the proceedings is no more helpful than their "intellectualization;" both encourage isolation. Affectivization isolates intelligence, just as intellectualization isolates affect. The goal of transactional analysis is to estabish the most open and authentic communication possible between the affective and intellectual components of the personality.

Transactional analysis does not pretend to be a restatement of Freudian, Jungian, or other psychology. Superego, ego, and id are concepts, whereas ego states are experiential and behavioral realities, and are even civil realities in a sense. The colloquialism here is that you can't find the telephone number of a superego, an ego, or an id, but you can find the telephone number of a Parent (such as the patient's father), or of an Adult (the patient himself), or of a Child (his telephone number when he was a little boy). The most fruitful application of psychoanalytic thinking finds its place in group treatment after the patient has been properly prepared by transactional analysis. It is also a profitable preparation for Jungian, Adlerian, existential, and other specialized terminologies and ways of therapeutic thinking. Transactional analysis, then, claims (and this claim has been filed elsewhere in more detail) [3] to be more general than any of these, and hence leaves room for all of them in appropriate contexts.

Transactional theory is simpler and more scientifically economical in its statements than many other psychotherapeutic theories, but its clinical use requires conscientious study, and in the advanced stages where it begins to overlap with psychoanalytic and existential therapies it takes on increased complexity. Nevertheless, its principles can be understood and appreciated by any well-trained psychotherapist, since it deals with the same phenomena as any other approach: human psychopathology. Many others have made observations in passing that resemble transactional statements. What is new here is the manner of ordering and dealing with these phenomena, and the systematic exploration and clarification of certain kinds of statements. The difference between an acute observation and a systematic theory is the difference between a poultice of bread with mold on it and a penicillin injection: they both contain the same essential ingredient, but one is more useful than the other.

Illustrations Two applications of transactional analysis will now be offered for consideration, one heuristic and the other clinical.

First, the therapeutic "poker face," which in unsophisticated circles is considered the hallmark of the trained therapist, is not always easy to justify. The reasons commonly given for maintaining this impassivity in group treatment can be sorted into five classes, which in increasing order of cogency and authenticity are as follows:

1. The therapist is "supposed" to keep a poker face, because everybody knows it is so and the books say so. This amounts to playing a role with the poker face as a physiological uniform.

2. A therapist may be subject to critical questioning at staff conferences if he does not keep a poker face, so that there is some implication that immobility or restrained token mimicry is as far as it is safe to go.

3. Sometimes it appears that the real reason for the poker face is that the therapist does not know what to do next and remains frozen hour after hour in the hope that some clue will be forthcoming.

4. In order for the patient to form a pure transference, it is essential that the therapist not reveal his own reactions to what the patient says.

5. The therapist does not react overtly because it is his task to keep from becoming involved in the patient's manipulations: first, so that he can retain control of the situation; secondly, so that he can observe the patient's reactions better; and thirdly, because it is important to know what the patient does when his manipulations fail.

The last explanation is the most valid one for those therapists who understand it clearly enough to know when relaxations are indicated. As to the other four, the first case signifies an act of compliance, the second an undue vulnerability, the third a deficiency in knowledge, and the fourth a misconception which does not distinguish clearly between psychotherapy and formal psychoanalysis. It will be noted that even in the fifth category, the therapist has not clearly defined his criteria for relaxing his immobility. This whole problem can be solved quite concisely in transactional terms.

From that standpoint, there are three types of therapy. In the first, as with certain schizophrenics, the therapist plays a Parental role and can exhibit his Parental ego state advantageously. In the second, as in analytic work with grown-ups, his task is to process data, which he can do most efficiently by maintaining a strictly Adult ego state. In the third, as in play therapy with children, the therapist may have to participate in the play at times, and will do that most naturally in his own Child ego state. It is immediately apparent that the prolonged maintenance of a poker face is appropriate only to the second type, and appropriate relaxations are clearly indicated by the nature of the other two kinds of therapy. Furthermore, relaxations are also indicated in "Adult" therapy whenever other considerations take precedence over data-processing; there may be occasions when reassurance, permission, or sagacity from the Parent (page 248) or humor or liveliness from the Child (pages 237 ff.) are indicated.

In the second example of transactional analysis, one supplied by Dr. Robert Goulding from a relatively new group of alcoholic patients, the rapid and clear-cut effects of structural analysis (the first phase of transactional analysis) are nicely demonstrated. Selma was originally Patricia's sponsor in Alcoholics Anonymous. When they came to the treatment group, Patricia reacted like a rebellious child toward Selma, and Selma fought back. With structural analysis, they soon perceived that it was Patricia's Child fighting with Selma's Parent. Patricia recognized her particular sensitivity, based on her own childhood, to Selma's mother Parent. Selma then recognized the irritating quality of Patricia's Child as reminiscent of her own little sister. Once this structure was clarified by them and historically validated, they lost interest in fighting and left the meeting arm in arm for the first time, laughing. This manner of exit also answered operationally their question "What can one do instead of drinking?" by giving them the experience of being friends with people even when sober.

The challenge in this situation lies in the fact that Selma and Patricia are getting better faster than they are supposed to and that this is happening without undue strain on either the therapist's or the patients' part. Rapid improvements with structural analysis may be quite stable and enduring if the patients have authentic insight into the structure of their transactions, and are not merely "making with the interpretations."

THE FORMAL ASPECTS OF
TRANSACTIONAL ANALYSIS

The formal exposition of the principles of transactional analysis has been set down in three previous volumes,[3,4,5] and will be given here only in the barest outline. Those principles were first derived from actual clinical material in treatment groups and only later stated formally and supported by documentation. This process will be reversed here; the principles will be given first and the clinical aspects clarified later.

STRUCTURAL ANALYSIS

Ego States Every human being has at his disposal a limited repertoire of ego states, which fall into three types. Parental ego states are borrowed from parental figures and reproduce the feelings, attitudes, behavior, and responses of those figures. Adult ego states are concerned with the autonomous collecting and processing of data and the estimating of probabilities as a basis for action. Child ego states are relics from the individual's childhood and reproduce his behavior and state of mind at a particular moment or epoch of his development, using, however, the increased facilities at his disposal as a grown-up. It is assumed that there are three organs which mediate the organization and implementation of these three types of ego states. The exteropsyche is concerned with Parental ego states, the neopsyche with Adult ego states, and the archaeopsyche with Child ego states.

The superego, ego, and id as defined by Freud are regarded as determinants of special characteristics of each type of ego state, but neither the ego states themselves nor the organs that "give rise" to them correspond to the Freudian "agencies." Superego, ego, and id are inferential concepts, while ego states are experiential and social realities. The descriptive study of ego states takes precedence over the study of the influences that determine them. In doctrinal terms, structural analysis precedes psychoanalysis. In structural language, psychoanalysis is essentially a process of deconfusing the Child ego state, but that ego state must first be isolated and described, and the Adult ego state must simultaneously be decontaminated and recathected so that it is free to assist with the subsequent analytic work.

The term "transactional analysis" is used to describe the system as a whole, which is divided into a logical and clinically useful sequence of phases: structural analysis, transactional analysis proper, game analysis, and script analysis. The diagnosis of ego states has been described elsewhere,[3] and is a special art to be cultivated by the therapist. A Parental ego state exhibited by a patient is referred to colloquially as his "Parent," an Adult ego state is called his "Adult," and an archaic ego state is called his "Child." Gratifying therapeutic results may be obtained from structural analysis alone, hence it is worth while for its own sake; the fact that it builds a solid foundation for further progress is an additional advantage.

The "Weak Ego" Two special features of structural analysis should be mentioned. First, there is nothing in this approach which corresponds exactly to the "weak ego" of conventional terminology. Every human being (except perhaps some with the most severe types of organic brain injuries) is regarded as possessing the complete neurological apparatus for neopsychic functioning. In certain cases the Adult ego state may be spoken of as "weakly cathected," but it is never dealt with as though there were some inherent defect in its structure. In clinical practice it can be verified that even mentally retarded people and "deteriorated" schizophrenics possess the complete apparatus for Adult ego functioning, and the therapeutic problem is to cathect this apparatus in order that it may take its normal place in the patient's psychic organization. As an analogy: if no radio is heard in someone's house that does not mean he lacks one; he may have a good one, but it needs to be turned on and warmed up before it can be heard clearly.

In this respect, then, structural analysis is more optimistic than other therapeutic systems, and this optimism is warranted by the results. If a patient is treated as though he had a "weak ego," he is likely to respond accordingly; if he is treated as though he had a perfectly good ego which only needs to be activated, experience shows that there is a good chance that his Adult ego state will become more and more active in his life: that is, he will become more rational and objective toward the outside world and toward himself.

"Mature" and "Immature" The second distinguishing feature is that the words "mature" and "immature" are never used in transactional analysis. Some of the reasons for this have already been implied in the previous paragraph. In general those are rather fatuous conceptions based on an essentially patronizing attitude. It is not that one person is "mature" and another "immature"; it is merely that one person chooses to exhibit his Child ego state more often than another. To take two rather clear-cut examples, an alcoholic may have a high capacity for processing certain kinds of data during his working hours, but when he relaxes his Adult ego state after work, he may behave in a child-like way. On the other hand one who is thought of as "mature" by his associates — a steady, "co-operative" community leader — may one day turn out to be an embezzler or a murderer, taking almost everyone by surprise. The question raised by these commonplace cases is as follows: is the responsible man who commits indiscretions when he is intoxicated to be called "immature," and the man who lives compliantly until he commits a crime to be thought of as "mature?"

Special Distinctions The structural analyst must be familiar with certain functional distinctions in the Parent and Child. What is loosely spoken of as "the Parent" may signify either the Parental ego state — that is, a reproduction of nurturing, angry, or critical behavior on the part of one or both parents — or the Parental influence — that is, behavior historically determined by borrowed parameters. In the Parental ego state, a woman is behaving as mother behaved; under the Parental influence, she is behaving as mother would have liked; and this includes specific maternal permissions or instigations as well as the specific maternal prohibitions generally included under the concept of superego. Hence this purely transactional, behavioral approach avoids the complications and limitations imposed by words like "identification" and "superego," impositions which are largely irrelevant to therapeutic progress, at least in group treatment. The Child similarly is exhibited in two phases: the adapted Child, who is acting under the Parental influence, as evidenced by such adaptations as compliance or withdrawal; and the expressive Child, who acts autonomously in expressing creative, angry, or affectionate tendencies.

Second-Order Structural Analysis At a late stage in treatment, second-order structural analysis may be indicated. This will reveal that the Parent has its own internal structure, such as that shown in Figure 7, where that aspect of the patient's personality structure is divided into "mother" and "father" segments, each of these in turn having Parent, Adult, and Child components, since the actual mother and father, being human beings, also have the usual repertoires of ego states. For patients in an advanced stage of structural analysis, each subdivision of Figure 7 may have clinical and historical significance. Correspondingly, the Child ego state, at the time it was originally fixated, already had Parent, Adult, and Child components, so that second order structural analysis may reveal an even more archaic ego state embedded in the Child ego state as currently exhibited by the patient. Thus a woman who ordinarily talks and acts like a ten-year-old girl may under stress feel and respond like a confused ("schizophrenic") two-year-old.

TRANSACTIONAL ANALYSIS

Complementary Transactions Transactional analysis consists of determining which ego state is active at a given moment in the exhibition of a transactional stimulus by the agent, and which ego state is active in the response given by the respondent. Complementary transactions are those in which the vectors are parallel; that is, the response complements the stimulus. A Parental husband speaking to a Child-like wife will expect a Child-like response from her, as shown in Figure 8A. An Adult stimulus anticipates an Adult response, as shown in Figure 8B. This principle gives the first rule of communication: as long as

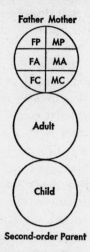

Father Mother

FP	MP
FA	MA
FC	MC

Adult

Child

Second-order Parent

Fig. 7. Structural diagram of a personality

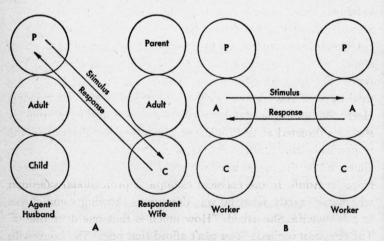

Fig. 8. Complementary transactions

the vectors are parallel, communication can proceed indefinitely. This is a necessary but not the sole condition for a "good" relationship; if the transactions become unpalatable enough, the relationship may deteriorate even though the vectors remain parallel.

Crossed Transactions If an Adult stimulus, such as an interpretation or comment, elicits a Child-to-Parent reaction, the vectors are crossed, as shown in Figure 6 (Chapter 6). This type of crossing is the commonest source of difficulty in social, occupational, and domestic life, and is known as Crossed Transaction Type I. In therapy it constitutes the typical transference reaction. An Adult-to-Adult stimulus eliciting a Parent-to-Child response forms Crossed Transaction Type II (Figure 9). This is the classical counter-transference reaction. It will be apparent that there are seventy-two varieties of crossed transactions, but I and II are the commonest types found in clinical work. The study of crossed transactions gives rise to the second rule of communication: if the vectors are crossed, communication is broken off, and the relationship is "bad"; or in its clinical converse, if communication is broken off, there has usually (or always?) been a crossed transaction.

Ulterior Transactions Both complementary and crossed transactions are simple transactions. Ulterior transactions are of two types. The angular transaction (Figure 10) is most commonly used by professionals who deal with people in their daily work. Here an ostensible Adult-to-Adult stimulus conceals another stimulus directed at the Child (or sometimes the Parent) of the respondent. The desired response comes from the respondent's Child, while the agent is in the clear because his stimulus was factually Adult. In the classical example a professional salesman who knew exactly what he was doing was showing some stoves to a housewife. She asked: "How much is that one over there?" The salesman replied: "You can't afford that one." The housewife declared defiantly: "That's the one I'll take." Here the salesman's

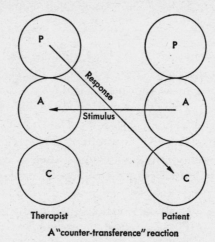

A "counter-transference" reaction

Fig. 9. A transactional diagram: crossed transaction type II

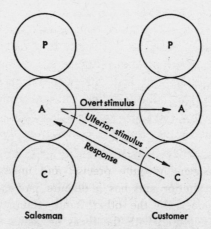

Fig. 10. An angular transaction

answer to her question (his transactional stimulus) was factual, since his estimate of her financial standing was correct. As a professional salesman, however, he knew that her Child would be listening to his Adult judgment and would respond on the basis of some child-like feeling (although he used other terminology). She disregarded his accurate factual statement of what she could afford and responded the way he wanted her to.

The second type of ulterior transaction is the duplex transaction (Figure 11) in which at the social or overt level — the level found on the tape recording or the transcript — the stimuli and responses are Adult-to-Adult; but it is evident to a sophisticated observer that below the surface there is another and more meaningful level, the psychological or covert level, where there is Child-to-Child or Parent-to-Child communication. This duplicity gives rise to the third rule of communication: the behavioral outcome of an ulterior transaction is determined at the psychological and not at the social level. In its pragmatic (e.g. research) inverse, this rule reads: No kind or amount of processing of the social level can predict the behavioral outcome of an ulterior transaction; prediction is universally contingent on a knowledge of the psychological level.

GAME ANALYSIS

A game is a series of ulterior transactions with a gimmick, leading to a usually well-concealed but well-defined pay-off. For a detailed discussion the reader is referred to the writer's volume *Games People Play*.[5] Clinical examples relating specifically to therapeutic situations, however, will be given in Chapter 14. The most important thing to remember is that the definition of a game is quite precise, and unless a series of transactions is ulterior and has a definite pay-off it does not constitute a game. On the other hand, transactional games should not be confused with the types of games dealt with in

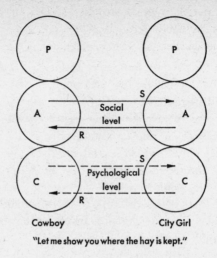

Cowboy   City Girl

"Let me show you where the hay is kept."

Fig. 11. A duplex transaction

mathematical game theory,[6] although there are certain similarities.[7]

SCRIPT ANALYSIS

The script, or unconscious life plan of the individual, may not
come to light except in very advanced groups. It will then be
found that the patient is actually spending his whole life in a
predetermined way based on decisions he made in early childhood, when he was much too young to make such serious commitments. These decisions remain unconscious, and choices of
partners and action are rationalized on grounds which are
actually irrelevant since the chief function of partners is to
play roles in the protagonist's script, and the ultimate goal of
human behavior (under ordinary civil conditions offering the
possibility of choice) is to bring about the desired culmination
of the script, which may be either tragic or constructive.

In clinical work the tragic scripts are the ones most often

found, since people with constructive scripts do not usually feel the need for psychotherapy. In general a script is based on a childhood theory that somewhere there is a kind of Santa Claus who will bring the individual a magic gift to crown his life. People wait varying lengths of time before they fall into despair about the appearance of this Santa Claus, and it is this despair which, other things being equal, determines when they seek treatment — some at 20, some at 40, and some at 60. Failing "Santa Claus," there are four alternatives from which the individual can choose. The most decisive is suicide in one form or another. The second choice is sequestration from society, along with other people in despair, in a state hospital or a prison (or sometimes in isolated areas or in certain types of rooming-houses found in big cities). The third alternative is to get rid of the people who are held to be responsible for the failure — by divorce, homicide, sending the children to boarding school, etc. The fourth alternative is getting better, which means to give up the hope of Santa Claus, to abandon previous destructive games, and to start anew living in the world as it is. It will be apparent that script analysis by its very nature has an existential quality.

TIME STRUCTURING

In order to analyse most profitably the proceedings of groups, there are two approaches. The first is descriptive, dividing the proceedings into discussion, description, and expression. Discussion is concerned with events that are removed from the current group meeting in time or place, including discussions of what happened at the last meeting. In some new groups a definite geographical and temporal progression can be noted. The members begin by talking about things that happened far away and years ago, in Philadelphia or in Alaska, and gradually approach the place and time of the current group meeting. When they arrive there, the discussion takes on a more personal nature, typically beginning with shoes and working upward.

Discussion is usually an evasive maneuver. Description is an intellectual way of handling feelings. In structural language the Adult tells the group what the Child is feeling, but the Child himself does not show in such a description. Expression means the direct expression of affect concerning the here and now at the time the affect is felt. Discussion and description are essentially pastimes, and expression may be part of a game or it may signify progress toward genuine game-free intimacy. The last distinction is crucial for therapeutic progress.

Time structuring in groups is based on particular needs. (1) The least differentiated is stimulus hunger, which drives the individual to social action in order to avoid sensory deprivation. (2) More specific is recognition hunger, an Adult's version of the infant's need to be touched, in which "verbal touching" replaces physical touching. The unit of recognition is called a "stroke," by analogy to physical caressing in infancy, where the units more literally take the form of strokes. (3) Structure hunger expresses the antipathy to monotony, stereotypy, and boredom. People are willing to pay almost any price to have their time structured for them, since few are capable of structuring their own time autonomously for very long. Hence the large salaries paid to entertainers. (4) A derivative of structure hunger is leadership hunger. One of the most important functions of a leader is to supply purposeful programs on the basis of which the members can structure their time. A psychotherapist satisfies this hunger, for example, by structuring the group in such a way as to promote the most economical, stable, and speedy recoveries.

The options open to a member for structuring his time at any kind of gathering (roughly in order of safeness) are as follows:

1. Withdrawal. There are three kinds of withdrawal.

a. Extraneous fantasies, in which the individual mentally leaves the gathering to indulge in fantasies of what he would do elsewhere.

b. Autistic transactions. These may be either *unadapted* or *adapted*. Unadapted autistic transactions are those which are impractical under the circumstances, such as fantasies of rape and killing involving members of the gathering. Adapted autistic transactions are found in inhibited individuals who may have something to say which is quite appropriate to the situation, but who are too shy to say it.

2. Rituals. These are stereotyped, predictable exchanges such as greeting and farewell rituals. The unit of ritualistic exchanges is the stroke.

3. Pastimes. Pastimes are similar to rituals except that the transactions are less stereotyped and take the less ceremonial form of multiple-choice sentence-completion transactions as in the pastime called "General Motors": "I like a (Chevrolet, Ford, Plymouth) better than a (Chevrolet, Ford, Plymouth) because (complete in 25 words or less)." The respondent then says: "Yes, very true, but might I just add one item: *I* like a (Chevrolet, Ford, Plymouth) better than a (Chevrolet, Ford, Plymouth) because (complete in 25 words or less)."

4. Activity. An activity is what is commonly called work. Since the kind of therapy group we are interested in here does not engage in such activities, they do not present a problem to the therapist. Briefly, activities are programed by the external material of the activity itself so that the transactions are based on the needs of the moment; e.g. "Pass me the hammer" is said when the external material demands that a hammer be used.

5. Games. Since the experienced transactional therapist will quickly break up rituals and pastimes to move on to games, and since, on the other hand, real intimacy rarely occurs in groups, most of the proceedings of transactional groups will consist of games and game analysis. These will be amply illustrated below.

6. Intimacy. Intimacy is a game-free exchange of internally programed affective expressions, and must be sharply distinguished from pseudo-intimacy, which is common in institution-

alized forms of group therapy where affective expression is encouraged without careful assessment of its authenticity. In the latter case the affective expression is largely socially (externally) rather than internally programed, and is usually part of a game in which the patient compliantly participates. It is different from the poignant experience which ensues when real intimacy, on the rarest of occasions, occurs in a group.

One advantage of transactional analysis, as previously noted, is that the technical vocabulary needed to handle the proceedings of a treatment group is relatively small. A clear understanding of four words — Parent, Adult, Child, and game — is the primary requirement for a short-term group or for the first phase of a long-term group, and selections from the secondary vocabulary (such as "script") can be added as need arises.

REFERENCES

1. Winkelman, N. W. "A Clinical and Socio-Cultural Study of 200 Psychiatric Patients Started on Chlorpromazine 10½ Years Ago." *Am. J. Psychiat.* 120:861–9, 1964.
2. Freud, S. *New Introductory Lectures on Psychoanalysis.* W. W. Norton & Company, New York, 1933, p. 212.
3. Berne, E. *Transactional Analysis in Psychotherapy.* (Chap. 5, ref. 5.)
4. Berne, E. *The Structure and Dynamics of Organizations and Groups.* (Chap. 2, ref. 4.)
5. Berne, E. *Games People Play.* (Chap. 9, ref. 21.)
6. Luce, R. D., and H. Raiffa. *Games and Decisions.* John Wiley & Sons, New York, 1957.
7. "Terminology of Game Analysis" *Transactional Analysis Bulletin* 1:24, 1962.

11
Basic Techniques

The therapeutic operations that form the technique of transactional analysis fall into eight categories. These have a certain logical order, which may sometimes have to be violated in clinical practice. Such operations are of two general types: interventions and interpositions.

INTERROGATION The therapist uses interrogation primarily to help him document points that promise to be clinically decisive ("Did you actually steal the money?"). To the patient's Adult, interrogations are thought provoking and in this respect resemble confrontations; they also signal to him the direction the therapist wishes to follow. The patient's Parent may evade the issue with prejudices, dogmas, or clichés ("You've got to look out for yourself") or may side with or against the misapprehended therapist in self-derogation ("It's silly to behave that way, isn't it?") or over-denial ("It's ridiculous to think I'd do anything like that"). The patient's Child may answer the truth compliantly or pleadingly, or may try to set up a game by answering approximately, tangentially, paradoxically, or falsely.

Do use interrogation when confident that the patient's Adult will respond.

Do not use simple interrogation if it is likely that the patient's Parent or Child will respond.

Sometimes use interrogation to test which part of him is responding or to find out how he will respond to a particular question.

Caveat: Rarely try to get more information than is needed for the immediate purpose, or you may find that the patient is happy to play "Psychiatric History."

SPECIFICATION Specification is a declaration on the part of the therapist, categorizing certain information. It may be assentive ("So you always wanted to buy expensive things"), which corresponds roughly to "nondirective" therapy; or informative ("That's more of the little girl in you"). The object is to fix certain information in his mind and in the patient's mind, so that it can be referred to later in more decisive therapeutic operations. The effects on the patient are similar to those of interrogation: Adult ("That's interesting, I never thought of that before"); Parent ("That's very immature," or "That's a ridiculous thing to say"); Child ("You're right again," or "Not exactly").

Do use specification when it is anticipated that the patient might later deny that he said or meant something, or as a preparation for explanation.

Do not use specification if it will frighten the patient's Child ("I get from that, Gene, that you have always had a sexual interest in other men").

Sometimes use specification to find out if the patient is a determined dodger or to see how far you can go without frightening his Child ("So, Gene, in both cases you refused to let him bring his girl along").

Caveat: Do not specify something that has not been specified, or the patient may be encouraged to play "Psychiatry — Psycho-analytic Type" ("Yes, I've always been masochistic").

CONFRONTATION In confrontation the therapist uses informa-tion previously elicited and specified, in order to disconcert the patient's Parent, Child, or contaminated Adult by pointing out an inconsistency. The patient is stirred up and his psyche is thrown out of balance, and this tends to cause a redistribution of cathexis. If this redistribution merely strengthens the inap-propriate ego state which is already in command, then the con-frontation has been badly timed or badly worded. The thera-peutic object is always to cathect the uncontaminated segment of the patient's Adult, and its attainment will be signalled by either a thoughtful silence or an insightful laugh. The thoughtful silence represents an unstable condition with two possible out-comes: a therapeutic one in which the patient may relinquish his previous position more or less permanently, and a counter-therapeutic one in which he may revert back to the former inappropriate ego state and become defensive or angry, per-haps using his newly activated Adult as accessory. The insightful laugh,* on the other hand, is pathognomonic of a decisive cathectic shift, with the release of psychic energy previously bound up in maintaining the inconsistency that the confronta-tion attacks; it therefore marks a therapeutic success of some stability.

To the patient's Child, a confrontation may represent a Pa-rental move in a game that stimulates defensive operations learned in early life ("But I didn't mean it that way" or "Now you have hurt me"). To his Adult it may represent an intel-lectual challenge for which he is grateful ("I never noticed that before"). To his Parent it may represent an incursion on Parental authority ("Well, I still maintain that . . .").

* See Chapter 12, pp. 288–9.

Do use confrontation if the patient is apparently deceiving you or playing "Stupid" (perhaps without being aware of it), or if you are genuinely convinced that he is incapable of tagging the inconsistency himself.

Do not use confrontation when it makes you feel smarter than the patient; in that case, you have probably been decoyed. If you find yourself using a confrontation beginning with a Parental "But" then you should consider that you have been outmaneuvered.

Sometimes use confrontation if the patient forces you to by playing a hard game of "Stupid," in order to find out why he so badly wanted you to do it.

Caveat: Do not confuse legitimate confrontation with a game of "Critique" — "You tell me how you feel and I'll tell you what's wrong with your feelings."

EXPLANATION Explanation is an attempt on the part of the therapist to strengthen (recathect), decontaminate, or reorient the patient's Adult ("So you see the Child in you was threatening to become active, and when that happens your Adult fades out and your Parent takes over, and that's when you shout at the children"). The patient may respond with either Parent ("Why do my children have to behave that way anyway?"), Adult ("That fits"), or Child ("Gee, I'll have to explain that to my husband"). In the Parent case, the patient's Mother has interfered to prevent the therapist reaching the patient, as she actually interfered when the patient was little, perhaps with the family doctor; in the Adult case, the patient is using her intelligence; and in the Child case she is intellectualizing. The distinction between "using her intelligence" and "intellectualizing" should be well noted. Sometimes when the patient uses her intelligence, the therapist may try to pretend that it never happened by calling it "intellectualizing." It should be a matter of pride with both therapist and patient to make this distinction accurately.

Do use explanation at every opportunity when the patient has been properly prepared and his Adult is listening.

Do not use explanation if the patient is still "Butting" ("Yes, but . . ."), "Cornering" ("They're not children, they're teen-agers"), or "Trapping" ("Ha! Yesterday you said . . .").

Sometimes use explanation if the patient is wavering between playing games and facing up, especially if the subject matter is intriguing to one of his Adult intellectual interests ("You can see the same thing in your own practice when mothers bring their kids to your office").

Caveat: Make your explanations as concise as possible — one or two simple declarative sentences — or you may find yourself involved in a game of "Psychiatry — Transactional Type."

ILLUSTRATION An illustration is an anecdote, simile, or comparison that follows a successful confrontation for the purpose of reinforcing the confrontation and softening its possible undesirable effects. Interrogation, specification, confrontation, and explanation are interventions. Illustration is more than that: it is an interposition, an attempt by the therapist to interpose something between the patient's Adult and his other ego states in order to stabilize his Adult and make it more difficult for him to slide into Parent or Child activity.

Illustrations may be classified on a time scale as *immediate* or *remote;* typically, an immediate illustration is supplied on the spot when a confrontation is immediately successful, as signified by a laugh of insight. In that situation, the illustration is apt to provoke further laughter, thus releasing further cathexis previously bound up in the inconsistency; in effect, it loosens up the patient's personality organization and thus facilitates reorganization of the area under attack. A remote illustration is supplied anywhere from ten minutes to ten weeks after the original confrontation. If the confrontation was successful, the patient is allowed more or less time to settle down into a new position, and the illustration then gives him an additional push in the direction desired by the therapist.

Illustrations are classified spatially as *external* and *internal*. An external illustration has the external environment as its subject; hence it is in the nature of a hint or analogy. An internal illustration is usually a comparison, since it refers to other members of the group, but it may also take the form of a simile or epigram. It is apparent that internal illustrations require considerable technical judgment and skill; they constitute direct transactions with the patient spoken to and indirect transactions with the other patient or patients referred to. Hence they represent a form of therapeutic economy and forcefulness. They must be timely for both the patient directly addressed and the patient indirectly addressed. The therapist has three choices: if Tom has been confronted, he may tell Tom he is like Mary (Mary, of course, listening); or he may switch and tell Mary she is like Tom; or he may address the whole group and refer to Tom and Mary impersonally. As an additional refinement, he may choose to tell Tom that Mary is like him, or Mary that Tom is like her, instead of the other way round. Because of such complexities, it is advisable for the beginner to become thoroughly familiar with the effects of external illustrations before he attempts his first internal one.

Illustrations should be humorous, or at least lively, and they should be intelligible to the Child of the patient as well as to his Adult; hence they must be couched in a vocabulary that a wise five-year-old child could understand. They should not include words of more than two or at most three syllables, nor words of Latin etymology. They may employ colloquialisms deliberately (but carefully) chosen to test Parental prudery.

To the Child, illustrations are seductive because they indicate freedom from Parental restrictions, especially the freedom to laugh, and freedom from literalness; they also imply permission for creativity. To the Adult they are pleasing because of their aptness and economy of thought. They may arouse more or less resentment in the Parent because of their obvious seductiveness to the Child, and such resentment will have to be dealt with sooner or later. If they are badly timed or ill-chosen, they may also arouse resentment in the Child because they hurt his feelings, particularly in people who are collecting hurts, injustices, or tokens of their own inferiority. In such cases, instead of the subject's Adult joining in the Adult laughter of the group, his Child interprets the laughter as Parental and seizes the opportunity to resent it. Imprudent illustrations may also cause depression in the Child because they threaten the protection he is getting from his Parent.

Do use illustration when you are sure that the patient's Adult is listening, that his expressive Child will hear you, that his Parent will not take over, and that the illustration chosen will be immediately perceived as directly relevant to the preceding successful confrontation.

Do not use illustration if you are talking to a self-righteous or literal Parent (as with many paranoids) or to a Child who is seeking justification for disjunctive feelings. Do not use it to elevate your own self-esteem by showing how clever or poetic you are. Do not use it in an attempt to rectify an unsuccessful confrontation. Do not use an illustration unless you feel that every patient in the group is prepared for it, or if not, that you are ready to deal with the consequences. If your creations are successful, however, it is not only permissible, but desirable for you to share the patient's enjoyment of them; just be sure that they laugh at your jokes before you do.

Sometimes use illustration to indicate that solemnity is not a necessary condition for therapy, or to test the progress of a self-righteous or literal patient.

Caveat: Remember the theatrical rule: a comedian should never stay on stage too long. And for a therapist, it is better not to go on at all than to fall flat.

CONFIRMATION Having interposed his influence to stabilize the patient's Adult, the therapist now waits for the patient to offer further material to confirm his confrontation. This will help him reinforce the ego boundaries still further. The patient's Child has only abandoned his inconsistency with some reluctance, and will try to salvage at least part of it in some covert way. The alert therapist will see what is happening and will meet the Child's new mobilization with a new confrontation.("Before, you were saying 'Isn't It Awful?' about your stomach pains, but you wouldn't go to see your doctor. Now you're saying 'Isn't It Awful' because your doctor put you on a diet, when you yourself were always going on diets. So I guess that confirms the impression that you always need to have an 'Isn't It Awful.'").

It is assumed that the patient's Child, if hard pressed, can outwit even the sharpest therapist. If the confirmatory information is too obvious, the therapist should ask himself why the patient allows himself to be unmasked. Is it his Parent betraying his Child? Or his Adult coaxing his Child to come out into the open? Or the Child continuing the game to save face, but making it easy for the therapist in the hope of being rescued, like a little boy chirping from his hiding place to give a clue in a game of hide-and-seek?

Confirmation may be heard by the patient's Parent as corroborating his opinion that the Child is not to be trusted. If that happens the Child will feel trapped by the therapist and accordingly resentful. For the Adult, confirmation has a strengthening effect because of its logical force. For the Child, it may be both entrancing (like a game of hide-and-seek) and reassuring because it demonstrates the therapist's strength and alertness, which inspire confidence.

Do use confirmation if the patient's Adult is established strongly enough tc prevent the Parent from using it against the Child, and the Child from using it against the therapist.

Do not use confirmation if either the original confrontation or the ensuing illustration was unsuccessful; nor if the patient is "Butting," "Cornering," or "Trapping"; nor if it makes you feel smug. Do not nag, pursue, or harry the patient with it unless you are testing his endurance.

Sometimes use confirmation tentatively to test the patient's reaction; or as an indirect transaction, to test another patient's reaction or to approach him indirectly, or to clarify his relationship with the patient you are talking to; for example, whether he will try to "rescue" the respondent or rather take sides with you.

Caveat: Again watch out for a game of "Psychiatry — Psychoanalytic Type."

INTERPRETATION   Everything that has been done up to this time has had as its primary object the cathexis and decontamination of the Adult. If this has been successfully accomplished, the patient now has at his disposal a strong, clearly defined, and competent Adult, while the Child has been only secondarily affected. At this point, the therapist has three choices. He can crystallize the situation so as to offer the patient immediate symptomatic relief and social control, which is the terminal phase of pure transactional analysis. Here the patient can get "better" and stay better as long as he can keep his Adult in the executive position "on top of" the still confused Child. The second choice is to postpone the crystallization until the Child has been deconfused by psychodynamic interpretation. This corresponds to the therapeutic plan of orthodox psychoanalysis. The third choice is a combination of these two: first the patient gets better by establishing Adult control, and after that condition has been stabilized, the analytic deconfusion of the Child is undertaken.

Curiously enough, the patient will co-operate with any of these three projects. He will willingly bend his efforts to the therapist's suggestion that they concentrate on further stabilization of his Adult. Or if the therapist tells him that he cannot get better until the sources of his original disturbance have been analysed, he will obligingly postpone his recovery until the analysis has been "completed." And if the therapist proposes that he can get better first and analyse his underlying conflicts after that, the patient will also comply if he has been properly prepared and is willing to give up the advantages of being disturbed. Experience favors the last alternative if it is practical, particularly if the patient is responsible for growing children, since in that case the children can have a "healthy" parent at home during the whole analytic phase; whereas in more leisurely approaches, decisive improvement follows analysis rather than preceding it, so that the children may suffer for months or years before the treatment takes hold on the mother or father.

Now let us review the situation from a structural point of view, to clarify the relationships between the three ego states. Everything which has been done so far (the first six steps) is structurally oriented toward increasing the cathexis of the Adult (e.g. specification), clarifying and strengthening its boundaries (e.g. confrontation and explanation), and decontaminating it from Child and Parent adulterations, so that it becomes firmly established in the executive position in the therapeutic situation. The net result is that the therapist has someone objective and logical to talk to. During this procedure, the Parental grip on the Child may also be loosened to some extent, so that the Child is more apt to listen to new Parental figures with new viewpoints (such as the therapist and the other group members) as well as to its own Adult. But in some respects the Child remains almost as confused as he was originally.

Structurally, interpretation deals with the pathology of the Child. The Child presents its past experiences in coded form to the therapist, and the therapist's task is to decode and detoxify them, rectify distortions, and help the patient regroup the experiences. In this an uncontaminated Adult is the most valuable ally. The Parent exerts a seductive influence against interpretations. The Adult scans them and tests them against the probable reality. The Child tries to ward them off because they threaten to deprive him not only of all sorts of gratifications, but also of the protection of his watchful Parent. In the typical situation it is the therapist's Adult plus the patient's Adult against the patient's Parent plus the patient's Child. Hence the clearer and more highly cathected the patient's Adult, the more chance of success. The same may be said of the therapist's Adult. At each step the Child must choose between offending the Parent and at the same time giving up old gratifications, or offending the therapist and at the same time giving up the possibility of new gratifications.

An Example A patient dreamed among other things that she was taking care of a squashed kitten. After the long recital of dreams was ended the patient asked facetiously: "How do you interpret my dreams, doctor?" By this she indicated that she had suddenly and too late realized that she was once again playing "Psychiatry — Dream Interpretation Type." But her rueful question also indicated that her Adult had now taken over. This offered the therapist an opportunity that he could make good use of. After a pause, he said: "About the crushed kitten, didn't you once induce an abortion on yourself?" The patient sniffed. After a short silence, she said "OK." After another short silence, she remarked: "I've always wanted to have a dog instead of a cat."

Here the sniff came from the Child, signifying that long years of suspense waiting for someone to call her to account for the abortion, were now ended. No external person had called her to account before because in her "culture" abortions were permissible. The "OK" came from the Adult, meaning "Now I realize how tense and guilty my Child has been feeling all these years as a result of that act, so now I am ready to do something about those feelings instead of pretending that they are not there." "I've always wanted to have a dog" meant "Now I am freed from Parental censure for the abortion, so I no longer have to expiate it by taking care of cats and I am at liberty to get a dog instead, as I've always wanted to do." Her associates ("culture") had said, "It would be silly to feel guilty about an abortion," to which her operational reply had been, "Don't think I'm that silly." Her suppression of guilt feelings had forced her into years of secret expiation. The therapist's message, which she understood well, was "Your Child does feel bad because your Parent has been beating on you ever since you did it. Have you had enough, or do you want to spend the rest of your life expiating to your Parent?" Her reply, which the therapist understood well, was, in effect; "I've nursed my comforting guilt feeling long enough; now I'm ready to cut loose from my Parent in this respect and strike out for myself." (The question of the underlying "real" Adult existential guilt feeling, as opposed to the libidinized expiative Child "psychodynamic" guilt feeling, could be dealt with later.)

Do use interpretation where and when the patient's Adult is on your side, when you are not directly opposing the Parent, and when you are not asking too much sacrifice from the Child or arousing too much fear of Parental retaliation or desertion. "Too much" means that the sacrifice plus the fear outweighs what her Adult and you can promise her in return for seeing things your way rather than the old way. For example, does she like dogs and your active world enough to give up cats and the comforting expiative world of her Parent?

Do not use interpretation when the patient's Adult is not in the executive position or is not properly prepared or is not on your side; nor when it is your Parent or Child talking instead of your own Adult.

Sometimes use interpretation to test whether the patient is playing a game of "Psychiatry." For example, in the case given above, if the patient had replied, "Oh, are kittens symbolic of abortion?" that would probably be the response of a precocious Child rather than that of an Adult. In that case the therapist might respond simply "OK!" to see whether the patient wanted to continue the game or call it off. An interpretation may also be employed as a last desperate resort in the hope that after the patient leaves therapy, perhaps long after, he may be able to stop warding it off and use it.

Caveat: In some cases, the therapist is more apt than the patient to intellectualize instead of using his intelligence.

CRYSTALLIZATION   The technical aim of transactional analysis is to bring the patient to a point where crystallizing statements from the therapist will become effective. A crystallization is a statement of the patient's position from the Adult of the therapist to the Adult of the patient ("So now you are in a position to stop playing that game if you choose to"). At this juncture transactional analysis has completed its task, with or without interpretation, in the area under consideration. Transactional analysis does not try to "make" the patient better, but to bring him into a position where he can exercise an Adult option to get better. The therapist is, in an existential sense at least, indifferent to which choice the patient makes; all he can do is make it possible for the patient to choose. There is, however, no use in trying to conceal from the patient that the therapist is biased by his own prejudices in favor of health and sanity; he may even advise the patient to choose getting better, but whether or not that advice is taken is up to the patient. If the therapist goes beyond mere professional advice, however, he becomes Parental, and the patient's "choice" is no longer an Adult choice, but an act of Child compliance or rebellion. That kind of choice is more of a resolution than a decision, and as all practical people know, resolutions are made to be broken; it is only Adult decisions which are made to be kept.

Logically speaking, if the patient at this stage asks, "Should I choose to get better?" the correct answer is "No." If the therapist should reply "Yes," then the patient's "decision" is no longer his own, and the only autonomous decision he can make is not to get better. If the therapist answers "No," then the autonomous decision becomes to get better. None of this applies, however, until the patient is in a position to make Adult decisions. Many therapists would decline to answer at all, but that is not necessarily the most productive response.

If the patient is properly prepared by what has gone before, then his Adult will receive the crystallization eagerly and enthusiastically. It will be taken as something he has been waiting for, a professional communication from the therapist's Adult that he is now able to get better, something he is not always competent to judge for himself. This notification is one way in which the therapist at long last earns his fee, by making such an announcement on the basis of the clinical judgment and experience that are his special advantage over a lay advisor.

At this stage the patient's Adult and Child are on good terms with each other, and the Child will also receive the crystallization gratefully, but with some trepidation and perhaps nostalgia as well, since it means abandoning permanently the old way and trying something new, still strange, and not yet fully tested.

What the Child is really abandoning by getting better is his Parent, and it is the Parent who is wronged by the whole procedure. Hence the Parent's reaction to a crystallization may resemble that of a certain type of mother when her son announces at the age of forty that he is finally leaving home to get married. She either hastens after the culprit (in this case, the therapist) or becomes an instant invalid. The able therapist should be able to cope with the enraged Parent who sees the Child slipping away into health; but a difficult and dangerous situation arises if somatic symptoms are used as weapons in a last-ditch fight. That is another reason why the final decision to get well is left to the patient. If he is pushed, he may get well psychologically, only to come down with a broken leg or a gastric ulcer. If it is left up to him, he will sense when the time is ripe to go ahead, and save himself from organic damage. Thus the therapist tells him when he is able to solo, but the patient decides when he will actually take off.

Do use crystallization as soon as you are sure that not only the Adult, but also the Child, and especially the Parent of the patient is properly prepared.

Do not use crystallization if the patient is showing renewed signs of somatic disease, or an unusual interest in somatic symptoms of himself or others, or a sudden access of courage or depression leading him into obviously hazardous situations.

Sometimes use crystallization if he merely *threatens* to acquire a somatic disease or to expose himself to undue hazards; then use it early in the session and be very alert for subsequent Parental reactions, and mobilize your utmost therapeutic abilities to deal with them competently.

Caveat: Do not confuse a Child "resolution" from the patient with an Adult "decision" on his part.

GENERAL PRECAUTIONS

The following general precautions apply to all eight types of therapeutic operations.

1. Never get ahead of the clinical material offered by the patient. Preferably, stay three steps behind. In confrontation, for example, offer the first item. If that is effective, the other two can always be used somewhere to good advantage. If the first is not effective, offer the second to find out whether the

patient really did not get the point or is just not receptive. In the latter case, you still have the third item in reserve and hence are still in control of the therapeutic situation.

2. Never miss a legitimate chance to forge ahead.

3. Never push against resistance except for testing purposes based on a well-thought-out concrete hypothesis.

OTHER TYPES OF INTERVENTION

The operations described above are those proper to a program of well-planned forward-moving transactional analysis, and provide the greatest economy of therapeutic time and effort for both patient and therapist. In special situations, however, the transactional analyst may have to fall back on other approaches, but he should not do so unless he can state his reasons clearly.

The most common situation requiring modifications is the treatment of active schizophrenics. Here the therapist may have to function deliberately as a Parent rather than as an Adult for a shorter or longer period, sometimes extending into years. Some Parental interventions, with their common names, are the following.

Support This may be simple stroking, whose content, providing it is tactful, is irrelevant. Its effect may be enhanced if the content is appropriately permissive or protective. ("Go ahead and do it.")

Reassurance Here the Parental tone of voice may be more important than the content. ("You're right to do it.") It is hard for reassurance to fail if the patient's Child feels exposed, but it may fail under two principal conditions of hypocrisy. (1) If the patient's actual parents gave hypocritical reassurance, the therapist's well-intentioned sentiments may produce an unexpected effect, either immediately or later. (2) If the therapist mistakes for the real thing his own hostile Child playing the role of a parent, the patient may also fail to respond favorably.

Persuasion This nearly always contains a strong element of seduction. ("Why don't you do it?") The therapist should be sure he knows what the patient expects in return for his compliance and be prepared to deal with the ultimate consequences either of having to deliver the implied reward or of paying the penalty for failing to deliver.

Exhortation Exhortation may in some situations produce gratifying results through compliance of the patient's Child. ("You've got to do it!") But insofar as this sets up an effective Parent-Child relationship between the therapist and the patient, and one which both may find gratifying, it may in the long run make it more difficult to accomplish the ultimate aim of therapy, which is to establish the patient's Adult in the executive. In this case, added to the patient's need to cling to the Parent-Child relationship, is the therapist's possible reluctance to give up such an appealing situation. All this applies *a fortiori* to the use of hypnosis.

Among the Child interventions which are used by some therapists, a few are legitimate — for example, in treating children. It is best not to use Child interventions without special training, as at a children's clinic. In some cases, uncertain therapists, at a loss what to do next, are beguiled by articles in the literature into attempting Child interventions which are ultimately based on trickery. No transactional analyst should allow himself to use any form of deception or dissimulation, for that amounts to deliberately starting a game with the patient. The therapeutic aim is to render the patient game-free, and it is doubtful if this can ever be most effectively accomplished by the therapist's setting up a game of his own. Certainly he has no right to complain if such a procedure backfires. Time spent in experimenting with gimmicks can almost invariably be better spent in observing and thinking about the natural and spontaneous behavior of patients.

CHOOSING AND TIMING
THERAPEUTIC OPERATIONS

The Therapeutic Forces The object of group treatment is to fight the past in the present in order to assure the future. There are four therapeutic forces at work in the group situation: the *vis medicatrix naturae,* the natural drive of organisms toward health; the biological salubrity of stroking or recognition from other people; corrective social experiences, confrontations, and encounters; and the operations of the therapist. The first three are continuously at work in any social situation, so that in these respects group treatment does not offer any advantage over other forms of social activity, such as Boy Scout work or lodge membership. Therefore, it is only by his therapeutic operations that the therapist justifies the time and energy he has put into his training, the fees he collects from his patients, and his status as a professional.

Learning To Operate Learning the science and art of therapeutic operation is similar to learning dancing or lumbar puncture. In learning a dance, the pupil first learns the individual movements, which he performs initially "by the numbers." At a certain moment, two or more of the movements coalesce into a single skilled sequence. Eventually the whole dance step becomes a gracefully flowing act of co-ordination, a unit in itself. As this happens with one step after another, the whole dance begins to take form as a series of smoothly flowing acts, blended into each other without perceptible throes of conscious ordering; the "numbers" drop out and the sequence becomes "automatic." This marks the transition from the science to the art, from a "digital" phase to an "analogue" phase, from arithmetic which adds one unit to another to calculus which takes the whole situation in a broad and fluent sweep.

Similarly, a medical student does his first lumbar punctures "by the numbers," consciously and with deliberation performing each step as a separate act, from the time he uncorks the antiseptic bottle until the fluid begins to drip. An old neurosurgeon, on the other hand, performs the whole procedure like legerdemain, so that there is a dexterous flow from the time he picks up the antiseptic until the needle slides unerringly into the proper space. An even simpler and more striking example can be seen in nursing care. The probationer goes through a short, somewhat staccato series of movements in handing a patient a pill from a medicine glass. An older nurse may accomplish this in a single, graceful, and remarkably economical sweep of her arm.

The beginner in therapy will find the same principle at work as time goes on. The procedure given below may seem complex and cumbersome to deal with "by the numbers," but with practice and experience the steps coalesce into what seems like a simple decision which is made in a split second; looking back, however, he may realize that he actually went through each step of the sequence in the proper order without being aware of it. For example, as an expert he may have observers in his group. If he makes an intervention that he "intuitively" knows is just right, one of the observers may later ask him why he did it, and he may be able to resurrect the whole thought process behind it — a narrative which might take ten or fifteen minutes to relate. Yet *in medias res* all this reasoning was condensed into a few seconds. The object of these prefatory remarks is to hearten the student so that he will not quail at this point before what looks like a formidable array. He may omit steps and trip over his own feet at first, but with practice he should some day be able to proceed smoothly, adeptly, and effortlessly.

Criteria for Action All operations are undertaken with only one goal in mind: curing the patient. This takes precedence over all other considerations, and especially over self-consciousness on the part of the therapist, such as wondering how it will look to the observers or sound at staff conference. It also takes precedence over the need to "do group therapy." The first question is therefore:

1. What am I trying to cure the patient of today?

The second question has to do with the rationality of the therapy and the therapist's timing in relation to himself.

2. Has the patient said or done anything which could form the basis for a therapeutic hypothesis?

A therapeutic hypothesis has two parts: the informational (psychological) aspect and the social (transactional) aspect. The informational or psychological aspect of the hypothesis attempts to answer the question: Has the patient said or done anything that promises to clarify a previously obscure aspect of his personality structure or dynamics? If so, what can I say to him that would, with the greatest economy of words on my part, elicit the maximum clarification from him? Or more succinctly:

3. What is my hypothesis about his personality?

4. How can I best validate it?

The social, transactional, or therapeutic aspect of the hypothesis is concerned with the effect of the operation.

5. How do I think he will respond to what I say?

The next two questions try to clarify the fifth one, and are the principal determinants in timing the intervention.

6. To which of his ego states should my intervention be directed?

7. Actually, at the present moment, which of his ego states is most likely to give the overt response to what I say?

In a straightforward therapeutic operation, the answers to questions 6 and 7 must be the same; that is, the ego state addressed must also be the one most likely to respond. Then the transaction will be complementary. If the answers to 6 and 7 are different, that is, if the ego state addressed is not the one most likely to respond, a crossed transaction must be anticipated. Except for certain types of confrontation, where a crossed response may be deliberately looked for, crossed transactions should be avoided. In any case, the answers to those two questions prepare the therapist for the patient's most probable response. In this way he can avoid being disconcerted and can keep control of the therapeutic situation, which is the key to success.

The answer to the next question is determined by the patient's therapeutic progress.

8. At this stage of his progress, which form of intervention is indicated?

The next criterion is concerned with the secondary factors, that is, the effect of the operation on each of the other patients in the group.

9. What will be the most probable effect of the operation on each of the other patients in the group at this time?

By rapid and accurate data-processing, the therapist may hit upon just the right wording to have the maximum therapeutic effect on all the patients present, or in risky situations, to have the minimum deleterious effect on each of the others. That is the strategy problem in group treatment.

The next question takes a rapid survey of the therapist's "emergency kit."

10. If the responses are not the most probable in each case, what are the more remote possibilities, and how would I deal with each of them?

If the answers to all these questions are satisfactory, the therapist will be ready to speak after he weighs one more decisive consideration, which is frequently neglected. If the operation is to be therapeutic, rather than merely academic, sensational, or confusing, it must be relevant.

11. Is the manifestation I am concerned with merely interesting, or is it pathological?

If it is not pathological, the whole project is dropped right there, since strictly speaking, the operation would then be irrelevant and would waste valuable time. Question 11 is specifi-

cally designed to stop in his tracks the type of therapist colloquially known as "Phallus in Wonderland."

These questions can now be conveniently listed in summary
form, and their application in practice illustrated.

1. What am I trying to cure the patient of today?

2. Has he said or done anything which could form the basis
for a therapeutic hypothesis?

3. What is the psychological hypothesis about his personality?

4. How can I best validate it?

5. How will he respond transactionally to what I say?

6. To which of his ego states should I be talking?

7. Which of his ego states will be most likely to hear
me?

8. Which form of intervention is indicated?

9. How will it affect the other patients?

10. What are the other possibilities, and how will I deal with
each of them?

11. Is the manifestation I am concerned with pathological?

If the probabilities estimated from these questions are satisfactory, then the therapist can proceed. More than that, on every
occasion when the answers to these questions are satisfactory,
it is his duty to proceed.

An Illustrative Problem   Let us now consider a commonplace
example: a woman who asks in the group whether she should
continue group treatment or go to Europe.

In transactional analysis, it is not necessary to know anything
about the patient's previous history except what relates directly
to the current momentary situation in the group. A patient is
"recognized" by a transactional analyst not according to the
usual historical criteria ("Oh yes, another paranoid 30-year-old
unmarried woman secretary with no siblings and a strict
father . . .," etc.) but rather by her operations in the group and
her future plans ("Oh yes, a secretive 'Ain't It Awful' player who

always looks tearful so that people won't ask her too many questions, and who is continually threatening to quit her job").

Sophia, the woman in question, was always ready to complain about how things were at the office, and each week she said she could not make up her mind whether to continue in the group or go to Europe. When the other members said that she was really trying to make her mind up whether to get better or to look for a magical solution to her troubles in Europe, she evaded the issue for a long time. On this particular day, she asked them again if she should stay in the group or travel. They replied rather effectively, wondering again how they were supposed to deal with a question like that, and politely asked her to explain its purpose. But Dr. Q thought from the way she broached the matter on this occasion that she was perhaps ready for a showdown, so he decided it was best to interrupt them and go to the heart of the matter. She had previously been asked several times why she did not want to get better, and had pretended not to understand the question. On the hypothesis that she was now ready to answer, Dr. Q therefore asked:

(a) "Why don't you want to get better?"

"Because getting better would mean doing the things my parents always wanted me to do, and I have to spite them," she replied, laughing nervously.

(b) "That reminds me of a story," said Dr. Q. "One night in the middle of winter a policeman found a drunk sitting on a doorstep, shivering and shaking and freezing, and he asked him what he was doing there. The drunk said, 'I live here,' so the policeman said, 'Then why don't you go in?' The drunk said, 'Because the door's locked,' so the policeman said, 'Why don't you ring the bell?' The drunk said, 'I did, but they didn't answer,' so the policeman said, 'Then why don't you ring again? You'll freeze to death out here.' And the drunk said, 'Oh, let them wait.'"

Almost everybody in the group laughed. Two nodded, and Jim said: "That's me, all right." Sophia also laughed. Then Dr. Q added:

(c) "Unfortunately, parents sometimes say things that are right. Are you planning to spend the rest of your life getting back at your parents, or do you think some day you'll get better?"

"Well," replied Sophia, "maybe some day I'll get better."

"Well, if you're going to do it eventually, why not do it now, and save all that time and grief?"

"I'll think about it," answered Sophia, whereupon Dr. Q immediately turned his attention to someone else.

The analysis of Dr. Q's operations is as follows (numbered according to the criteria given above):

1. His current task was to cure the patient of playing "Ain't It Awful." To accomplish this in effect required her to shift her commitment from proving that the world was causing her troubles, to finding out how she could change her way of experiencing that world. As long as her indecision continued, so would her anxiety attacks.

2. She asked her usual question in an unusually tentative or "testing" way which indicated that perhaps she thought the game was up. This gave rise to the hypothesis that the time was ripe.

3. The psychological hypothesis was that cathexis had moved from her Child to her Adult so that her Adult was now strong enough to consider her situation objectively and her Child was tranquil enough to refrain from interrupting—a situation which, while it was not ideal, was at least favorable.

4. This could best be validated by directly undercutting her Child's position to see whether she would abandon it or try to re-establish it.

5. The probabilities were that she was ready to abandon it, although she might possibly reply: "But I don't understand. I do want to get better."

6. From the way she answered the remarks of the other members, it appeared that Dr. Q could talk to her Adult.

7. Dr. Q anticipated that her Adult would give the overt response. In order to obtain the desired result, it was necessary for her Child also to listen to the question rather than trying to ward it off, and the prospects seemed encouraging.

8. Since she was not yet committed to therapy, it was advisable to begin at the beginning with an interrogation, although she had learned enough so that a rather sophisticated question (a) was possible.

9. Several of the other patients were at the same stage, so that the question (a) was meaningful for them also, and it was unlikely that they would take umbrage at it. The rest of them were already committed, and would feel pleasantly superior and helpful.

10. If Sophia warded off the question (a), it could be redirected to one of the other members (Jim) who had already indicated that he was giving the matter some thought. If anyone did take umbrage, it was almost certain that Jim would come to the rescue by indicating that he was prepared to discuss the matter.

11. Her indecision was an integral part of her pathology, and a commitment to therapy was crucial to her recovery. Hence operations in this area were a profitable investment of time.

The initial operation, then, consisted of an interrogation (a). Sophia's reply was in itself a sharp specification, and contained a self-confrontation (as evidenced by her nervous laugh), and also a structural explanation, since it was evident that she realized it was her Child who was spiteful. In order to emphasize this Adult realization and also to engage her Child in it, Dr. Q supplied an immediate external illustration (b). Her ensuing laugh was a confirmation. Since the immediate goal was a transactional one rather than an analytic one, no interpretation

was attempted. Instead Dr. Q moved immediately to crystallization (c). Her response was satisfactory, since it contained
no "buts" and all he could ask of her was what she said: that
she would think about it. There was evidently no value in pursuing the matter further at that time, so that Dr. Q proceeded
immediately to someone else's problems.

Dr. Q's therapeutic plan was to bring about a decisive alteration, under Adult control, of Sophia's (Child) view of herself
and the world around her. That would enable her to enjoy her
surroundings and eliminate her anxiety attacks. She would then
be in a position to take her trip to Europe and enjoy it. After
she returned, she could come back to the group if she wished
so that her situation could be stabilized by analytic procedures
designed to relieve some of the latent paranoid pressure from her
Child. Some of the other members who had got better first and
analysed afterward sensed what he had in mind. They seemed
to be in favor of his plan, and did their best to further it.

Dr. Q's operations — the interrogation (a), the illustration
(b), and the crystallization (c) — were the results of intuitive
instantaneous decisions. Afterward, however, he was able to
rationalize them in detail according to the eleven given criteria.
Undoubtedly the complete rationalization took place in some
preconscious rapid action "computer" at the time the decisions
were made.[1] In this example, the operations proceeded in the
most logical order from interrogation through to crystallization.

Mention should be made here of the "bull's-eye," an operation
that has a therapeutic effect on the Parent, Adult, and Child
of the patient simultaneously.[2] That is an ideal to be striven for.

REFERENCES

1. Berne, E. "Concerning the Nature of Diagnosis." *Int. Rec. Med.*
   165:283–92, 1952.
2. Berne, E. *Transactional Analysis in Psychotherapy* (Chap. 5, ref.
   5), p. 236.

12

The Transactional Theory of Personality

The transactional theory of personality is also a theory of life. For the transactional analyst to plan his work systematically he must be familiar with the sequence of events by which each human being has arrived at his current human condition. He learns to understand both the theoretical and clinical significance of these developments, and to infer from clinical manifestations where the individual is and how he got there. As in many professional matters, things which may seem obscure or esoteric at first will become clearer and more universal as the therapist acquires experience in the transactional approach.

EARLY TRANSACTIONS

The First Five Years It is assumed here that each normal human infant is born into the world with the capacity to develop his potentialities to the best advantage of himself and of society, to enjoy himself and be able to work productively and creatively, and to be free of psychological disabilities. In the first few days of life, however, he may already run into trouble. Some pediatricians claim that they can predict intuitively from the mother's personality whether or not her newborn baby will suffer from colic. The baby's life centers on getting his nourishment from the maternal breast and there are numerous possibilities for variation in this respect: anatomical, depending upon the structure of the mother's nipple; physiological, depending upon the copiousness of her milk; and psychological, depending upon how she handles the nursing situation. In some parts of the world there are external aggravations which it is hardly possible for a middle-class therapist to appreciate fully — wars, riots, epidemics, famines, and chronic undernourishment and dietary deficiencies. In the stable classes, the external complications which affect nursing infants are likely to be more intimate, arising from the father, the grandparents, the pediatrician, and the needs of the other children. Another kind of problem is posed by the suspension of breast feeding in favor of the bottle. The ultimate effects of some of these influences upon the development of personality can be inferred in part, but systematic studies have only recently begun.

Outstanding in this respect is the clinical work of Spitz [1] on maternal handling, a problem which is now of widespread laboratory interest, principally through observation of monkeys [2] and rats.[3] The phenomenon of imprinting [4] also remains to be clarified, particularly in its human implications. The indications so far are that handling has some effect on the functioning of the adrenal cortex, which in turn may influence many of the qualities of the organism's emotional and social life. For the transactional analyst the problems of nursing, handling, and imprinting are of deep social significance, but it is not yet possible to make clinical judgments in this area with any feeling of confidence or reliability. It is probable, however, that an early matrix for depressive and schizophrenic manifestations is laid during this period, the primal reaction occurring in the form of marasmus or anaclitic depression. The psychodynamic aspects of such early pathology have been most thoroughly discussed (in the pre-experimental era) by Melanie Klein [5] and her followers.

The next period of interest, within the limitations of our present knowledge, is the moment when the infant comprehends, in some sense, that the breast is not part of himself but has an independent existence. Taken at face value, that would be a true scientific discovery on his part based on inductive observation. This shift in attitude, whatever its inner structure, marks the beginning of neopsychic functioning. Concurrently, perhaps with some causal relationship, the infant may be learning not only that the breast or bottle are out of his absolute control, but also that even his limited influence depends to some extent on his control of himself. If he bites the nipple, it is quickly brought to his attention that this can have unhappy consequences, and may result in the loss of the breast.* Similarly with the bottle; he must acquire some control in sucking because if he does not and clamps down too hard, for example, the bottle will stop functioning. The loose use of certain words in this connection is not prejudicial from the clinical viewpoint — "comprehends," "observation," "learning," "control," "attention." Whether the infant "learns" by conditioned reflexes, or by something approaching "thought," for example, is not the issue here. What is important are the traces left by very early experiences, and the possible developmental influence of such "engrams" or "mnemes."

The next series of transactions which may determine the individual's subsequent development arises from the fact that he must control his own body in a way that is acceptable to the people around him. There are several types of situations which are crucial here. A common example is the too-early bowel training. Some mothers attempt to bowel-train their infants in the first few months of life, presumably before the nerve tracts which make for natural control have been ripened, so that it requires

* It is probable that the anlagen of games are formed during these earliest transactions. See E. Berne, "Recent Observations," *Transactional Analysis Bulletin* 2:74, July 1963.

unnatural effort on the infant's part to comply with the mother's demands. Since bowel training is not instantaneous it involves long, complicated series of transactions stretching over days, weeks, or months, leaving room for the development of a large variety of maneuvers and games on the part of both the mother and the child.*

The next decisive epoch begins at the point where the child perceives that the external environment is placing restrictions upon his relationship with his mother. In transactional terms, he discovers that there are other "people" in the world whom he must encounter in his dealings with her, whether because they are more powerful than he is, like the father who displaces him at various times of day and night, or because she seems to prefer them, as in the case of newborn siblings. It may be assumed that by the age of two or three he is able to construct well-formed fantasies concerning such matters and what he would like to do about them, but we may also assume that there are serious distortions in his perceptions and data-processing. The final common pathway is the operations and games he evolves in his attempts to deal with such rivalries.

The Family Culture   The schematic progression which has been outlined here is usually not without its overlap, so that the games revolving around food, those revolving around bowel training, and those concerned with possession of the mother may become interwoven and offer an interesting challenge for the game analyst if the individual presents himself for treatment in later life. There are certain special tendencies that may profoundly affect the clinical situation. Thus the interest of the whole family may be invested principally in food, and the emphasis may be at any point in the alimentary tract. It may be chiefly concerned with intake, as with gourmets; with assimila-

---

* The reader is reminded that the words "parent," "adult," and "child" (uncapitalized) refer to actual people, while "Parent," "Adult," and "Child" (capitalized) refer to ego states.

tion, as with diet faddists; or with excretion, as with stool-watchers. The last case represents a residue from the problems of toilet training, and leads into the second category, those families that tend to take execretory activities very seriously and devote a large amount of their attention to them, generally on the principle that lots of excretion is good, and that no excretion is bad or even fatal. This interest comes to its fullest flower in the colonic irrigation addicts.* In a more subtle way it may result in equating thought control with bowel control, so that in effect thoughts are treated transactionally very much as bowel movements are. A third type of family may focus principally on rivalry and bickering, so that games revolving around favoritism, with bad behavior and good behavior as trade goods, may occupy a good deal of attention. The quick way to make a preliminary appraisal in these areas is to inquire what the patient's family used to talk about at the dinner table.

So far this account resembles the psychoanalytic approach, although it is a little more literal, a little simpler, and concentrates more on the social apparatus than on the psychic apparatus. Now the divergencies begin to grow wider.

THE TIME OF DECISIONS

As the child grows older, his transactions with other people become more and more channelized by his family experiences, perhaps from a kind of operant conditioning. He has learned the hard way that he cannot have everything he wants when he wants it, that he must control his body to meet the demands of other people, and that he has rivals and lives not only in a

* In every large city (as the Yellow Pages of the telephone book will attest) there is a surprising number of people who earn a good living doing nothing but administering colonic irrigations. One active clubwoman habitually talked at cocktail parties about "a certain colonic" she had had years previously, which had released "a certain piece of mucus" whose shape she would describe in detail.

powerful though perhaps affectionate world, but also in a competitive one. At this point (usually from his fourth to seventh years) he begins to settle on certain compromises which will affect his relationships with people in later life. These solutions require making decisions, taking positions which justify the decisions, and warding off influences which threaten the positions.

An Illustrative Case A typical example is illustrated in the following clinical extract. A little girl (Rita) used to run to greet her father every night when he came home from work, but as time went on she became bewildered because he seemed to be two different people. Some evenings he was fatherly and kind, but on other occasions he would talk to her roughly and even push her out of the way. As the unpleasant occasions became more frequent, she grew dispirited and often did not go to greet him at all. Sometimes when he arrived in a good mood he would reprove her for her neglect, and she would feel that she had made a mistake. Then she would try again. But as his drinking grew worse she became more and more discouraged. Rita began to hide in her bedroom when she heard him at the door. One day he staggered into the house and made a particularly vile scene with her mother. The little girl, frightened, bewildered, and forlorn, burst into tears and decided that never again would she love a man. This decision, which she adhered to for the next 30 years, was made at the age of 6 years, 2 months, and 23 days, on January 2, 1931, at 5 o'clock in the afternoon. The time could be set accurately by her memory of the houses they lived in, the fact that it was right after New Year's Day, and that it happened in the dusk of a winter's afternoon. This decision, made when Rita was much too young in judgment, knowledge, and experience to enter into such serious commitments, determined her whole future.

It will have been noted that she had made several tentative decisions in the same direction before, but always with some reservations. The final outcome was truly the result of "a moment of decision." That moment was also a moment of fixation, for the child who actually existed on that snowy day was the same Child who revealed herself in her individual and group treatment sessions, with the same multiform possibilities for feeling and action. Something in her became walled off, and her Adult and later Parental accretions had to grow around this sequestered little girl. That, then, clinically and historically, is what constituted "the Child" of this particular patient.

Once having made her decision, however, certain difficulties arose. How was she to solace herself and justify herself for the times when her father came home in a good mood, eager for her greetings, which she gave on such sober evenings with considerable reserve? In order to maintain her decision she had to take a certain position regarding her father, namely, that in spite of his amiable appearance when he was sober, he was nevertheless fundamentally bad. This position in time extended to nearly all members of the male sex who were senior to herself, or from whom she could evoke a Parental attitude. The not-OKness of such men she epitomized in the slogan "All men are beasts." Decent men bored Rita until she could provoke them; they threatened her position and with it her decision, since if all men were not beasts, perhaps she should allow herself to love one. In effect, a benevolent man threatened a life-long psychological investment, which, like most investors, she could not bring herself to abandon. In order to avert such threats it was necessary for her to prove that even benevolent-looking men were, like her father, fundamentally bad.

This whole development was elucidated as a result of Rita's relating the following incident. She went to a bar one evening when her much older husband was busy. There she met a man who "seemed decent enough," and during the evening they became quite friendly. The man asked her to come into the garden which surrounded the roadside tavern. She consented readily, being fully aware of what he had in mind, but when he attempted to kiss her, she slapped his face and said, "You're a swine." She also called him some even more offensive names, whereupon he hit her. She was then able to come for her interview the next morning with a bruise on her face, demonstrating to the therapist that all men were beasts, just as she had known all along. This incident, of course, was closely related to her attempts to involve the therapist in a related game. The game-like quality of her relationship with the man in the saloon is quite evident; in fact, she seduced him into going outside and then turned on him unjustifiably. Of the "decent" men present, she had picked the one who looked most impulsive. Hence it may be seen that one function of games is to stabilize the patient's position.

It should also be noted, however, that the seductive maneuvers of this lonely woman constituted an attempt to establish an intimate relationship, which she was unable to carry through. Some clinicians might call her operations "character defenses." But they were much too dynamic and ongoing for such a static term, and they resulted in a well-defined payoff whose visible sign was a purple bruise. This account illustrates the background and course of the game known as "Rapo — Second Degree," also called in game analysis "Buzz Off, Buster."

Reorganization of Character Not only are the patient's day-to-day relationships based on games designed to strengthen the position by which she maintains her decision, but the whole course of her life is similarly determined. In Rita's case, for example, her marriage was interrupted by frequent separations, justified by bitter complaints that her fatherly husband was inconsistent and that it was impossible to love him. In this respect she followed in her mother's footsteps. Thus she re-enacted in her own grown-up life both her mother's trouble and the drama she herself had experienced as a child in her separation from her father, with suicide in mind as the only way out in the long run. This proclivity for re-enactment determined the course of her therapy. The "Buzz Off" games with her husband eased off as she tried to run through the same script with the therapist, offering to cast him instead of her spouse as the villain if he were willing to play the part. Thus another function of her games was to further her long-term suicidal script, the protocol (or original version) of which had been written by her seventh year, and which she had played out in an appropriate form, called a palimpsest, during her adolescence, and was now producing in another more ruthless adaptation ("The Broadway Version") in the course of her marriage.

The point of critical clinical significance in all this is that both character formation and much overt symptomatic psychopathology arise from conscious decisions made at an early age. Since they are decisions, they can be un-decided. At the time they were made they offered the best solution available to the patient in view of her possibilities at that period. One of the primary objects of therapy is to stabilize and decontaminate the Adult so that these decisions can be reconsidered. If the patient can bring herself to abandon her position and her life-long investment in it, then it becomes possible for her to review her solution and find another, more constructive one.

Actually, children do pretty much what their parents want them to. Rita's father wanted her to like men and then not to like them, and that is what she did; in fact, she was only repeating her mother's behavior. If the primacy of the Adult is established during therapy, not only can the Child's decision be reconsidered, but the Parent can usually be brought to terms as well.

The Constancy of Games The first time the therapist describes subversive elements in the patient's operations, the patient may be puzzled. Eventually she may accept his confrontation on some one occasion that she was coming on just the way the therapist specified. Perhaps it is a few weeks before she is willing to concede that she has played the same game again. As treatment proceeds, thenceforward, it becomes more and more apparent to both therapist and patient that she is playing the game much more often than at first seemed evident or even possible. Finally, after a varying length of time, the revelation comes that what at first looked like non-game-playing behavior, or perhaps like an assortment of different games, turns out essentially to be variations of the same game. It suddenly becomes clear to both the therapist and herself (though not necessarily simultaneously) that she is playing this game not only on a few occasions, but all day long, every day. This moment of revelation is a decisive one both for the therapist's planning when it occurs to him, and for the patient's recovery when it occurs to her. For that is the moment when she becomes aware of her phenomenological Child, feels it subjectively in its clearest form, and reveals it to the therapist.

This is the phase when it becomes possible for the patient truly to relinquish the game by an Adult act of re-decision. If she succeeds in doing so, she is then faced in the most poignant way with an existential question: If I give up that way of structuring my life, what am I going to do instead? And further: If I refuse to play the game, what will my family do instead? These are not questions for other people to answer. Here the patient is on her own and all that the therapist and the other members of the group can do is to stand by encouragingly (or perhaps critically) until she finds a more constructive way of life, but that way can only be found on her own initiative.

Diagnostic Problems The preceding considerations determine the order of the therapist's diagnostic questions to himself and eventually to the patient. First he must determine her predominant ego state when she is playing her favorite game or games.* The next thing to be established is what roles the other

---

* This is the key to everything that follows. Until he can distinguish ego states, the therapist can make only empirical guesses which may *sound* like transactional statements, but are lacking in precision and reliability. The structural analyst has the same advantage over other therapists as the solid-state physicist has over the empirical metallurgist.

people are supposed to be playing and the nature of the transactions involved. After that, the therapist wants to know which
position these games are reinforcing, and what script they are
furthering. In this manner he can discover what motivates the
patient in her social relationships. Thus he prepares the way for
the decisive insight which hopefully will enable her to abandon
her investment in an illusory striving and replace it with something better adapted to the world in which she finds herself, and
more constructive for herself and her intimates.

CLASSIFICATION OF POSITIONS

Clinically, the therapist is working backward from the phenomena to their origin, from the phenotype to the genotype. The
genotypes we are presently concerned with are positions, and
here it is worthwhile to shift from empiricism to logic. It is
possible to make a logical classification of positions that is of
considerable assistance in clarifying the therapeutic approach.

The Nature of Decisions   First it is necessary to understand
the nature of the decisions which make positions necessary. A
healthy decision is an adaptable but inflexible statement of
purpose (heavily influenced, as already noted, and often paradoxically, by overt or covert parental urgings): "I will discover
the real Troy"; "I will devote myself to God"; "If I am unable to
bend the heavens, I will move Hell." In these examples the decision stands in the face of all sorts of vicissitudes which the
individual is able to weather and even profit from because of
his adaptability. A pathological decision is a verb absolute, a
determination of conduct in psychiatric patients (and that is
what makes them patients) that leaves no room for adaptation
because of its absoluteness, its "never" or "always": "Never again
will I love anybody" or "I will always watch out for myself
first."

The full statement of a decision should include its origin: (a)
"Never again will I love a man — because father beats me un-

fairly when he is drunk"; (b) "Never again will I love a woman
— because mother deserted me for my baby brother"; (c)
"Never again will I risk loving anyone — because mother showed
me I was unlovable." A position is a corresponding predicate
absolute, such as (a) "All men are evil," (b) "All women are
untrustworthy," (c) "I am never lovable." On the position are
based scripts and their derivative games, e.g. (a) "Second-
Degree Rapo" as illustrated in the case of Rita; (b) "If It
Weren't For Her"; and (c) "They'll Have To Take Me as I Am."
Thus the logical classification of games is to order them according to the positions they are designed to defend.

The Four Basic Positions The subjects of all positions are
particulars of the polarity "I — Others," and their predicates are
particulars of the polarity "OK — not-OK." The basic "convictions" for all positions are then the following four [6]:

1. I (we) am OK   3. You (They) are OK
2. I (we) am not-OK   4. You (They) are not-OK

These convictions yield the cadre for all possible positions,
thus:

1. I am OK, you are OK   3. I am not-OK, you are OK
2. I am OK, you are not-OK   4. I am not-OK, you are not-OK

Every game, script, and destiny is based on one of these four
basic positions. It is evident that only position 1 is intrinsically
constructive, and therefore existentially possible. Position 2 is
essentially paranoid, 3 depressive, and 4 futile and schizoid.
Typical games played from each are: 1 — "Homely Sage"; 2 —
"I'm Only Trying To Help You"; 3 — "Alcoholic"; 4 — "Look
What They Did To Me." The basic statements of the cadre can be
elaborated in various ways so as to yield almost innumerable
variants. As to subjects, "I" may be enlarged to "we," and "you"
may stand for "you," "they," "men," "women," "children," "everybody else." As to predicates, "OK" may stand for "rich," "helpful,"

"religious," "clean," or any other "good," while "not-OK" may stand for "poor," "ignorant," "childish," "sloppy," or any other "evil." Each of these particulars will give rise to its own peculiar repertoire of demonstrative games.

Choices of Action Furthermore, each of the basic positions, whatever its elaborations in detail, has certain connotations of action. For the patient who is pushed to the limit of his endurance, the alternatives are doing nothing, getting better, getting rid of people, becoming psychotic, or committing suicide. It is easier to clarify these if they are considered in reverse order.

The position "I am not-OK, you are not-OK" (4) leads ultimately to the choice of aesthetic or spiteful suicide. The aesthetic suicide may be justified with elaborate philosophical rationalizations, and this is an important determinant of the schizoid's interest in philosophy; the spiteful suicide is usually concealed only by mere gestures at rationalization, which are easily relinquished by the patient in favor of a frank declaration of the revenge motive. An exhibitionistic suicide may be attempted as a desperate, pathetic, and often vengeful effort to get attention from a parent, living or dead—even if it is only a gruesome stroke of recognition which will say "Well, you finally did something to attract my notice!"

The indications are that the aesthetic suicide results from lack of stroking during early infancy, leading to a deeply rooted depression (more precisely, despair) with feeble attempts at restitution manifested by schizoid behavior. When these fail the patient makes the final choice. He may postpone the action indefinitely, but once the choice is made he settles down into a relaxed spectatorship of life, perhaps having a last fling or collecting further justifications for the act in an attempt to wring the most out of it. In the female any of these types of suicide may follow an illegitimate impregnation, which is exploited by the Adult of the patient (under the influence of the Child) to emphasize the futility, to enhance the revenge, or in the exhibitionistic type, to add to the gossip. Such a choice of suicide is referred to in transactional groups as "killing yourself" or, colloquially, "knocking yourself off," and the justifications are called "trading stamps."

The position "I am not-OK, you are OK" (3) may result in the choice of sequestration: that is, the individual cuts himself off from the OK people by making use of one of the institutions provided by society for not-OK people, such as state hospitals, prisons, and dreary rooming-houses. With melancholic patients the sequestration again takes the ultimate form of suicide. Every individual in this position takes some sort of shelter, whether the position is manifested as social insecurity or deepest melancholia, or something in between. His feeling is "I am less OK than those others, and therefore cannot mix freely with them." Colloquially, this is called "resigning from the human race," and the therapy, of course, consists in having the patient renew his application for membership so that he can get back the membership card, which he may have relinquished at any time between earliest infancy and his teen-age years. In milder cases certain compromises are possible. For example, in every city there are OK saloons and not-OK saloons, and there are subclasses of not-OK saloons, such as those frequented by homosexuals, criminals, beatniks, or down-and-outers. There each of these types can cling to a tenuous membership in his own kind of not-OK crowd, and can obtain some degree of recognition if he wears the uniform and adopts the culture of that crowd. In clinical practice, most patients in the sequestration category are toying with the idea of hospitalization ("The last thing I want, what I am most afraid of, is going to a mental hospital"). Hence this choice is colloquially known as "going crazy," with "deathing out" as a melancholic alternative.

Among people who transact their everyday living from this position one of the commonest predicates, carried from childhood, has to do with money and its connotations: "There are

Poor People and not-Poor People, and I am one of the Poor People." If such an individual happens to acquire a lot of money, he does not become a not-Poor Person, but merely a Poor Person who happens to have a lot of money.

The position "I am OK, you are not-OK" (2) in relatively healthy people may lead to certain choices of profession such as missionary or district attorney. These are professions dedicated to the elimination of "badness" in general. In less healthy individuals, the choice is to eliminate specific people in order to get rid of the "bad" challenges or responsibilities they bring with them. The results range from socially acceptable religious or political action at one pole to homicide or infanticide at the other. The mother who kills her offspring is saying "Anything rather than going crazy." She refuses to go to a physician, psychiatrist, clinic, or hospital, or even to stand in front of her house and scream so that she will be carried off. By not taking any of these actions, she indicates that she has made another kind of choice. That is why *Medea* as conceived by Robinson Jeffers and Judith Anderson is unconvincing. The sound and fury fail to conceal the fact that there are many alternatives available besides infanticide, and that the lady is merely taking advantage of everybody's gullibility to act like a sulk. In everyday life, this choice leads to a variety of easily engineered ways of getting rid of troublesome people, such as divorce. In the case of children, they may be relegated to boarding school. Another device is to send them to a zealous but innocuous psychotherapist. If the psychotherapist is not innocuous enough, it is very easy to get rid of him. Colloquially, then, this alternative is called "getting rid of people."

The fourth choice, based on the position "I am OK, you are OK" (1), in clinical practice is referred to as "getting better." When he makes this choice, the individual has eliminated suicide, sequestration, and getting rid of people as solutions for situations of personal stress and as climaxes to his script. His transactions with society are then based on the premise that they can be mutually enjoyable for himself and others.

Let us consider for a moment in this light the "healthy" decisions mentioned at the beginning of this section. The decision "I will discover the real Troy" and others like it are a sophisticated adolescent or latent-period version of an earlier decision which reads either "I will discover something," or "Never again will I give up," or most likely a combination of the two which gives it its adaptability. The basic position is "I am OK (intelligent and persistent), you are OK (intelligent and persistent)." Through various vicissitudes this becomes modified into "I am OK, you are OK, they are not-OK." From this position either of two games can be played: "You'll Be Glad You Knew Me" (constructive) or "I'll Show Them" (dubious).

"If I am unable to bend the heavens, I will move Hell" can now be analysed as follows. The decision is "I will bend the heavens," or whatever form that would take in the first few years of life. To defend this decision, the position must be "I can do it," which comes out "I am OK (capable), you (parents) are OK." This becomes altered into "I am OK, you are OK, they are not-OK (because they will not let me bend the heavens)." The frustration imposed by "them" threatens the original decision and its concomitant position; this necessitates a "neurotic" period of reorganization, with the ensuing compromise "Then I will move Hell," which restores the original situation. In the case of Semmelweis, the original decision is something like "I will never let women die," and the position is "I am OK (loving women), you are not-OK (killing women)." When the others go on killing women, the original decision becomes impossible, and hence staying well becomes impossible; he is therefore left with the choices of suicide, homicide, or psychosis. Theoretically, if he had been able to shift into "If they won't let me save women, I'll save men," he would, after the period of "neurotic" reorganization, have stayed well.

An Illustrative Example A seventeen-year-old boy (John) was hospitalized for a severe anxiety attack. After he was discharged he had some difficulty in finding a therapist whom he could trust, but when he did he was able to discuss his sexual conflicts, and improvement in many spheres soon became apparent. Couched in the usual clinical language, as above, this history sounds rather commonplace. From the transactional point of view, however, it reads differently. When John found a suitable therapist, they concentrated not on the sexual determinants of his anxiety attacks, which were indeed present, but on the structural and transactional aspects of his behavior. He said that his Child was going to the therapist in order to demonstrate to his parents that he was crazy and that it was they who had driven him crazy. Once his game ("See What You've Done To Me") had been analyzed, he abandoned the choice of going crazy and was no longer afraid of being sent back to the hospital.

His mother and father then went on a vacation, and he told the group that he had a strong temptation to attempt suicide. The group did not try to support, reassure, or persuade him; instead, they went matter-of-factly to what they had come to regard as the core of such matters — the transactional aspects as related to his parents, to them, and to the therapist. The result was that he abandoned this project also.

We next find him with a gun that accidentally goes off and misses a companion, but he does not feel that this represents a transaction. While waiting for a more favorable opportunity to investigate this incident further, the therapist proceeded with the analysis of John's sexual conflicts. After a long interval, during which he made some progress in this area, John finally confessed that he had often had strong desires to bash or shoot people. His willingness to confess was based on the fact that he was ready to give up the idea of such violent measures as possible solutions for his difficulties.

A few days after that he came in and said that at the garage where he worked he had made a valuable improvement on an automotive device and had already started the preliminary work on engineering it for commercial manufacture.

While sitting in his therapy group, John had listened with interest when other patients discussed their attitudes toward the four choices described above. The therapist now proceeded as follows. First, he interrogated him briefly about the invention to identify its psychodynamic connotations for future reference, but went no farther in that direction. Instead he remarked that it was no accident that the patient had done some original thinking that particular week. He reminded John of how he had first come with the intention of proving he was crazy; of how he had abandoned that in favor of suicide; of how he had abandoned suicide in favor of killing someone else; and of how only the previous week he had abandoned the last alternative. Since the game aspects of these three choices had been effectively brought to his (Adult) attention ("See What You've Done To Me" and "See What You Made Me Do"), he could not, without considerable sacrifice of Adult integrity, return to any of them; therefore he was left with only one alternative, and that was to get better.

Dr. Q also mentioned that John's original project of proving he was crazy was what had kept him coming for treatment, and hence had made his recovery possible. Dr. Q had played along with him by granting in all honesty that he was perhaps a little bit crazy. "That hooked you long enough to give me a chance to get you interested in yourself." John laughed at that and said: "I sure outsmarted myself." By this he meant that he had come to the psychiatrist only to prove that he was crazy, and not intending to go any farther than that; but that by thus exposing himself to psychotherapy, he had ended up in improving in spite of himself. "Himself" in this context means all the decisions he had made to the contrary in early childhood, such as "Never again will I trust anyone." (His mother had divorced his father and remarried when he was five, and for a long time afterward John refused to let his parents touch him.)

This patient's case brings out the fifth alternative, which is an alternative but not a choice: the prolonging of indecision by continuing with the same old games. This is known colloquially as "doing nothing," and is merely a way to serve time in the hope that something will happen; in transactional language, waiting for "Santa Claus" or death to solve the problem. Only after the patient abandons his games as a result of game analysis is he faced with the necessity of choosing a decisive course of action, and as in the case of John, he may toy with each of the other alternatives before he makes the choice to get better. The transactional group's slogan at this point is, "You'd better start enjoying yourself before rigor mortis sets in." * The good prognosis in John's case was due to the evident fact that he did not cling tenaciously to one position (as a paranoid or melancholic, for example, might have done), but could be shaken loose to shift from one to another until it was possible for him to settle on the most productive one.

Clinical Accompaniments There are certain clinical phenomena that accompany each choice and the shift from one choice to another. If the patient has already abandoned some of his games when he comes for treatment he appears with feelings of futility, fear, failure, guilt, anger, disappointment, depression, or unreality. Usually, however, he enters the group playing such initial games as "Wooden Leg," "Psychiatry — Psychoanalytic Type," "Ain't It Awful — Paranoid or Depressive Type," "Little Old Me," or "See How Hard I'm Trying." If the therapist becomes involved in these, the patient is likely to feel elated and slightly triumphant, and there may be some temporary improve-

* This slogan comes from a similar injunction received by a patient in a dream. It is contrary, perhaps, to the monastic apothegm: *"Nihil sic revocat a peccato quam frequens mortis meditatio,"* which is sometimes inscribed on the walls of autopsy theatres.

ment. The patient may then continue to come in order to recharge the good feelings by playing a little game every week. On the other hand, if the therapist refuses to play, the patient does not know how to proceed and falls into the state known in transactional analysis as despair, which is very close to Kierkegaard's "despair" and Thoreau's "desperation," and which can be clinically differentiated from depression. Despair is precipitated by a dialogue between the patient's Adult and the outside world which is overheard by the patient's Child, while depression is a dialogue between his Parent and his Child with little Adult intervention. If the patient is already in despair, the therapist's refusal to play his residual games will intensify his bad feelings.

Because of the discomfort of despair, the patient seeks among the three solutions possible for him at that stage. He may "get worse," that is, make more concerted efforts to involve the therapist in a game; or he may consider suicide or seek oblivion with drugs or in a drunken stupor; or he may get rid of the troublesome therapist by quitting. If none of these solutions promise to fill his needs, he is then faced with the necessity of looking at the outside world to find an answer: by sequestration (hospitalization) or by getting rid of some troublesome people and responsibilities. This phase is marked by confusion, bewilderment, and resentment. If these solutions in turn are somehow made unavailable, he is left with only one alternative, and that is to get better. At this point the confusion lifts and is replaced by somatic anxiety attacks. In effect, these mean that the patient is now facing the archaic fears previously warded off by playing games. This is the initial decisive step toward recovery. He is now willing to look squarely at the world for the first time in many years, and what he sees frightens him. Since these fears are based on Parental distortions that have been communicated to the Child, the structural task at this point is to divorce him from his Parent and replace it with an Adult, perhaps using the group and the therapist as a kind of transitional object between his own Parent and his still ineffective Adult.

While the patient is testing the possible ways of relieving his despair, there may be rapid shifts in symptomatology. There are likely to be outbursts of depression when he contemplates suicide, of schizoid behavior in a bid for hospitalization, and of anger when he lashes out at the people who bother him. The therapist, with the help of a sophisticated group, may resolve each of these transitory phases rapidly so that the patient can move on to face the real issue, which is his reluctance to commit himself to getting better.

Deconfusing the Child Once the patient is convinced that the other alternatives are less profitable, he starts to get well.* It may take anywhere from two weeks to two years to reach this point, depending on the patient's ability to give up the gratifications yielded by his games. All the material previously gathered may then be used for analytic work in order to stabilize and promote the recovery by deconfusing the Child.

Thus, as John improved rapidly in his social, occupational, and sex life, and also in the quality of his transactions with the therapist, at a certain point Dr. Q suggested (during an individual session), "In order to keep it this way, we should go back to the sexual confusions you were telling me about and see if we can get them straightened out. In spite of the way you're getting along these days, I think your Child is still not seeing things clearly. Think of all the inventions you might be not making because of that." In order to illustrate the principle that you never know whether you are seeing things clearly or not, and you may be quite satisfied with the world as you see it without realizing that there are many things you are not seeing, he thought of asking John: "How do you think I would see things if I got a new pair of glasses?"

Instead, on a hunch, he said to the patient, who was lying on the couch: "Do I wear glasses?" John, as has already been

---

* The reader may still ask "Yes, but how do you convince him?" That is like asking "How do you grind a lens?" You read about lenses, experiment with lenses, and best of all, get a job with a lens-grinder.

implied, was an unusually intelligent and alert young man, and had sat in the group, usually directly facing the therapist, for an hour and a half each week for more than a year. In answer to the question the patient at first hesitated and then finally said: "I would say no. I think if I were describing you to someone I would say you didn't wear glasses." The therapist said, "Turn around and take a look," and to emphasize the point he removed his glasses. The patient took one look at the therapist's bare face and said, "Yes, you do wear glasses." He then burst out laughing and said "Okay. Let's go ahead." This confrontation, successful to an unexpected degree, was of considerable help in the subsequent proceedings.

This case is intended to illustrate the point that by using the transactional theory of personality and life, the patient can get better first and explore his sexual conflicts later, thus gaining in some cases several years of productive living, which under the conventional approach might have to be postponed until after the analytic phase was over. John's capabilities improved considerably before the systematic investigation of his Child conflicts was undertaken. His Adult readiness to proceed with that phase was evident in his response, so that now the therapist had an ally in dealing with the shrewd and apprehensive Child.

The proceedings also give some examples of how transactional analysis deals with aspects of identity, maturation, insight, and awareness. Thus on the one hand the transactional view of personality complements more specialized theories, while on the other it dovetails with more general philosophies such as those of Erikson [7] and the existentialists.

SOME COMMENTS ON PSYCHOBIOLOGY

The theorist in psychobiology is reluctant to make any statement until he has precise information, whereas the clinician is entitled or even obligated to make operational formulations using whatever contributory findings are at hand, since his duty is to do the best he can for the patient in the state of knowledge at the moment the patient comes for treatment. Such formulations, however tentative they may be, are useful instruments of clinical expediency. The chief requirement is that they reconcile ongoing experimental findings with clinical experience, and ongoing clinical experience with experimental findings.

Ego States Of considerable interest to structural analysis is Penfield and Jasper's observation [8] that electrical stimulation of certain areas of the human temporal cortex leads to the reexperiencing of past events in a totality whose sense corresponds exactly to what is here called an ego state. Penfield and his co-workers speculate that in this respect the brain functions like a tape recorder to preserve complete experiences in serial sequence, in a form recognizable as "ego states"—indicating that ego states comprise the natural way of experiencing and of recording experiences in their totality. Simultaneously, of course, experiences are recorded in fragmented forms and in discrete modality and phase forms in other parts of the brain; but this is not directly relevant to the present discussion.

Transactions Transactional analysis is interested in the finding that stimulation of the reticular activating system [9] promotes what is here called neopsychic or Adult ego state functioning. In the absence of such stimulation, phenomena often occur which would here be called manifestations of the archaeopsyche, or of Child ego states.[10] It is assumed, therefore, that deficient sensory stimulation in early life, as described by Spitz [1] and by Harlow and Harlow,[2] results in an instability of the neopsyche and the corresponding Adult ego state. The endocrinological effects of handling or of lack of handling [3] are also of interest to the transactional analyst.

Games Game analysis is grounded on the principle that the human organism can accept, up to a point, visual, auditory, and symbolic recognition signals as a substitute for direct tactile stimulation of corresponding quality. This is the biological advantage derived from playing games. Thus soft looks and a smiling face may have partial effects similar to those resulting from physical caresses, a fact heavily exploited by female game-players. Verbal teasing may have partial effects similar to those of physical prodding or tickling.

Physical Intimacy The infant at first requires tactile stimulation, but very soon auditory stimulation becomes acceptable as a supplement. In some individuals in later life tactile stimulation may be refused in favor of auditory recognition. Verbal recognition, however, does not seem to have such profound biological effects as tactile recognition. Social organization is based on tactile restraint, and leads to insufficient gratification in this area. Even if tactile recognition and stimulation is freely given, as in love and marriage, it is rarely assimilated as unreservedly as that offered originally by the mother, and hence there is usually a large or small residue of what may be termed "tactile hunger."

This tactile hunger has both quantitative and qualitative aspects. The quantitative aspect has to do with the duration of the stimulation and its cumulative effects. As to the qualitative aspects, the human skin is a highly efficient organ for the absorption and emission of certain wave lengths of radiant energy, which no doubt contribute to the gratification of cuddling, so that tactile hunger is most completely satisfied by the contact of "complementary skins" over the largest possible area.* The mother who cuddles her baby is in contact with a relatively large percentage of the infant's total skin area. In our society, however, a certain percentage of bottle-fed babies never come into contact with the unclothed body skin of their mothers.

As the individual grows older, tactile and other stimulus hun-

---

* "We ourselves are at all times glowing or emitting invisible 'light' . . . infra-red is constantly being emitted, absorbed, and re-emitted . . . as . . . objects exchange radiant energy with their neighbors." Human skin is an almost perfect emitter (and absorber) of long wave-length infra-red.[11]

gers become interwoven in a complex symbolic way with social situations, privileges, restrictions, responsibilities, and demands. From below, the primary hungers filter through and give rise to a dissatisfaction with life as it is and a hunger for "fulfillment." The postponement of this fulfillment results in an attitude which is colloquially called "waiting for Santa Claus."

THE SANTA CLAUS FANTASY

In the Santa Claus fantasy, the individual bases his behavior and his plans on the assumption that if he behaves a certain way he will eventually be presented with a unique object that will bring him the highest degree of happiness. This object in its most primitive form is aptly described, perhaps, as a magic orb, "the golden orange of the world studded with rubies and diamonds and full of ambrosias and elixirs," the sort of vision some people describe as accompanying complete orgastic fulfillment or a successful experience with certain intoxicating ("psychedelic") drugs. Some of the characteristics of this magic orb indicate that it probably recapitulates or is derived from some early infantile sensory experience.[12,13]

Whatever reward the Child in the patient is expecting for his good behavior, he is doomed to disappointment. For most, Santa Claus never comes: if there is a knock on the door, at best it is only the milkman. For the others, when he does come he leaves not the magic orb which the original childhood tales of Santa Claus led them to expect, but only a tinsel ornament, a piece of paper, or a big little red wagon which can be duplicated in any auto showroom. Healthy people learn to resign this quest in favor of what the real world has to offer but, to some extent, feel the despair that comes from such resignations. The neurotic clings to the assumption that if he plays his cards right he may some day come into sole and permanent possession of the magic orb.

THE BASIC PROBLEM OF PSYCHOTHERAPY

At the deepest level, the patient comes to the therapist in the hope that if he behaves in a certain way and follows the instructions of the therapist, the therapist will eventually present him with the magic orb, and in that way he will obtain its permanent possession. If the therapist is unaware of this, he may be at a loss to account for many of the phenomena that occur during treatment and for many of his results, and hence be unable to plan his treatment effectively. As soon as he perceives that the clinical evidence supports this basic premise, however, he will realize that one of his chief duties is to inform the patient at an appropriate time and in an appropriate way that he is not capable of gratifying this particular need. The message need not be given in its specific form but in any terms which fulfill the transactional requirement of telling the patient, "There is no Santa Claus." Although he has already been told this before he comes for treatment, he has not necessarily given up hope, and the therapist may be his last resort in an attempt to restore his illusions.

The therapist who is able to confirm for himself what has been outlined here will as a result feel considerable sympathy for his patient and a corresponding regret for the unpleasant duty that lies before him. In certain cases it is possible to soften the blow by telling the patient that, although he can never really earn possession of the magic orb, he might be able to catch an occasional glimpse of it if he can form a game-free relationship with a member of the opposite sex. Aside from such intimate relationships, however, the patient will have to learn to be content with whatever trophies he can obtain from the real world. The reason he can be "cured" is that while one part of him clings to the Santa Claus fantasy and would rather live in a fairy-tale world than give up hope, some other part of him knows that it is an illusion. On the other hand, if he has already given up hope and is ready to die, become psychotic, or kill someone as a result, the therapist can offer him the whole real world to replace the lost illusion—new lamps for old nostalgias, a fresh red apple for a vanished orb.

Transactionally, what actually happens in this framework is as follows: the patient comes to the therapist with the idea that the therapist has the patient's cure at his disposal, probably locked in his desk. It is only because the therapist is demanding, stingy, mean, or selfish that he does not hand it to the patient immediately at the first interview, but the patient has little doubt at first that if he behaves well enough for long enough, it will be given to him, very much as Santa Claus would give him presents when he was little. At a superficial level the cure may be visualized as a kind of diploma or piece of paper, but at a deeper level it is seen as the magic orb. Thus the patient may comply with everything that the therapist asks until he loses patience and suddenly rebels because he is not getting the reward he expected. Other patients rebel from the beginning, with the attitude "Why should I have to follow the rules to get what I want?" But when they see that this rebellion does not pay off, they may calm down and become more compliant, only in the end to rebel again.

In both cases the actual transactions are variants of the game "Gee You're Wonderful, Professor," based on the position that the therapist is a magician. The patients actually behave as though the therapist had a sign out in front of his office saying "I am a magician and I have magic orbs." The operations of various types of patients can thus be classified very much like the operations of people who go to a fortune-teller. Some are skeptical and try to unmask the fraud, while believing in it; others have a superstitious awe of the therapist's powers. They make fun of him, deride him, praise him, resent him, or respect him, but always eventually they become angry or sad when they do not get what they came for.

If the therapist can weather all this, he will end up with a patient who is willing to accept what the world and his intimate relationships can offer him, rather than seeking something mythical and unattainable. Even in those cases, however, there will be a residue of archaic dissatisfaction, and the patient will always part from the therapist with an implied question: "Is that all?" The good therapist will therefore resign himself to the fact that all he can offer his patients is the world, and nothing beyond that. The Adult of the sensible patient will agree with him and only as their gazes meet at the last parting will the patient's eyes be saying "Is that all?" and the therapist's eyes be replying "Yes." And on those terms they must say farewell.

A *Caveat* What has been said above about Santa Claus and the magic orb is in no way an attempt to establish a kind of "single basis" for psychiatric disorders. It is only intended to emphasize, on the basis of clinical experience, one important question that has to be settled in order to ensure a stable result. This applies whatever the patient's "cultural" background; hence the therapist need not be distracted unduly by "cultural" factors, which at the clinical therapeutic level are of relatively little significance.*

TRADING STAMPS

Transactional trading stamps are the currency of what are colloquially known as transactional "rackets," chiefly guilt, fear, hurt, and anger, and often inadequacy, stupidity, or bafflement as well.[14] When the patient is young, his parents teach him how to feel when things get difficult: "In our family, when things get difficult, we feel guilty (afraid, hurt, angry, inadequate, baffled)." These feelings become rackets when the patient learns to exploit them and collect them in his games and script, usually because they have become sexualized. For example, much "justi-

---

* Cf. Berne, E., Chap. 4, refs. 4 and 5. Also "Cultural Factors in Group Therapy," *Int. Ment. Health Res. Newsletter* 3: 3–4, June 1961.

fiable" grown-up anger belongs in this category, the payoff in the game called "Now I've Got You, You Son of a Bitch." Here the patient's Child is full of suppressed anger. He waits until someone does something that justifies his expressing it. Justification means that his Adult goes along with his Child in saying to his Parent, "No one can reasonably blame me for getting angry under such conditions." Thus relieved of Parental censure, he turns on the offender and says, in effect, "Ha! No one would blame me, so 'Now I've Got You,'" etc. In transactional language, he gets a "free mad" (a "red trading stamp"). If he saves them up instead of cashing them in on the spot, he may eventually get enough to feel entitled to a "free" homicide.

A patient went home from a group meeting one day and briefly explained trading stamps to her 12-year-old son. He said, "Okay, mom, I'll be back soon." When he returned, he had a small roll of perforated stamps for which he had made a dispenser, and a little paper book with the pages divided into squares. The legend read: "This page when full of stamps entitles you to one free suffer." The boy understood perfectly the principle involved: if people do not spontaneously frighten you, provoke you, insult you, or entice you, then you can initiate a game in order to make them do it; in this way free frights, mads, suffers, or guilts can be collected.

The "store" where transactional stamps are redeemed has the same assortment of prizes as a regular trading-stamp store: big ones, little ones, and toys. For "100 books," say, the patient can get one of the big ones: a free suicide, a free homicide, a free psychosis, or a free quit (divorce, leave therapy, quit job). For "10 books" he can get a toy (unsuccessful) suicide. For "1 book" he can get a "little" prize, a free sexual fantasy or drunk. An alcoholic, for example, by starting a game of "Uproar" at home, may provoke his wife into giving him 10 insult stamps, which entitle him to a guilt-free evening at the corner saloon and a seat at any tavern seminar on the psychology of women. Some patients, particularly paranoids, collect "counterfeit" stamps. If no one will provoke them, they imagine a provocation. People who save one "color" often tend to pass the other colors by; one who collects mads ("red stamps") may not be interested in collecting guilts ("brown stamps") and will actively reject "gold stamps" (affectionate or admiring strokes). Like paper stamps, transactional stamps are usually collected in the course of buying "groceries," that is, they arise out of legitimate transactions as a by-product; thus while the Adult goes about its business, the Child is eagerly watching for bonuses. For a patient to get better, he must throw away his old stamps, and either stop collecting or start to collect "gold" ones, which will entitle him to some free happies. That is one factor hindering recovery; few collectors of trading stamps are willing to throw them away.

HUMOR

As already noted, there is no evidence that solemnity in psychotherapy leads to sounder or more rapid clinical improvement. It is not only the archaic Child in the patient who subscribes to the belief that the therapist is a magician; the therapist himself tends to concur in this belief, and every magician knows better than to laugh in the presence of his own wizardry. The exception is that certain ritualistic jokes, peculiar to each situation, are permitted.[15] Hence therapeutic solemnity arises from a *folie à deux*, which may have its place in some kinds of therapy, but is inconsistent with a rational approach. The transactional analyst is well aware of the biological and existential function of humor, and does not hesitate to exploit it. It is only necessary for him to distinguish Parent, Adult, and Child forms of laughter, and that is not always easy. Parental laughter is indulgent or derisive. The Child laugh in the clinical situation is irreverent or triumphant. The Adult laugh, which is therapeutic, is the laugh of insight, and arises from the absurdity of circumstantial predicament and the even greater absurdity of self-deception.

The laughter in transactional analysis groups is based on the paradigm of the Tokyo Taxi.[15] The first wild ride in such a vehicle leaves the shocked passenger with three options: either to struggle to maintain his equanimity, a struggle which is hardly worth while; or to cower shakily in a corner; or to laugh. Those who laugh arrive at their destinations just as quickly as the others and they have two advantages over them. First, they have enjoyed the experience more, and secondly, they will be less boring when they recount it.

The therapist should remember that while death is a tragedy, life is a comedy. (Furthermore, even one's own death is not always a tragedy as such; it may only become tragic in its effects on others.) Curiously enough, many patients reverse this dramatic principle, and treat life like a tragedy and death like a comedy. The therapist who follows them is once more a party to a *folie à deux*. Human beings, according to the existentialists, are in a predicament all the time; and even those who subscribe to other philosophies must admit that they are in a predicament a good deal of the time. The biological or survival value of humor is to deal summarily with predicaments, thus releasing the individual to go about the business of living as effectively as he can under the circumstances. Since most psychogenic problems seem to arise from self-deception, Adult humor has a most rightful place in the materia medica of the psychotherapist.

THE GOAL OF TRANSACTIONAL TREATMENT

In practice, the whole transactional theory of personality — the effects of early experiences, decisions, positions and their consequences, the Santa Claus fantasy, the collection of trading stamps, and the value of metaphor and humor — are summarized in the transactional-analytic position "I am OK, you are OK," expressed in the following language: Every human being is born a prince or a princess; early experiences convince some that they are frogs, and the rest of the pathological development follows from this. Many pathological maneuvers and attitudes are expressed in frog-prince jokes. For example, the psychotic says, "Now that you've kissed me, I've been transformed back into a prince" (although he hasn't); the sociopath says, "If you kiss me, I'll become a prince" (although he knows he won't); the neurotic says, "I'm no worse looking than any other frog." *

In these terms, there are two kinds of therapeutic goals. The first tries for something called getting better, or "progress," which in effect is making more comfortable frogs; the second aims at getting well, or "cure," which means to cast off the frog skin and take up once more the interrupted development of the prince or princess. Transactional analysis aims for the latter. It does not try to make a braver schizophrenic who will socialize, get a job, and "improve" so that he is doing pretty well (for a frog); it aims to transform schizophrenics into nonschizophrenics, to make princes from frogs. The patients learn from bitter experience that "progress" is not enough, that the only thing that will give permanent and satisfactory results is to get well, which means getting back their memberships in the human race. For the therapist, this is basically a matter of giving them cogent permission to do so. They started out as princes, but their parents discouraged or forbade them from continuing so and insisted that they become something less. The therapist, with the help of the group, has to rescind that deleterious intervention, and give them permission to become what they started out to be. Hence the value of Maxwell Jones's work,[17] which in extension allows the patient to attend the staff conference on his own case, a clear indication to him that there are not two races of humanity, "people" and "patients," but that he can in due course take his place with full rights among the people.

---

* Thanks are due to Dr. Donald Young, of San Francisco, who first focused my attention on the frog-prince lore, which fits the clinical circumstances well and is congenial for patients to talk about.

REFERENCES

1. Spitz, R. "Hospitalism: Genesis of Psychiatric Conditions in Early Childhood." *Psychoanalytic Study of the Child* 1:53–74, 1945. See also "Hospitalism: A Follow Up Report" and "Anaclitic Depression." Ibid. 2:113–17 and 313–42.

2. Harlow, H. F., and M. K. Harlow. "Social Deprivation in Monkeys." *Scientific American* 207:136–46, November 1962.

3. Levine, S. "Stimulation in Infancy." *Scientific American* 202:80–86, May 1960.

4. Hess, E. H. "Imprinting in Animals." *Scientific American* 198:81–90, March 1958.

5. Klein, M. *The Psycho-Analysis of Children.* Hogarth Press, London, 1949.

6. Berne, E. "Classification of Positions." *Transactional Analysis Bulletin* 1:23, 1962.

7. Erikson, E. H. *Insight and Responsibility.* W. W. Norton & Company, New York, 1964.

8. Penfield, W., and H. Jasper. *Epilepsy and the Functional Anatomy of the Human Brain.* Little, Brown & Company, Boston, 1954, pp. 127–47.

9. French, J. D. "The Reticular Formation." *Scientific American* 196:54–60, May 1957.

10. Heron, W. "The Pathology of Boredom." *Scientific American* 196:52–6. January 1957.

11. Barnes, R. B. "Thermography of the Human Body." *Science* 140:870–77, 24 May 1963.

12. Jung, C. G. *The Integration of the Personality.* Farrar & Rinehart, New York, 1939.

13. Fodor, N. *The Search for the Beloved.* Hermitage Press, New York, 1949.

14. Berne, E. "Trading Stamps." *Transactional Analysis Bulletin,* 3:127, April 1964.

15. Berne, E. *The Structure and Dynamics of Organizations and Groups.* (Chap. 2, ref. 4.)

16. St. Cyr, C. "The Tokyo Taxi." *Transactional Analysis Bulletin* 1:23, 1962.

17. Jones, M. *The Therapeutic Community.* (Chap. 9, ref. 13.)

13

The Relationship Between
Transactional Analysis and Other
Forms of Treatment

As already noted, the design of transactional analysis is such, both clinically and theoretically, that it can be used to provide a suitable context for the introduction of any other form of rational therapy. In order for the therapist to exploit this flexibility to the best advantage, he should have an adequate understanding of the relationships between transactional analysis and other popular forms of treatment.

TRANSACTIONAL ANALYSIS AND PSYCHOANALYSIS *

At the present time, other things being equal, psychoanalysis is the preferred treatment in those conditions it was designed for, namely, the transference neuroses — phobias, hysterias, and obsessional neuroses — together with character abnormalities that have been developed instead of these diseases.† Everything other than these, such as narcissistic or psychotic conditions, is more or less unsuitable. These restrictions were laid down long

* This discussion is based on twelve years of psychoanalytic training with the New York and San Francisco Psychoanalytic Institutes. The writer, however, is not a member of any Psychoanalytic Society.
† Note the word "diseases" which W. J. H. Sprott and James Strachey used in translating Freud.[3]

ago by an unquestioned expert in the field, and later developments have confirmed that Freud was right: outside of the clearcut transference neuroses, psychoanalysis is "more or less" unsuitable. But since it has been the most widely taught of the therapeutic approaches, it has been employed for every kind of psychiatric disorder, and the question of its suitability has gradually been less emphasized by its practitioners, although not by others. Transactional analysis, in qualified hands, has turned out to be a happy remedy for this defect in the treatment of conditions outside the classical triad. Even in the transference neuroses, it may be the best treatment when circumstances do not favor the employment of the psychoanalytic procedure, as is the case with the majority of all patients in psychotherapy.

An Illustrative Anecdote A phobic patient (Elsie) who had been in transactional group treatment for two years requested individual treatment. When the therapist suggested that she lie on the couch, she manifested considerable resistance. After she finally did decide to lie down, she very soon reported a strange feeling. "I'm afraid you're going to touch me — maybe I want you to — then I could reject you." She recognized all this with astonishment as archaic and Adult-ego dystonic.

Her previous treatment had prepared her for this kind of objectivity, which is similar to that described by Fenichel: the division of the ego into an observing portion and an experiencing portion.[1] In transactional analysis, such objectivity is deliberately encouraged during the initial structural stage, before "interpretations" are made; as rapidly as the clinical material and situation allow, an "observing portion" is dissected out *in toto* before anything else is done. The plan is that from the very first the patient should have available an "objective" part of the ego (the Adult), whose objectivity can be extrapolated as a therapeutic ally to view judiciously all sorts of unexpected phenomena.

In Elsie's case her previous therapeutic experience of 100 group sessions (arithmetically about one-sixth of 150 hours) with a few individual sessions here and there, enabled her to recognize forthwith the social aspects of her archaic feelings. The therapist and other group members had suspected that certain things that had "happened" in her life were the natural outcome of a game of "Second-Degree Rapo." For example, she had gone to her clergyman for comfort, and he had ended by trying to make love to her. She pushed him away and told a neighbor about it in confidence, only remembering "too late" that the neighbor was an elder of the church. If no one actually made a pass at her, she had to imagine that they would. There was no need for the therapist to point out the connection between the clergyman incident and her thoughts on the couch. Her previous denials of sexual interests were no longer tenable. Indeed, her first fifteen minutes on the couch (following two years of transactional group treatment) made a deep impression on her.

This case illustrates three ways in which transactional analysis resembles psychoanalysis:

1. It splits off an objective part of the ego (the Adult) which can often be swiftly stabilized and brought into play in many different areas. This preparation, besides having its own significant therapeutic effect, serves well if the patient is switched from group treatment to specialized individual treatment.

2. At an appropriate time, it takes an active interest in archaic reaction patterns as they occur in the treatment situation. (In this case, as in others, the emergence of archaic reaction patterns in their pristine form did not seem to be impaired by the activity required of the therapist in a transactional group. The probability is that the therapist's authenticity, rather than the number of words he says per hour, is the decisive factor in promoting candidness on the part of the patient's Child.)

3. It encourages the patient to relate these patterns to other behavior in the immediate and remote past.

With these preliminary remarks in mind, we can now proceed

to a more formal consideration of the relationship between the two approaches, and especially of the ways in which they differ.

PERSONALITY STRUCTURE

Structurally, transactional analysis speaks of Parent, Adult, and Child, which are more personal than the superego, ego, and id spoken of in psychoanalysis. The former represent psychological, historical, and behavioral realities, while the Freudian terminology is a conceptual one.

The Superego Freud [2] defines the superego as "a special agency in which (the) parental influence is prolonged." The superego may be compared to one aspect of the transactional Parent, the "Parental influence." Both the superego and the Parental influence modify behavior on the basis of past experiences with certain individuals; in staff-conference dialect these are called "parental figures," or more vulgarly, "authority figures"; transactionally they are known as "Parental people." The superego arises through the *processes* of incorporation, internalization, introjection, and their cognates. These processes are interposed, so to speak, between what the Parental figures actually did and the patient's behavior. The concept of Parental influence deals directly with the patient's actual transactions with Parental people, regarding the processes involved as not directly relevant to clinical application outside of formal psychoanalysis. Thus, if a patient avoids using obscene words, the transactional analyst asks as his primary concern: "Who told you not to use obscene words?" and can get a direct reply. This reply is as immediately meaningful to the patient as it is to the therapist.

In general, the superego is prohibitive. To explain dishonesty, promiscuity, or alcoholism in terms of the superego, some writers first postulate the influence of such an agency, and then infer that it is defective, and that such "bad" behavior is due to "superego lacunae." "Parental influence" includes not only prohibitions, but also permission, encouragement, and commands. Thus the transactional question about "bad" behavior is: "Which of your parents gave you permission, encouragement, or orders to indulge in such activities?"

The concept of the superego refers to an agency, force, or psychic instance. It does not directly describe what happened. "Parental influence" is an inference that arises out of the immediate clinical situation and clarifies for the patient on the spot what happened to him and who did it. The "Parental influence," however, is only one aspect of the transactional Parent. The other is the overt exhibition of a Parental ego state. If the patient raises a finger in admonition, the transactional analyst asks, "Which of your parents raised his finger?" thus approaching the problem, as a matter of policy, in the most direct and pragmatic way. The phenomenon of a Parental ego state takes nurturing behavior in its stride by asking, "Which of your parents spoke to children with that kind of considerateness?"

The Parental ego state can be discussed psychoanalytically by referring to the processes mentioned above: incorporation, internalization, introjection, and also identification. Transactional analysis deals with it at a transactional or operational level without using intervening concepts.

The Ego   The psychoanalytic ego has reality testing as one of its principal functions. The "Adult ego state" of transactional analysis is described as a state of mind focused on data processing and probability estimating. Actually, "reality testing" has two meanings, the first relating to accuracy, and the second to pathological distortions. Consider the following proposition from a gastroenterologist: "It is not necessary for a healthy person to take an enema every day." This is both accurate and undistorted. If a woman of peasant origin says, "You must move your bowels every day or you will die of autointoxication," she is inaccurate, but is not necessarily distorting her environment; her data processing and probability estimating may be dealing efficiently with the restricted information available to her and the few superficial clinical observations she has been able to make. On the other hand, if a metropolitan housewife says, "Almost everybody takes an enema every day," she is not only inaccurate, but there is some special factor at work in her selection of friends and of reading matter, and she is obviously ignoring information available to her. Her data processing and probability estimating are distorted by archaic influences. In psychoanalytic terminology she might be described as having a weak ego. The transactional analyst would say that she had a strongly cathected Child ego state that was contaminating her Adult ego state; that is, the ego state in her that deals with matters of excretion (the Child) is highly cathected, but it is the wrong ego state for making accurate judgments of physical reality. The strength of her Child is shown by its dominating influence over her thinking, with its preoccupation about enemas. This Child ego state is not her id, it is a matrix into which her id flows. The gastroenterologist might be equally preoccupied with enemas, but in a different ego state; in his case the id flows into an Adult matrix.

Psychoanalytically there is more tendency to speak of these three people in quantitative terms ("strong ego" and "weak ego"), and transactionally more tendency to discuss them in qualitative terms (Adult data-processing and Child distortions). Parent, Adult, and Child are all part of the "ego system," whereas the psychoanalytic ego can be to a certain extent equated specifically with the Adult ego state. The transactional analyst would not recognize the concept of "a weak ego," but he would be willing to consider the proposition that "one ego state is more strongly cathected than another in this person."

The Id Freud [3] describes the id as "a chaos, a seething cauldron of excitement . . . it has no organization and no unified will . . . nothing which can be compared to negation." The transactional Child is highly organized, is not necessarily seething, and is quite able to say "No"; and in fact has a strong tendency to do so when this suits his unified will. Thus the Child is a well-organized ego state, in contrast to the unorganized cauldron of biological drives which is the id. Where psychoanalysis speaks of the id under the inhibiting influence of the superego, transactional analysis speaks of the Child under the inhibiting, permissive, or provocative influence of the Parent. Child and Parent are distinct personalities, each with its own separate and complete organization; they are not necessarily opposed to each other, they are simply in many respects inconsistent which each other. They have a strong psychological and civil reality; from old directories, as already noted, one could find the addresses and telephone numbers of the original child and parent who are perpetuated in the patient as ego states.

Reconciliation Structurally, the two systems can be reconciled by regarding superego, ego, and id as determinants in the formation of Parent, Adult, and Child ego states: the Parental ego state being most heavily influenced by the superego, the Adult ego state by the ego, and the Child ego state by the id. Many anomalies can be accounted for in transactional analysis by assuming that more than one determinant is active in the formation of a single ego state, and conversely, that a single determinant can be channeled to any of the three ego states. Thus, the id supplies the motive power for the Parental ego state in the nursing situation. Such mothering behavior is derived from the same biological substratum as the more popular sexual and hostile drives of the id which influence Child ego states. The principle of determinants is thus a fruitful structural link between psychoanalytic theory and transactional analysis.

METAPSYCHOLOGY

Freud speaks of bound and freely mobile cathexis.[2] Such a two-state concept does not satisfactorily explain many phenomena, particularly those connected with the feeling of "Self." In the classical compulsion neurosis, for example, there is a divorce of that part of the personality which has the executive from the part which has the feeling of "Self." In order to reconcile these paradoxes, transactional analysis takes a somewhat different view of psychic energy, breaking it down into three components: bound, unbound, and free. A latent or inactive ego state is said to be cathected with bound energy; when an ego state becomes active, its indigenous energy is unbound; the free cathexis, meanwhile, may move across the boundaries from one ego state to another. In this model, the feeling of Self resides in that ego state which at a given moment is charged with free cathexis, while the executive command of mobility is taken by that ego state which has the greatest charge of active cathexis (where active = unbound + free). Usually the two coincide, but sometimes they do not. Thus transactional analysis deals with a three-state model of cathexis, in contrast to the two-state model of psychoanalysis. This difficult matter has been more fully dealt with elsewhere by the writer.[4]

TRANSACTIONS

Reactions versus Transactions Psychoanalysts are concerned with transference reactions and, to a growing extent, with counter-transference reactions. Such "reactions" are treated in transactional analysis as "transactions." "Crossed transaction type I" (Figure 6, Chapter 6 — Adult-Adult stimulus crossed by Child-Parent response) corresponds to the classical transference reaction, while "crossed transaction type II" (Figure 9, Chapter 10 — Adult-Adult stimulus crossed by Parent-Child response) represents the commonest form of counter-transference reaction. Transactional analysts assume as a matter of course that crossed transactions type II (implying counter-transference) might occur just as frequently as any other type of transaction in the treatment situation unless steps were taken to avoid them. By dealing with such responses initially on the spot at the transactional rather than the psychodynamic level, the transactional analyst is prepared to take immediate reparative measures when they do occur, and is not dependent on the difficult process of self-analysis to indicate remedial procedures. But he still has self-analysis available for consideration in his leisure time as a way of dealing with undesirable proclivities.

Types of Transactions Transactional analysis originated from, and is designed for, group treatment. That situation elicits a much larger variety of transactions than individual treatment does. Hence the transactional analyst must be prepared to analyse with precision any type of transaction whatsoever. In the transactional diagram, this includes nine types of complementary transactions, 72 types of crossed transactions, and a large assortment of ulterior transactions (theoretically, 6480 types of duplex transactions, plus all the possible types of angular ones). Fortunately, most of these are rare, and the bulk of his analysis is concerned with about a dozen types that occur most commonly. In general, psychoanalysis focuses principally on crossed transactions type I and has no specific procedures for dealing with most of the others.

GAMES

At first sight, games (in the writer's experience) are usually described by psychoanalysts as special types of character defenses, thus tending to minimize their ongoing nature, and especially their transactional elements: the con, the gimmick, and the payoff. For example, anal aggressive character defenses are familiar phenomena, but it is also necessary to take into account the fact that the act of aggression is merely one move in an ongoing series of transactions in which the payoff is of decisive importance. Thus, in the game of "Schlemiel," the aggression is a gratifying way of passing the time while waiting for forgiveness, but it is usually easier for the Schlemiel to inhibit his impulses than it is for him to forego the forgiveness once he has committed himself. Where other approaches merely describe certain initial tendencies, the transactional approach makes it possible to predict with considerable confidence whole sets of transactions in sharp outline, and makes such insights available as a matter of course to even the most inexperienced therapist.

Defenses and Gratifications To the transactional analyst, the defensive function is only one aspect of games. Along with the defensive advantages, there are various gratifications derived from playing games. These can be roughly divided into types, and in general each type may be regarded as exerting an equal force in prolonging the game. Since the defensive aspect is more difficult to deal with (at least in group treatment) than the gratifications, the transactional analyst concentrates on the latter. If the archaic gratifications lose their attractiveness through insight or compliance, the patient gives up the game, abdicating its defensive functions along with the other advantages, thus laying bare the underlying pathology. Concurrently this may result in marked social improvement, eliciting new types of gratifications more firmly rooted in current reality, which may exert a powerful therapeutic effect. This shift may be highly appreciated by the patient's intimates and associates, such as his wife and children.

A simple example is the game of "Veteran," a variant of "Wooden Leg," where the most obvious payoff is in money. If the patient can be induced to give up his pension, along with the social exploitation of his symptoms, the whole matter can be approached differently, often with the enthusiastic co-operation of his family (unless they too are heavily involved in the game). Once the patient is shaken loose from his stereotyped social behavior by removing the gratifications, the defensive function is much more easily yielded than if that is attacked first. As an analogy, the problem of felling a tree with a shovel may be used. It is quite possible to dig through directly to the taproot, leaving most of the other roots intact, and then attack the axial root, after which the peripheral roots will be weakened. But this involves cutting through a very thick root and doing it in the dark, so to speak, by digging under and through other roots. A

much simpler system is to cut the peripheral roots first, whereupon the tree may fall of its own weight without the worker
having to do anything to the most difficult root of all, the taproot.

SCRIPTS

The Repetition Compulsion   The script has some relationship
to the repetition compulsion of Freud, and even more to what
he calls the "destiny compulsion." [5] Freud relates these to the
death instinct, and indeed, death is the long awaited fulfillment
of many scripts. There is no term in psychoanalysis for the original experiences that pattern the individual's life; transactional
analysts call these the "protocol." What is repeated then in the
script is some version of the original protocol. In some cases
this re-enactment may take a whole lifetime, so that although in
principle the script is repetitive, there may not be enough time
for an actual repetition. In other cases, however, the whole
script is re-enacted many times, as with women who marry one
alcoholic after another, or with men who lose one job after
another.

The Infinite Regress   In a more subtle way, the script is also
re-enacted as part of itself, and these re-enactments in turn contain versions of themselves (like the famous fleas, which had little
fleas upon their backs to bite them, which in turn had lesser fleas,
and so ad infinitum). Thus the whole life of a patient is his script
on a grand scale; his yearly re-enactments (e.g. losing his job)
are lesser versions contained in that matrix; and during the year
he may run through the whole script each week in some minor
version. Indeed, a keen observer may see a patient run completely through some adaptation of his script in a single group
session. Some apparently trivial incident, lasting only a few
seconds, may reveal to a perceptive therapist the whole story
of the patient's life. An example of this is described elsewhere
by the writer,[4] where the manner in which the patient reached

for an ashtray typified her whole destiny. The advantage of formulating the principles involved in formal transactional terms is that even an inexperienced therapist then knows what to watch for and how to deal with it.

Scenes and Acts Like some psychoanalysts, transactional analysis speaks of the "transference drama" (rather than of transference "reactions"), and recognizes this as a special adaptation of the script. This concept offers considerable sweep and coherence in dealing with archaic manifestations. Thus Oedipus becomes not merely a "character" who exhibits "reactions," but the protagonist in a dramatic build-up. Furthermore, the script analyst is able to recognize scenes and acts, and with his experienced sense of dramatic tension, he can recognize an unfinished drama. Thus if a patient gets married or gets a divorce with his Adult in good control, the script analyst does not feel satisfied until he has decided whether the patient has actually abandoned his script to live an autonomous life or whether his Adult behavior merely signifies the intermission before the curtain goes up on the next act.

THE THERAPEUTIC ATTITUDE

Transactional analysis is an actionistic form of treatment, where psychoanalysis is to a much greater extent a contemplative one. The transactional analyst says, "Get better first, and we can analyse later." Surprisingly enough, in most cases the patient will oblige. He does so in spite of the fact that to get better means to give up his archaic gratifications, but he is willing to do that when and if he becomes convinced that there are better ones available. Afterward, he may wisely wish to analyse the origin and significance of his abandoned games in order to ensure stability for his reorientation. Thus the transactional patient and his family benefit from the accomplishments that take place before the deeper analytic phase of his treatment, so that it is of relatively less consequence how long he remains in treatment after that. The psychoanalyst, on the other hand, may imply, "After you have been analysed, you will get better." Again the patient obliges, but under those conditions feels he does not have "permission" to get better until he is "analysed," and that may take years — years which may be decisive in the progress of his career and the development of his children.

In transference language, the psychoanalytic contract often reads to the patient as follows: "If you come regularly and tell father everything according to the procedure he prescribes, then your cure will be forthcoming." The "cure," as previously noted, is conceived of at some archaic level as some splendid object that the therapist keeps in his desk. The long analytic process then becomes in his mind a condition imposed arbitrarily by the "bad" therapist, who requires the patient to undergo it in order to prove that he is worthy of the glorious prize. Under such conditions, an energetic patient often feels resentful and rebellious, and makes whatever difficulties he dares, gauging carefully how far he can go without jeopardizing his prospects. Thus all sorts of troublesome games occur, which from the psychoanalytic point of view are called resistances. It is easily understandable that many patients even perversely prolong the analysis.

The transactional contract reads: "If you get better first and give up your symptoms, then you may come if you wish and talk to father for an hour each day." The patient may still be reaching for his golden orange, but he has already met the therapist's demands. His continued attendance is not a condition, but a privilege. Thus he proceeds with the analytic phase in a much more agreeable frame of mind than under the other contract, and makes fewer difficulties. Since he is enjoying life meanwhile, the therapist at least offers him something in place of the magic orb, so that question is easier to deal with when it comes up. This does not mean that the analysis of resistances is forfeited, but only that they are softer and more accessible. For instance, they may change from hard psychotic paranoid ones into deadpan humor. Such a shift can be brought about with gratifying frequency by the use of transactional analysis. One reason may be that the psychoanalytic contract is (from a paranoid point of view) a persecutory one, while the transactional contract is more easily seen as an indulgent one.

In both cases, the termination of treatment will be the same, since neither therapist can supply the magic orb. Whatever treatment procedure is used, the patient (i.e. his archaic Child) will end up feeling disappointed, and as already noted, his final comment to the therapist, spoken or unspoken, as he departs from his final session will be "Is that all?"

TRANSACTIONAL ANALYSIS AND
EXISTENTIAL ANALYSIS *

Insofar as actual living in the world is concerned, transactional analysis shares with existential analysis a high esteem for, and a keen interest in, the personal qualities of honesty, integrity, autonomy, and authenticity, and their most poignant social manifestations in encounter and intimacy.

PERSONALITY STRUCTURE

In structural terms, the problem of autonomy revolves around the Parental influence and the life-type known as the "jerk." A jerk is someone whose parents forbade him to be happy unless certain conditions were met, and since the conditions are impossible to fulfill, he spends his life in a miserable conflict between rebellion and attempts at compliance. The result is that apologetic clumsiness replaces authenticity in his social behavior,

* This section is based on presentations by and discussions with Dr. Arthur Burton, of Sacramento, California, and his colleagues of the Western Society of Existential Psychiatrists and Psychologists. (See *Transactional Analysis Bulletin* 1:19, 1962, and 2:43, 1963.)

and the struggle for autonomy is replaced by a self-defeating struggle for approval.

In milder cases of existential impairment, contamination of the Adult by the Parent, as in certain political extremists, leads to a prejudiced and distorted view of reality and of other people, resulting in spurious transactions. Since in most cases transactional analysis takes the side of the Child and the Adult against the Parent, it tends to promote autonomy in the jerk and to increase authenticity in contaminated personalities.

Integrity depends on clear data-processing of internal dialogues by the uncontaminated, Adult, and clear insight into the subversive nature of those social institutions that impair authentic encounters between individuals. Hence strengthening the Adult promotes integrity.

Transactionally, the most authentic people in the world are young infants whose vision and relationships have not yet been seriously impaired by "the jazz." In effect, transactional analysis attempts to re-establish in the patient the clear awareness and the candid intimacy of childhood as exemplified by the early relationship between the child and his mother. The patient learns to exercise Adult insight and control so that these childlike qualities only emerge at appropriate times and in appropriate company. Along with these experiences of disciplined awareness and disciplined relationships goes disciplined creativity.

DYNAMICS

The Self, in some existential sense, is recognized and highly regarded by transactional analysts. The Self is experienced as that ego state in which the free energy resides at a given time. At the moment the person is expressing Parental anger, he feels "This is really me" even though this Self resides in a borrowed ego state. At another moment, when he is objectively adding his client's accounts, he again feels "It is 'really me' adding these figures." If he sulks just like the little boy he once actually was, he feels at that moment "It is 'really me' who is sulking." In these examples, the free energy, which gives rise to the experience of "really me," was residing in the Parent, Adult, and Child, respectively.

The transactional patient learns to control his free energy to a considerable extent, so that he can shift his "real Self" from one ego state to another by an act of will: shift from Parental anger to attend to his Adult business, or from a Child's sulk to give Parental tenderness to a sick spouse or offspring. At first he relies heavily on external stimuli to bolster such shifts, but he learns more and more to effect them through autonomous acts of volition. He also learns to appraise his own authenticity: is it *really* his real Self who is being Parentally tender, Adultly candid, or freely imaginative, or are these spurious acts of compliance, rebellion, or hypocrisy?

The inherent paradox that "the patient" can control his "Self" is so far no more resolvable in transactional terms than in philosophical or existential ones. What transactional analysis offers is a method for exploiting this paradox to increase autonomy and authenticity. The "Self" and "free energy" are left open-ended as an experience and as a construct, respectively, whose ultimate reduction and definition belong outside the province of psychiatry. This is an invitation to philosophers, theologians, poets, and creative and interpretive artists of all kinds to participate with psychotherapists in giving meaning to ultimate values.

GAMES

Games are by definition exploitative, and hence from an existential viewpoint inherently bad. The ideal of transactional analysis is the game-free relationship. Pragmatically, however, it is recognized that such relationships are hardly possible outside of a small, select circle; in other society, games offer the most interesting possibilities for structuring time. As long as the individual can exercise the option of deciding which games to play, how far to go, whom to play with, and when not to play, he can maintain his authenticity. If he violates that, he may be beset with feelings of guilt, disappointment, or chagrin. He is then faced with the question of integrity. If he indulges such unworthy feelings, he has lost it. When he recognizes that they result from his own lack of insight, prudence, experience, or self-restraint, he has regained it.

Rackets Self-indulgence in feelings of guilt, inadequacy, hurt, fear, and resentment are colloquially called "rackets." Such self-indulgences are most likely to occur when specific unpleasant feelings become sexualized. ("It's a funny way to have an orgasm," says the transactional analyst, or more kindly, "Sex is more fun than fear or resentment." *) The patient has two ways to avoid these indulgences if he wishes. First, he can stop playing the games of which these feelings are the payoff. Secondly, if he chooses to play or is seduced into playing them, he can shift afterward from the self-indulgent (Child) ego state into another one. The patient will only "go straight," however, if he is committed to an implicit or explicit "contract of authenticity." This contract, which reads "I am here for you to help me eliminate spurious transactions and reactions," is attractive to most patients.

The problem of legitimacy in connection with such feelings has not been completely solved by the transactional analyst, but certain preliminary statements can be made and certain basic positions outlined from which to survey the possibilities. The crucial test is the transfer of these feelings from the Child ego state to the Adult ego state. The Child feels guilty for what he himself has done. The Adult feels guilty for being like those others and for belonging to a race which is capable of doing such terrible things. For the Child, guilt is a kind of bastard self-

---

* It is true that the dodo became extinct as a result of this philosophy, but I am talking about psychopathology, and not about survival kits.

indulgence with the transactional advantage of "copping a plea" (if you feel guilty, you are more OK, especially to the "helping professions"); for the Adult, it is a legitimate commitment to an ethos. The authentic person simply does not do precisely those things which he knows with certainty he is going to regret afterward; or at least if he does do them, he does not then use "Mea culpa" as a plea for forgiveness or to start a game of "Kick Me." ("I apologize for burning down your house and running away with your wife.") For the Adult, a mistake is not something to feel bad about, it is something to learn from.

Similarly with the currently fashionable feeling of "hostility" (it is awfully hard to be OK nowadays without it). The transactional analyst starts from the basic position that there is no such thing as Adult anger, that anger is a "racket" indulged in with Parental permission or encouragement. Interestingly enough, it was not a pugilist, but the intelligent seventeen-year-old patient (John) discussed in the previous chapter who convinced the at first incredulous writer that this was true. To the Adult, pain and frustration are problems to be solved; to the Child, they are provocations to be taken advantage of. ("Now I'm entitled to hit you!" he says.) In the Adult ethos, indignation at what has been done to other people is permissible; only from this position can the individual authentically decide whether he is entitled to be indignant about things that have been done to him personally. The same applies to disappointment, which will be considered shortly.

In the face of such a hard look, the patient is tempted to cry: "But the feeling, the feeling, what do you do about that?" This question can be answered, but answering it is a real test of the therapist's ability. If the patient can see that he considers himself "entitled" to his feelings mainly because he has laboriously collected enough "trading stamps" to justify them, he may be able to regard them more objectively, and even to relinquish them in favor of more authentic and rewarding ones.

THE SCRIPT

Nearly all human activity is programed by an ongoing script dating from early childhood, so that the feeling of autonomy is nearly always an illusion — an illusion which is the greatest affliction of the human race because it makes awareness, honesty, creativity, and intimacy possible for only a few fortunate individuals. For the rest of humanity, other people are seen mainly as objects to be manipulated. They must be invited, persuaded, seduced, bribed, or forced into playing the proper roles to reinforce the protagonist's position and fulfill his script, and his preoccupation with these efforts keeps him from torquing in with the real world and his own possibilities in it. Thus while the patient John was intent on proving that he was crazy and that the psychiatrist was a "kook," he never noticed the doctor's glasses, said many things that were only half-honest, was unable to exercise fully his creative powers, and was afraid to laugh or enjoy himself in the treatment group.

The person who is freed from his script will see the world in a new way (or rather in an old and long-forgotten way). A biologist who had spent some years doing "research" into mothering behavior in mice, as his script called for, later in his career bought his young son some pet mice. One day during his script-struggle he was idly watching a young mouse-mother among the pets, when suddenly for the first time in his life he saw a mouse. As he put it, "I never realized in all those years that mice were people." It is also likely that there for the first time in his adult life he also saw a mother.*

A script-free person is prepared for game-free candid intimacy if he meets someone like himself who is game-free, or who can

---

* A similar situation, in which a whaleman, in a situation of acute stress, suddenly realized for the first time that whales are people, is described by James Michener in his book *Hawaii*.

become so under the right circumstances. Such a meeting is probably the highest form of what existentialists call an "encounter." Thus in transactional terms an encounter is a preparation for intimacy.

THE THERAPEUTIC PROBLEM

Transactional analysts distinguish, perhaps in a way congenial to existential analysts, between depression and despair. Depression results from a dialogue between the Parent and the Child; despair results from the failure or the therapeutic interruption of a game or script: it is a dialogue between the Adult and the external environment which is overheard by the Child. In order to prevent despair, the patient tries to re-establish the game, becoming more frustrated and more angry at the therapist's efforts to prevent this.

Disappointment is something different from either depression or despair. The original protocol of any script is formed at such an early age that it always contains a magical element. At the most archaic level it is a quest for the magic orb, in life or in death, and that is one thing that brings the patient to the therapist. The patient's varying attitudes as the treatment progresses are fundamentally reactions to the therapist's failure to produce, and to the patient's doubts as to whether the failure is his or the therapist's.

In the long run, the patient must undertake the task of living in a world in which there is no Santa Claus. He is then faced with the existential problems of necessity, freedom of choice, and absurdity, all of which were previously evaded in some measure by living with the illusions of his script. The fundamental feeling is one of disappointment, and whether or not it is contaminated by resentment depends on the skill of the therapist. Perhaps that is his ultimate existential task: to divorce disappointment from anger.

TRANSACTIONAL ANALYSIS AND
GESTALT THERAPY *

The strongest link between these two approaches is their mutual interest in what is popularly called "nonverbal communication." The transactional analyst and the gestalt therapist, however, both go far beyond the limits of pasimology and mimicry to observe all sorts of physiological manifestations. Their devotion is first to observation, and only as a derivative of that to "communication." Both pay keen attention to carriage, posture, muscle tonus, tics, auxiliary movements, gestures, involuntary sounds, perceptible secretions, and vasomotor phenomena. The transactional analyst is especially interested in sphincter tonus and activity as described by the patient. All these phenomena are first dealt with structurally as manifestations of Parent, Adult, or Child ego states. The pointed index finger may be a Parental admonition, an Adult indicator, or a Child's accusation. Gestures are for the most part imitative of an actual parent; sphincter phenomena are symptomatic of archaic attitudes and impulses, since it is the Child who controls the involuntary nervous system and can make voluntary symbolic use of the sphincters as well. In addition, the evidence is that the Child (archaeopsyche) also controls autonomic nervous system influences on the voluntary musculature, such as those manifested in postural tonus. This is most dramatically illustrated in cases of psychogenic hoarseness [6] and cerebral palsy.

Insofar as such physiological phenomena are "communications," and act, or can be exploited, as transactional stimuli which elicit social responses that some part of the patient easily antic-

---

* This section is based on case presentations by and discussions with Dr. Gene Sagan, of Berkeley, California. (See *Transactional Analysis Bulletin* 1:20, 1962.)

ipates, they can be analysed transactionally as well as structurally.

In any case, the transactional and the gestalt therapeutic approaches to somatic expressions are similar. The patient is confronted with the phenomenon, and an attempt is made to analyse it. The psychological function of the phenomenon can be more easily clarified if its exhibition can be arrested. Both approaches are actionistic in this respect: the patient is requested *not to do it,* in order to see what happens when he does not. The results are analysed historically, phenomenologically, structurally, and socially.

TRANSACTIONAL ANALYSIS
AND PSYCHODRAMA *

The psychodramatist may deliberately arrange for the patient to re-enact part of his life history. The transactional analyst regards what happens spontaneously in a sedentary group meeting as a re-enactment of all or part of the patient's script (not "symbolically," which evades the issue, but actually, in a cogent, condensed, and not very heavily coded form). The script theme "Rush, Stumble, and Quick Recovery," which may be stretched over months or years in everyday life, can be inadvertantly but convincingly enacted in a few seconds in a treatment group. The concept of "differentiation" in the group imago concerns a kind of spontaneous casting of auxiliary egos.

Play The transactional analyst may also perform certain kinds of "experiments" that resemble psychodramatic techniques. For example, if a patient tells a story about her husband with the obvious implication that the therapist should tell her whether she is right or wrong, the therapist first says, "Yes, you are

* This section is based on the observation of several demonstrations conducted by Dr. J. L. Moreno.

right." After a pause, he asks, "How do you feel now?" He then says, "No, you are wrong," and then asks, "How does that feel?" The interesting thing is that he may do this several times with the same patient, or explicitly state beforehand that he is trying an experiment, yet the patient's responses will be just as spontaneous and reliable as if she did not know what he was up to. This is an important observation that throws new light on the relationship between the Adult and the Child of the patient, and on the nature of play.

Ego States versus Roles Regression analysis, in which the therapist, in order to activate and decontaminate the patient's Child, cathects his own Child ego state, resembles psychodrama in some respects. In this procedure, it should be noted, the therapist does not *play the role* of a child, he *becomes* the child he once was. He does not imitate children, he takes on the identity of his old archaic self. This differentiation is critical in distinguishing between roles and ego states. There are several ways in which people who are uncomfortable with their own Child ego states can brush off structural analysis. One such way is blandly to proceed as though ego states were synonymous with roles. Like an actual child, a person in the Child ego state may play very well the role of an adult. (This is known technically as a "precocious Child.") This role-playing may persist for years before the true Adult ego state in such a person can be cathected therapeutically.

TRANSACTIONAL ANALYSIS AND
SUPPORTIVE THERAPY

From the transactional point of view, supportive therapy is regarded as intrinsically spurious. Parental supportive statements (known colloquially as "throwing marshmallows" or "gumdrops") are fundamentally patronizing, and transactionally they are brush-offs. Functionally they can be translated, according to patients who become objective about their own Parental ego states, as follows: (1) "I am glad to have an opportunity to patronize you; it makes me feel worthwhile," or (2) "Don't bother me with your troubles; take this marshmallow and keep quiet so I can talk about mine." When the Child in the respondent no longer needs marshmallows, he can afford to (and if he is honest does) let his irritation at such clumsiness become evident.*

The transactional analyst may elect to use a supportive Parental approach with certain schizophrenics, particularly those who were orphaned in childhood. The more experienced he is, however, the less persistently he does so. In any event, as soon as the patient's Adult is sufficiently well established, the therapist takes pains to uncover the patient's concealed resentment at having been patronized. In this he is prudently guided as to timing and dosage by Federn's dictum that one does not analyse the transference with schizophrenics and tries to maintain it in a positive state. This procedure, therefore, is only followed in long-term therapy and when the therapist is competent to handle the risk involved.

TRANSACTIONAL ANALYSIS
AND GROUP ANALYSIS

While the transactional analyst is a conscientious student of group dynamics, he does not allow peripheral phenomena to distract him from his contractual obligation to cure the individual patient as economically as possible. He promotes whatever beneficial effects can be derived from the dynamics of the whole group, and he intervenes when the group situation is having a significantly deleterious effect. Like the group analyst, he is in a

---

* The essence of "supportive" statements is best shown in a cartoon from the *New Yorker* showing two frogs, one saying to the other: "Don't be silly, you're no worse looking than any other frog."

particularly good position to perform these functions effectively because the clinician has opportunities to investigate aspects of group psychology that are inaccessible to nonclinical workers.

The nonspecific effects of group membership arise from stroking and recognition, which may have important therapeutic results. Mutual confrontation within the group increases authenticity. The demands of orthodoxy and "finding common ground," on the other hand, decrease it, while confrontation of the group by a threat from the outside world may actively encourage spurious reactions (paranoid, for example).

"OVERNIGHT" GROUP MEETINGS

A recent development is the very long group meeting lasting 12 to 48 hours, called variously "continuous group therapy," "extended group therapy," or more colloquially "the marathon" or "the pressure-cooker." For the transactional analyst, the most cogent feature of such meetings is the interpolation between two segments of a period to sleep, and perchance to dream; if this policy is followed, they are most pertinently called "overnight" group meetings. Without such an intermission, there is little chance to assimilate the events and experiences of the day, and to put into effect and solidify on the spot any changes which result. Otherwise, perhaps, there is some weakening of the Adult through fatigue, so that there are more frequent and more emphatic incursions of Child activity, but this is of the nature of mere abreaction without the opportunity for reorganization that the intermission for sleeping makes possible.

In many cases the patients are most enthusiastic following such a meeting, with statements like "Gee, things happened in these two days that would have taken years to happen in our ordinary [90-minute] meetings." There is some feeling that perhaps Sartre was a little hasty in writing his play "No Exit," since being shut up in a room with six or ten other people for a prolonged period may be an enlightening and inspiring experience, rather than the hell that Sartre portrays, even for those couples who complain of a hellish relationship to begin with.* In such a situation, the therapist can use his complete armamentarium: psychoanalytic, existential, gestalt, psychodramatic, supportive, group-analytic, and transactional. He should not, however, make a point of being eclectic, as that may become disconcerting or even boring. There should be some clear contract, and transactional analysis offers an excellent matrix for such prolonged sessions, while from time to time, whenever it is indicated, he can introduce other types of pertinent interventions and interpolations.

On the basis of the limited experience available at the present time, the following suggestions are offered:

Location Some therapists prefer a summer resort or conference ground where the patients can live together for a week end. It is quite practical, however, to use the regular meetingplace in the therapist's office.

Physical Arrangements This is an excellent opportunity to dispense with the table. The patients should sit in a circle, and the therapist where he has a clear view of what is going on.

Food and Drink Food should be available, buffet style, preferably in another room to prevent undue distraction. There is no need to break up for meals, and if the meeting is interesting enough the patients will not want to. Liquor should be forbidden by common consent, but soft drinks and coffee should be readily available.

Sleep A tentative time should be set for ending the meeting for the night, but this can be extended if indicated. The meeting should resume promptly at the time set the next morning, so that lateness will show up clearly. The participants should not go

* Perhaps Sartre's characters, like Medea's family, suffered mainly because they did not have a therapist available, rather than because of some ineluctable fate.

home for the night, but should stay at the resort or, in the city, at hotels and motels: this avoids interrupting the continuity with home problems and family games.

Fees The patients will recognize the devotion of the therapist, and an appropriate fee is the regular fee for ordinary meetings multiplied by the number of "periods," a period being a morning, afternoon, or evening. Thus if the meeting lasts an afternoon, an evening, and a morning, or an evening, a morning, and an afternoon, a suitable fee is three times the usual fee.

The Therapist's Relief The therapist should absent himself for two or three hours toward the end of the proceedings and occupy himself with some nonclinical activity. This relaxes his Adult so that things have a chance to fall into place, and gives the patients an opportunity to see what happens without him.

Precautions The therapist should not overestimate the fragility of his patients, but if he decides (not "feels") that someone is being pushed too hard, he does two things. First he offers his protective (but not over-protective) Parent to calm the Child of the threatened one; then he gets a hook into the Adult of the patient and keeps it there as long as he judges necessary. The patients will take their cue from him; if anyone tries to sabotage the operation, they will very likely take care of the saboteur by turning on him.

Aim It should be emphasized once more that the aim of group treatment is not to "do group therapy," but to get patients well. As an analogy, there is a big difference between "doing a neurological" and setting out to discover whether there are localizing neurological signs: the first may turn into a mere ritual, while the second is a well directed Adult procedure.

REFERENCES

1. Fenichel, O. *Problems of Psychoanalytic Technique.* Psychoanalytic Quarterly, Albany, 1941, pp. 52 ff.

2. Freud, S. *An Outline of Psychoanalysis.* W. W. Norton & Company, New York, 1949.
3. Freud, S. *New Introductory Lectures on Psycho-Analysis.* W. W. Norton & Company, New York, 1933, Chap. 3.
4. Berne, E. *Transactional Analysis in Psychotherapy.* (Chap. 5, ref. 5.)
5. Freud, S. *Beyond the Pleasure Principle.* International Psycho-Analytical Press, London, 1922.
6. *Transactional Analysis Bulletin* 4:27, April 1965.

14
Clinical Games

The therapist who has a clear understanding of therapeutic games may save himself and his patients weeks, months, or even years of partly misdirected effort. It is a fact, however, that some professional schools in effect train their students to play these very games, so that their graduates find it hard to decline the seductive pseudo-therapeutic gambits offered by their clients. Those who work in institutions or organizations run the additional risk of becoming corrupted by one of the many organizational games. Some of the commoner variations of games that arise in the treatment situation are outlined below. The realistic therapist will eventually discover that these summaries, though they may be incomplete, are neither cynical nor irresponsible. For a fuller consideration, the writer's book on this subject [1] is recommended.

"I'M ONLY TRYING TO HELP YOU" (ITHY)

This game begins when a patient presents his "helpless" Child to a Parental (and especially maternal) therapist. The therapist may find the patient's "needs" irresistible and offer advice, which the patient either does not take or follows with unpleasant consequences. The patient's stubborn or reproachful attitude at this point causes the therapist to think or say, "But I'm only trying to help you!" This indignant or hurt counter-reproach confirms the therapist's position that people are really ungrateful; no matter how many hours you spend bending over a hot stove, etc. At staff conferences and discussions with ITHY colleagues, the position is corroborated further by the corresponding Parental pastime, whose slogan is "We're only trying to help them, but it's hopeless (thank goodness)." This offers outside support for the therapist's position, alleviating any guilt she may feel for having exploited the patient, and relieves her of the responsibility for curing him, since no one really expects results with such "impossible" people as she finds on her chronic case load.°

The patient, on his side, is intuitively aware of what is going on. He knows that whatever he does will be gratifying to the therapist. If he takes the proffered advice, or feels "better" because of her support, he provides her with the satisfaction of having successfully "dealt" with him; if he does not, he has helped her maintain her reproachful position. If he is an old case who has been transferred from one therapist to another or from one agency to another, he knows the strategy of the game better than the therapist and is in complete control of the situation.

The competent Adult therapist only offers advice or "support" to the patient when she can predict with a high degree of confidence whether or not the patient will accept it, whether he will use it to succeed or fail, and what the probable effects on the treatment situation will be in each of the three alternatives (Not Accepted, Reported Success, Reported Failure). With these precautions, the therapist is in control of the situation because

° This game is typically feminine because at the most archaic level it is based on a life theory which reads, "Good food will cure anything, and that is what I have to offer." Hence the resentment many female social workers feel toward male psychiatrists, and vice versa.

she has already prepared for the patient's next move; whereas the patient, who is used to dealing with "pigeons," is at a disadvantage if he wants to set up a game. He may thus be confronted with the possibility of actually having to get well — a prospect he is likely to find distressing.

Real helpers do not reproach others for their bad results. A surgeon who is unfortunate enough to have a fatality in his practice does not meet the bereaved ones by saying in an aggrieved tone, as though the patient had deliberately frustrated him by dying, "But I was only trying to help him!"

"It's Delicious" A variation of "I'm Only Trying To Help You" is called "It's Delicious," with the slogan "If I like it, I don't understand how you can dislike it." The prototype is the mother who tells her child that he must eat the food because it tastes good (to her); if he refuses, she calls him stubborn. The obverse of "It's Delicious" is "You'll Get Holes in Your Teeth." Such a parent thinks her own prejudices must be shared by her offspring.[2] This game was played in its classical form in the therapeutic situation by a social worker who remarked in a horrified tone to a "delinquent" girl, "Oh, if you do that, you'll go to jail." Here this usually Adult social worker slipped into her Parental ego state with the attitude "I think jail is terrible, therefore everybody thinks jail is terrible." Her game-wise supervisor did not share her surprise and chagrin when the girl ended up in jail in exactly the way the social worker had warned her against. The girl did not share the worker's horror of prison. Instead, her reaction to the warning was "Oh, so that's how you get into jail." That was the information she was looking for, and she knew what to do with it.

SWYMD A derivative of ITHY is "See What You Made Me Do," which may be played by either the therapist or the patient. An experienced patient who knows how to take advantage of the therapist's eagerness will contrive to cause confusion in her paper-work or schedule, and then cynically enjoy her efforts to keep from looking at him reproachfully with the accusation "See what you made me do." On the other hand, the patient may follow the therapist's advice in a certain matter, but be careful to sabotage it, which earns him the privilege of coming in a rage to his next interview so that he can cry angrily, "See what you made me do!"

"Now He Tells Me" Another way in which the patient can get his revenge on the therapist who plays ITHY is called "Now He Tells Me." The patient compliantly accedes to all the therapist's efforts to help him and makes excellent "therapeutic progress." At the end of an hour in which they have had an enlightening discussion about the patient's psychodynamics, he remarks, "Oh, by the way, I've decided not to come back any more." Or if he elects to continue the game, he may announce after they have been "analysing" his "money problem" for a few months, "Oh, by the way, I forgot to tell you. Since our last session I withdrew the family savings and invested in a surefire company to sell beds to Bedouins." The therapist's consternation is his payoff for weeks of patient planning. Patients are often reluctant to talk it over with their groups before making a dubious investment just because they know that it is dubious and that the other members will probably talk them out of it, thus spoiling the game and holding them up on the road to self-immolation.

"PSYCHIATRY"

"Psychiatry" is not always played as a game with a well-defined payoff. As a mere pastime, it occurs in three popular forms. "Mental Health" is based on the thesis that if only the right procedure can be found, everything will be all right. In "Psychoanalysis," the patient tells a dream, and then the therapist is supposed to interpret it; or she relates her early sexual experiences and the therapist is supposed to ask questions or raise his eyebrows significantly. If he fails to respond correctly, the patient looks puzzled or disappointed. In "Transactional Analysis" she talks glibly about her Parent, Adult, and Child, and the therapist is supposed to look appreciative or impressed. There are, however, other forms of "Psychiatry" that are more game-like.

"*Archaeology*" * The slogan of "Archaeology" is "If you don't dig hard you can't get better." The patient and therapist dig harder and harder, and if the patient does not get better it is because he is not digging hard enough or in the right places, or was not a suitable candidate for psychoanalytic treatment in the first place. As a final punishment, he may be put on the "chronic case-load" list. A more pointed variation is called "Tell Me This." The patient relates an anecdote, say about his childhood, and the therapist asks a question. If, as he secretly hopes, the patient cannot answer, his reaction is "Well, if you can't answer *that* question, you can't blame me if you don't get better." If the patient is experienced and skillful, however, he does answer the question. This throws the therapist off balance, because he does not know what to do with the answer anyway, and now he has no excuse for not making the patient better.

"*Furthermore*" This game is played by the therapist and the other members of the group with a patient whose riposte is "Let Me Explain." (This is also a favorite marital game.) Someone throws an accusation at the one who is "It," and he responds with "Let me explain." The moment he stops talking, someone else begins "Furthermore, you also, etc.," whereupon he again says "Let me explain." When he stops once more someone is ready with another "Furthermore . . . ," and this procedure is repeated indefinitely. An alert observer soon notices that the other players do not listen to the explanations of "It"; they are ready with the next "Furthermore" long before he has finished.

* This name was suggested by Dr. Norman Reider of San Francisco.

and are only waiting for him to take a deep breath so that they can have at him. An even more alert observer will see also that the one who is "It" does not really listen to the accusations; he is ready with his explanation before his accuser has stopped talking. In fact, he may very well be answering some other accusation rather than the proffered one. A variant of "Furthermore" is "Calmly" or "Mature," in which the "furthermores" and "let me explains" are heavily disguised in rational-sounding polysyllables on both sides.

"Critique" "Critique" may also be played by any number, but the therapist usually takes the lead. The patient describes his feelings, and the therapist tells him what is wrong with them. The payoffs for "Furthermore" and "Critique" are golden-colored Smug stamps made of iron pyrites.

"SCHLEMIEL"

In its social form "Schlemiel" is a game in which a visitor comes to the house and has messy accidents, such as spilling his drink on the rug or splashing his hostess's evening gown with gravy, and then says "I'm sorry!" The spilling and messing are pleasant ways for the Schlemiel to pass the time until the payoff, which consists of the forgiveness he gets after he says "I'm sorry." It is easy for the therapist to become involved in a game of "Schlemiel" with a patient who arrives late for his appointments, is late in paying his bill, or causes him other inconveniences. The unwary therapist will accept the patient's apology and give him the desired forgiveness. By doing so, he impairs his therapeutic effectiveness, since he has given the patient the upper hand by letting him win the game. Many patients who understand game analysis have said quite frankly that one reason they continued in therapy was because the therapist refused to play their games. If they had been able to con him into playing, they might have come for a while to enjoy the games, but would have quit eventually on the grounds that he was incompetent to help them if they could consistently outsmart him.

On the other side, it is quite inexcusable for the therapist to be the schlemiel. If he makes a mistake and wishes to discuss it, that is one thing, but if he says "I'm sorry" in order to get the patient's forgiveness, that is another. In unusual circumstances, he may say "I'm sorry" as a matter of courtesy, but if he puts himself in such a position more than twice, it is time for him to retire to his tent and meditate. The best solution is for him not to make mistakes, at least not the kind that require a social apology.

Illustrations The therapist who is habitually late for his appointments cannot afford to apologize, for if he does, the patient (unless he is a jerk and lacking in insight) will understand that he is being laughed at by the therapist's Child. He must either become punctual, or else state the situation frankly to the patient's Adult in some such terms as: "It is evident that I cannot get here on time; the reasons for this are irrelevant to your treatment, but the fact is one of the realities of the treatment situation. It may be an unfortunate one, but let us see what we can get out of it by investigating your reactions." This is an attempt to make the best of a bad situation, and very often it pays off. It is true that if the therapist is a "nice guy," the patient may forgive him all sorts of sins, but this indulgence should not be exploited.

A similar contingency may arise when the therapist likes to take his own telephone calls during working hours. There are two sides to this question. If the therapist does not take his own calls, there is a kind of unreal isolation during the treatment hour; if he does take them, the interruptions may be too long or too frequent. He can always compromise by taking his own calls and telling the caller he will return the call shortly. If the patient objects, there is no need to apologize; the therapist can say, "That's the way I prefer to do it, and perhaps we can learn something from your reaction." The results in the long run may be satisfactory to both parties.

ORGANIZATIONAL GAMES

Organizational games, from the present point of view, fall into four classes: management games, case-load games, "Wooden Leg," and "I'm Only Trying To Help You." There is no implication that every organization plays all of these. A game-free organization will play none of them; others play some of them; and a game-ridden one may play all of them.

"Good Management" The principal management game is called "Good Management." A currently fashionable form is to have a psychiatrist on the staff of an industrial or government organization, since everybody knows that nowadays that is part of good management. The psychiatrist is then exploited in various ways, but is steered away from situations where he may actually be able to change something. The chief administrator may use him as a pawn in games of "Let's You and Him Fight"; he lets the psychiatrist tell the unpleasant things to his executives, so that he, the chief administrator, does not run any risk of unpopularity or of being accused of bad relations or bad management. In any case, the psychiatrist's lectures and other activities are summarized numerically in the Annual Report.

There is a growing number of organizations which make legitimate use of a staff psychiatrist or other consultant accustomed to taking clinical responsibility. Even at worst "Good Management" is potentially a constructive game, since a competent, strong-minded, and tactful consultant can often actually initiate some worthwhile changes.

Closely allied to "Good Management" is "Good Research." [3] In this game, research proposals (in the social sciences) are couched in the language most likely to elicit a grant, with only secondary consideration of the effects of the proposal on the patients to be "researched." At the same time, by the strategic use of acceptable jargon, it is demonstrated that the proposal contains exactly what the patients need: 2 computers, 15 observers, etc. The patients who become involved in this game tend to be good sports about it. This demonstrates one research conclusion that is by now firmly established by repeated tests: that most patients, if properly appealed to, are good sports. An honest research worker who is involuntarily dragged into this game may nevertheless get some useful research done by skillful interpretation of the proposal. In order to be sure of a second grant, however, it is usually necessary to demonstrate that the original hypothesis was correct and therefore needs further investigation. It is a foregone conclusion, therefore, that almost everyone who does research on group therapy will show that his approach is useful. The writer knows of not a single published case of grant-supported research which demonstrates that the researcher's approach to group therapy is *not* useful. (This topic has already been discussed at the beginning of Chapter 8.)

Case-Load Games   In general, case-load games are bureaucratic, being concerned with budgetary considerations and job tenure, rationalized with "I'm Only Trying To Help You." They are divided into under-load and over-load phases. In order to justify these games, game-playing "helpers" take the "broad view" that social problems are essentially unsolvable in the present, but that at some future time the answers will be forthcoming. In this comfortable situation, the helper makes strenuous efforts to solve the problems, but need not succeed because he is protected by the carefully nurtured hypothesis that they are essentially unsolvable.

The games revolve around the strenuousness of the player's efforts in the face of odds that everyone is supposed to acknowledge as insurmountable. Hence there is an institutionalized reservation that only a small percentage of clients or patients can be helped, and that these cannot be helped except over a very long period. It is considered respectable, so to speak, to dispose of a modest number of clients, say 10 per cent each year, but no more. Anyone who exceeds this quota is open to suspicion. Experience shows that in game-ridden organizations, zealous workers are very likely to be reprimanded or to be removed from their positions. Indeed, it is possible to predict the point at which that will happen, if not with mathematical rigor, at least with mathematical symbols.[4] A consultant may likewise be regarded with disfavor in some organizations if he implies that a larger percentage of clients can be helped than is generally supposed, or that they can be helped more rapidly. There are good reasons why some administrators become uneasy in the face of increased effectiveness.

The Under-Load Phase Many workers preserve their psychic equilibrium by continually demonstrating the ingratitude of people or the Augean enormity of the social problems which frustrate their Herculean efforts and require rivers of money instead of the grudging trickle they are allotted. Hence when there is an under-load in a game-ridden organization, some of the staff-members may become acutely uncomfortable (which they attribute to secondary factors), so that there is a cry for larger case-loads. External budgetary requirements and the desire to keep the staff at maximum size or even to enlarge it, contribute to this discomfort.

In considering under-load problems, the clients of the organization may be divided into two classes: chronic and acute. It is permissible to rehabilitate, cure, or discharge a modest percentage of the acute clientèle, but any serious inroad on the chronic case-load is regarded with disapproval because it could result in contraction or elimination of the organization. For this reason the rehabilitation, cure, and discharge of a chronic client is treated as a special event during lean periods. The worker may be cautiously commended, but many searching questions are asked, and the general air of skepticism does not encourage others to follow suit.

The Over-Load Phase During the under-load phase, the policy of "reaching out," offering services to the community, and undertaking promotional campaigns is followed. The slogan is "We Want To Help," which is rendered to the individual client as "We're Only Trying To Help You." If these efforts are successful, the organization swings into the over-load phase. With an over-load, there is a long waiting list, everyone is pressed for time, and no one is expected to do anything beyond the usual routine. Quantity takes precedence over quality, and there is no time for skepticism. The organizational game during this phase is "SNAFU." All sorts of things are going wrong because the case-loads are much too high for anyone to expect good management. At this point it is common to appeal for funds to enlarge the facilities of the organization and to obtain more workers.

Illustrative Examples A large organization was established by a state health department to deal with the problem of alcoholism. As these ample facilities became over-loaded, a whole new approach was designed, requiring the expenditure of several million dollars and the hiring of a large number of new workers. The flow chart of the proposed reorganization was presented in an elaborate, well-defended diagram, showing where the patients would be admitted, where they would go next, where the community and the various professional influences entered, and so on. There was, however, one notable omission: there was no arrow showing how the patients got out of the whole set-up, so that once in (according to the diagram) they could only go round and round in a tortuous closed path. When this defect was pointed out by a game-analyst there was considerable anger on the part of those in charge of the organization, who said that they had other things to worry about at the moment and would take care of that later.

In another civil service organization, where the workers were too rational to play "I'm Only Trying To Help You," they were perfectly content to have a chronic under-load except when budget time approached. Then they would begin to "reach out" into the community, seeking to increase the case-load so that they could justify a continued need for funds. After the budget had been passed they were faced with the task of reducing the case-load so that they could resume their former pursuits of study and research without being too distracted by the needs of their patients. Thus there was a yearly cycle: scientific productivity, followed by community activity; then a period of grumbling and efforts to relieve themselves of the cases they had acquired, in order to return to the productive phase. The administration of this particular establishment carried on its manipulations without any attempt at concealment from the staff. This caused disillusion and resentment among some of the idealistic young clinicians who were in training there.

Group therapy offers special opportunities for playing case-load games. An under-load cuts down the number of groups and thins out the complements of the remaining ones. The uneasy therapist tends to become more active in order to prove the worth of his efforts, and plays a harder game of "ITHY." An over-load of cases favors the activation of more and larger "therapy" groups, which may be used in a game of "See How Hard I'm Trying." The slogan here is "Look, I'm so busy I have to treat ten people at once." Or a worker who is tired of playing "SNAFU" may start groups on the principle: "I can't help them, but maybe they will be able to help each other, and if they don't, then no one can blame me."

"Wooden Leg" This is a game in which the patient challenges the therapist with an established disability, classically "What do you expect of a man with a wooden leg?" It is difficult for the therapist to win this (i.e. get the patient back on his feet) without the patient's consent. The organizational varieties of "Wooden Leg" are typified by "Indigent" and "Veteran." In such cases the therapist is faced with case-load games played by external organizations which he is quite unable to cope with,

such as state welfare departments and veterans organizations. The patient or client is aware of this, so that from the beginning he has the upper hand. Thus if a therapist elects to work in certain game-ridden organizations, he must compromise on a standard "ITHY" type of therapeutic contract, which on his side reads, "I will try to help you providing you don't get better (because that would threaten my position that people are ungrateful)," while the patient's side reads, "I will do anything you say providing I don't have to get better (because that would threaten my pension)." If the therapist attempts to break this game up, the patient can bring enormous political and journalistic pressures to bear. Hence, the effective treatment of people on relief or on pensions is transactionally impractical until they can be persuaded to give up their pecuniary advantages and their organizational shelters in favor of getting well. The "Wooden Leg" element enters in its grossest form with the challenging plea: "What do you expect of a (man with a low back pain) (ambulatory schizophrenic) (ex-serviceman)?" * The implication is clear that if the therapist does not accept the plea, there are powerful people behind the patient who will give him his comeuppance. The "wise" therapist resigns himself philosophically to this dreary defeat. The contractual problem in such organizational desperation often involves a technical point which will now be taken up.

GROUP APPARATUS VERSUS THERAPIST

In all institutions a therapist must play two roles. On one hand he has a contract with the organization and certain responsibili-

---

* In the Moscow Psychiatric Institute (1960) the "ex-serviceman" plea was accepted as a justification for alcoholism. According to recent (1965) press accounts, however, there has been some change in the Soviet thinking about drinking. Among other things, the policy of paying "alcoholics" while they are hospitalized has been questioned. In general, the Soviet Union is one of the most interesting fields for the study of organizational games.

ties toward it, and on the other he has a contract with his patient or client. The two usually have many incompatibilities. A correctional officer, for example, has a police function and in some states carries a gun and a badge, while at the same time he may be expected to act as a therapist. Rehabilitation workers also may have police duties, such as reporting irregularities (even those elicited in the course of "therapy"), and in at least one state they are expected to participate in "early morning raids" on the homes of their clients in order to detect further irregularities. These are inherently impossible situations for doing effective or even ethical psychotherapy, unless and until the patient can commit himself to giving up playing all games with the therapist and the mother group.

Solutions There are, however, some procedures that clarify the situation, even if they do not resolve it. The first is for the officer or worker to make it very clear to the patient that he has two separate functions: one as an arm of the apparatus of the organization; the other as an independent contractor with the patient. He can state quite clearly that these are incompatible, but that he must perform them both. He can undertake to notify the patient which role he is playing at a given moment, in an attempt to keep them from becoming intermixed. This device is rarely completely satisfactory, but it may be the best available in certain situations. Another compromise is adopted in some private hospitals, for example, where one physician is responsible for the patient's psychotherapy, and another for all administrative problems, and the two roles are kept discrete. In theory this is a good solution, but in practice it does not always work because a shrewd patient can often involve his two mentors in a game of "Let's You and Him Fight," or some other three-handed game. As already noted, the Child in each patient is generally more adept than any professional person at manipulating people, and is also more determined because he is playing for more personal, and therefore higher, stakes. Again, therefore, it requires co-operation on the part of the patient for this solution to work. Up to the present, these are the best compromises that can be found for organizational therapists.

Private Practice   The therapist in private practice can become involved in a similar situation in treating compensation cases of various kinds. The courageous therapist can avoid contamination of his therapeutic contract by refusing to accept any responsibility toward the compensating agency. He can demand that the patient choose him either as a therapist or as a medical expert, and decline to play both roles simultaneously. This puts him in an unfashionable and even perilous situation.

Illustrations   In the case of a veteran, for example, the therapist may state that he is not an arm of the Veterans Administration and is merely making his therapeutic services available to the patient with the VA paying the cost; he owes no responsibility whatsoever to the VA other than curing the patient, which is what he is being paid to do, rather than helping him prolong his neurosis. Such a statement may occasionally arouse indignation initially, particularly in patients who move from one therapist to another, since it upsets their plans to exploit the new therapist as they have the others. In the long run, however, the patient may be grateful to the therapist for breaking up his game of "Veteran" in order to do effective psychotherapy. Similarly, in legal compensation cases, he can give the patient the choice of having him either as a therapist or as a witness, but not both. Not all attorneys are sympathetic to such an attitude and the therapist might find himself in some disfavor as a result of this. If he is firm, he may convince the patient's attorney that as a reluctant witness he would not be of much value in the case, but he is nevertheless open to subpoena. In addition, since this attitude is inimical to the currently fashionable flirtation between psychiatry and the law, the therapist might also be regarded askance by some of his own colleagues. Psychiatrists who have successfully avoided such contaminating influences, however, are gratified at the results and feel that the risks involved are well taken if they are to fulfill their treatment obligations properly.

The Rationale of Autonomy If a therapist consents to be a compensation witness (even if it only involves writing a brief note), it is evident that his attitude toward the patient will be different from what it would be if he were a completely free agent. For if he succumbs to administrative pressure, he is playing "I'm Only Trying To Help You," and may even be seducing the patient by offering to do so. He is in effect saying: "I'll do anything to help you, even go to court — which is irrelevant to your getting better, and in fact in most cases is inimical to your getting better; it will also influence what you tell me, but nevertheless I will do it." In most cases, however, it is the patient who has seduced the therapist. In more commonplace situations, such as pension cases, it may not even occur to the therapist to question the subtle implications of his involvement with the patient's paperwork and the possible games it represents. In general, a therapist who has any relationship whatsoever with a patient other than that of pure therapist lays himself open to becoming involved in games, not only with the patient, but also with the patient's allies or enemies. To that extent his therapeutic effectiveness is impaired.

Clinical Examples A patient (Wilbur) who had been in combat in the South Pacific and had been on a pension for almost twenty years was introduced to a private therapy group. He did not attend regularly and played a hard game of "Psychiatry — Group Therapy Type" which he had learned in another city. The other members of the group found this irritating and somewhat boring. When the therapist brought up the question of his getting better, he said that he had given up hope. Somehow at this point the payment of the therapist's fee by the VA was brought into the discussion. It became clear that the patient regarded the therapist as a servant of the VA who was working for the money, and that he was dropping into the therapy group as he would into a massage parlor whenever he felt uneasy. The therapist said that he had no official position with the VA, was not their employee and was merely at his own option and choice performing services for them which he could terminate at any time. Some of the other patients did not understand at first what Dr. Q was trying to convey, and rallied defensively around Wilbur, saying that he had done his duty for his country, etc. The therapist said that that was quite true and that Wilbur had the privilege of resting on his pension, his laurels, and his symptoms for the remainder of his life if he chose, but in that case he, Dr. Q, did not see what he had to offer Wilbur, since he was not running a psychic massage parlor. On the other hand, Wilbur also had the privilege of choosing to get better, and in that case he, Dr. Q, might have something to offer him. The other patients were at first indignant, but after two or three weeks they began to see the point.

Wilbur himself was sufficiently impressed so that it was possible for the therapist to propose that when he attended a group session the VA would pay for it, but if he stayed away he would pay for the missed session out of his own pocket. Wilbur's acceptance of this proposal was at first somewhat equivocal, and Dr. Q kept after him until he made a clear and unambiguous commitment to this plan. He always had the option of withdrawing from the group whenever he chose and going to another therapist. He elected to continue under the terms offered by Dr. Q, but dropped out after a few months when the other patients became too persistent in questioning his symptoms.

Another therapist followed a similar policy with a patient who was a plaintiff in a suit for damages. It was evident that the lawsuit was retarding therapeutic progress. The psychiatrist had explained to the patient at the very outset that he could be either a witness or a therapist but not both, and the patient had agreed to employ him as a therapist. Now the patient wanted to go back on their agreement on the grounds that he could not restrain his lawyer from issuing a subpoena. The therapist said that that was the patient's problem, and that if he were subpoenaed he would be a very reluctant witness and probably of no further use as a therapist. Here again the patient elected therapy and induced his lawyer to proceed with the case without the psychiatrist's testimony. It should be noted that this put the lawyer in the same dilemma as the patient. He had to choose whether he wanted his client to get better at the risk of impairing his suit, or wanted to win the suit at the risk of impairing his client's recovery. It is difficult to say which choice would make him a more honest lawyer. At any rate, he chose the first alternative. He did not subpoena the psychiatrist and managed to win the suit without him.

TYPES OF THERAPISTS

As already mentioned, each therapist has his favorite game which it is his duty to become aware of and take steps to avoid during his therapeutic operations. Beginners, however, do not always have sufficient insight to do this properly. Every supervisor becomes familiar with certain typical game-like attitudes prevalent among psychiatric residents and psychology and social work trainees. A descriptive characterization of some of the commoner ones is given below. The descriptions are of extreme cases, but most residents have a little of each of these in them, and it is a good idea to break up these tendencies in the second or third year so that the underlying talents can begin to manifest themselves free of such hampering attitudes.

Phallus in Wonderland * This man approaches his patients as though they were exotic creatures from another planet, and is continually astonished because they behave the way the book says they will. He is a staunch admirer of his own skill and

* The writer first heard this expression, under the most poignant circumstances, from E. H. Erikson.

perspicacity, and if nothing really happens with his patients he knows that his public will understand. He is a devoted disciple of Freud, and as one of the sorcerer's chosen apprentices he is fascinated by the strange antics of parapeople and their interesting reactions to his incantations. It takes a ruthless supervisor to shatter his dreamy world by telling him that patients are people too, and that in fact he may be the paraperson and they the real ones.

The Delegate This man knows the answers, and if his patients do not get better no one can criticize *him*. He has the whole weight of psychoanalytic tradition behind him. Although Freud has not yet sent him a personal message to that effect, he knows that the old man would not find fault with anything he has done. If he runs into misfortune with a patient, he is sure that his sympathetic colleagues would agree that sometimes it is like casting pearls before swine. The supervisor has to tell him that it is more like doing twirls without a spine.

The Smiling Rebel This man is late for conferences and appointments, but it does not bother him, so why should it bother anyone else? He is doing his own thinking. His teachers are parapeople who are so preoccupied with their own square ideas that they miss things obvious to him. Some day he will be grown-up like them, and then the public will listen to what he has to say. In the meantime he can quietly carry on his experiments, throwing in a word occasionally to let people know he has something cooking without necessarily telling them precisely what it is. Someone has to tell him that he is already grown-up and must be punctual. He really ought to tell his supervisor about the experiments.

The Patient Clinician He is never flustered and never raises his voice. Psychotherapists are parapeople, but they are entitled to laugh occasionally just like real people — only for a few seconds, however, and then they must get back to work. He says what he has to say calmly and deliberately, but often his colleagues are not as rational as he is and do not follow his advice. Patients usually follow it, but if they do not they must be gently persuaded to see the error of their ways. He gets along well with alcoholics and in fact has often thought of taking a drink himself. Since he will probably get along in his own way, it is perhaps best for his supervisor to listen and say nothing.

The Jargon Juggler Nobody knows the homosexual sadistic Oedipal incorporation resistance better than he does. His patients are wonderously transistorized robots with human bodies just like his own, and they are completely unaware of their underlying motivations. The one who says, "Hello, I just came from work and I'm sort of tired, do you have a cigarette?" does not realize that he has initiated an interview, traveled from his place of employment, complained of fatigue, and attempted to manipulate the therapist. Naturally, after his phallic drivenness, the patient regresses to hypochrondriacal self-pity, sucking on a breast-baby-feces symbol cigarette borrowed because of maternal transference. All this may be very true, but the beginning therapist is only guessing. The supervisor has to tell him to take one thing at a time, not to guess, and above all to try to say it in Anglo-Saxon words of no more than two syllables.

The Conservative This man knows better than to break a silence, or to interrupt when a patient may be about to prepare to express affect. His patients often complain that the group sessions are boring, but they do not realize what a serious matter psychotherapy is. He himself is not bored because he is too busy gripping the arms of his chair or keeping his back muscles tense. There is nothing exactly wrong with his staff presentations but somehow they lack impact. No one criticizes him because there is nothing to criticize, and besides they have all made more mistakes than he has. The supervisor has to encourage him to experiment: break a silence occasionally and see what happens, or take the initiative away from the patients maybe just once every two or three sessions, and observe the effect.

The Hypochondriac He cannot try anything new because it makes him uncomfortable. It does not occur to him that he is not there to be comfortable, but to treat his patients. He rationalizes his neophobia on the grounds that he cannot do a good job if he is uncomfortable. When he was on surgery (one assumes), gloves and gowns made him uncomfortable, and he explained to the chief that he could not do good surgery unless he was comfortable. Perhaps the chief said, "Oh, my, I wouldn't want one of my residents to be uncomfortable, do come into the operating room bare-handed in your street-clothes." More likely the chief said, "If you're uncomfortable with surgical techniques, perhaps you had best transfer to some other branch of medicine, such as psychiatry." The supervisor should tell him that if he is not comfortable with the best possible technique, he should either get comfortable, or else transfer to some other branch of medicine, such as surgery.

REFERENCES

1. Berne, E. *Games People Play.* (Chap. 9, ref. 21.)
2. Cf. Greenburg, D. *How To Be a Jewish Mother.* Price, Stern, Sloan, Los Angeles, 1964.
3. San Francisco Social Psychiatry Seminars. "Consultation by Mail." *Transactional Analysis Bulletin* 2:87, 1963.
4. Berne, E., R. Birnbaum, R. Poindexter, and B. Rosenfeld. "Institutional Games." *Transactional Analysis Bulletin* 1:12, 1962.

15
Diagnostic Categories

There are specific problems that often arise with patients in certain of the standard diagnostic categories, and these will now be considered from the transactional standpoint. The diagnostic terms are taken from the table of contents of the *American Handbook of Psychiatry*.[1] In addition, some special treatment situations will be considered.

MINOR MALADJUSTMENTS

This term is often justified, particularly with adolescents. Once the patient is in treatment, the maladjustments may tend to become magnified in the therapist's mind, and hence in the patient's mind as well. Furthermore, once the therapist has "diagnosed" beyond the initial complaints, he may feel duty-bound to continue therapy in many cases. By analogy, a surgical patient may be subjected to complete X-rays of his bones. If any abnormalities show up, the surgeon runs a certain risk in ignoring them even if they are not of proximate clinical significance. Thus some psychotherapists come very close to inducing a kind of psychological hypochondriasis in their patients. Every human being has idiosyncracies, and these must be differentiated from exhibitions of harmful psychopathology. The Rorschach and the

Minnesota Multiphasic Inventory (MMPI) are common provocative agents in this respect.

There are two kinds of parents who are apt to bring their
children to psychotherapists for what are actually "minor" maladjustments. The first is the one with a fixed Parental ego state,
Big Daddy or Good Mommy. When their son does not conform
to their standards, they feel shamed before the neighbors or the
school faculty, and their attitude is a combination of "Ain't It
Awful?" and "Why Does This Have To Happen to Me?" With
a weaker parent of this type, it may be "See How Hard I've
Tried." Another type is the one with a fixed Adult ego state
who plays "Mental Health." When their offspring do not respond
to their carefully planned techniques, such parents may also end
up with "See How Hard I've Tried." Both these types of parents
are apt to become resentful if they feel that the therapist is
criticizing them. He should therefore be careful not to say anything to the child which may be taken home to use as ammuni-
tion against the family. If the therapist deals directly with the
parents, he may have to mix any pellets of objective appraisal
with more or less copious quantities of marshmallow. If the
whole family is taken in treatment, initial adherence to these
principles requires exquisite judgment on the therapist's part.

WAR NEUROSES

It is probable, in military as in civilian life, that anyone who has
killed, seen killing, or seen a friend killed, will have significant
sequelae for many years, perhaps for life. (Simply being shot
at or wounded is rarely traumatic in this sense.) Such sequelae
should never be neglected in the treatment of any combat (or
concentration camp) veteran, even twenty or thirty years after
the event. They may be concealed beneath a heavy overlay of
current situational reactions, or come out more openly in a hard
game of "Alcoholic" or "Veteran." There are also rare cases

where a noncombat veteran who is not receiving any form of compensation from the Veterans Administration may play a variant of Veteran, "Ex-Service Man." Thus a forty-year-old paranoid who was brought to each treatment session by his mother refused to discuss his situation with the therapist because the therapist was "taking money from an ex-service man." Of course he said it was irrelevant that the therapist had been in the service too.

All such cases have "died" to some extent psychologically during their military service, and have not lived since. They must be shaken from the steadfast position they took in those bygone days and be induced to live once more in the present, before much else can be done. The conscientious noncommissioned officer who feels guilty over the death of a member of his squad or platoon is particularly difficult to re-orient.

NEURASTHENIA AND HYPOCHONDRIASIS

These people are playing a hard game of "Ain't It Awful." After a decent interval, the therapist should bluntly refuse to play. He can start with "I've heard that before." His second move is "Okay, so what else is new?" He must then offer the patient something to replace the game; typically, he can point out that marital sex is more fun than "Ain't It Awful," although in some cases this requires considerable preparation, and if the patient is unmarried this solution is not available and the position is difficult.

Under favorable circumstances, and with proper timing, some of the swiftest and most gratifying results in group treatment can be obtained with these people. A woman who had spent years going from one doctor to another with a variety of complaints was handled so adroitly by the other members of the group, with the therapist's guidance, that within four weeks she had stopped playing "Ain't It Awful" and had no further need for medical consultations. She substituted a happy home-life instead, and eighteen months later was still carrying on merrily, without medical care, in another city. It was well established in the group that she had learned "Ain't It Awful" from her mother; and since her "divorce" from her mother was not complete, her social life remained somewhat stereotyped. Further treatment was therefore recommended.

HYSTERIA

The favored game of conversion hysterics in group treatment is "Do Me Something," with the motto "I know all you say is true, but this knowledge isn't helping me, so what are you going to do about that?" Since the proper treatment for this condition is orthodox psychoanalysis, the therapist may be able to do little in the group. If he chips away the advantages of the game, the patient may "forget" to have her symptoms, but usually she drifts away to seek medical, surgical, or dramatic treatment such as hypnosis or narcoanalysis.

Hysterical characters show poor adaptive capacities in the group. They start their exhibitionistic games abruptly without feeling out the other members. Thus a woman played "The Stocking Game" at her first session, lifting her leg to show a run in her stocking so that the men would get sexually excited and the other women jealous (or excited too). A widow came dressed in modish but demure widow's weeds, and then sat so that the other members could look up her skirt. If the group treats such a patient roughly, or pointedly ignores her, she may not return. A mild "unobtrusive" response of the desired quality (which the patient will notice with gratification) may help to keep her coming until a confrontation is possible. The therapist can then tell her to pull her skirt down, and can deal at an effective Adult level with her protestations of innocence.

PHOBIAS

Since the phobia resides in the Child, phobic patients do well if Adult control can be established, and can become quite successful in their outside endeavors. But this structural improvement is unstable and recurrences are not uncommon. Thus they may continue in group treatment for years (as they often do in individual psychotherapy). The most effective procedure is to analyse their games until they are almost game-free. Since the games protect them from their phobias, this increases the instability. When they are protected by only a thin layer, a single session on the couch may produce remarkable results, laying bare the archaic structure of the Child's relationship to the therapist, which may emerge in its pristine state even after a long term of preceding group treatment. (This is illustrated in Chapter 13 in the case of "Elsie.") After such a glimpse, the knowledgeable therapist has many new advantages in dealing with the patient in the group. Nevertheless, these cases remain difficult, and the therapist should not expect too much of himself or the patient if orthodox psychoanalysis is not available. He should remember that psychoanalysis was specifically designed for just this type of problem, and anything short of that treatment is necessarily makeshift and opportunistic.

ANXIETY STATES

For the group therapist, anxiety states are divided into two classes, somatic and social. Somatic symptoms tend to disappear as the patient's Adult becomes engaged in transactional analysis, and when they do occur the patient finds them relatively innocuous and unhampering if he has attained Adult social control. By social anxiety is meant clinging and lingering. These patients like to linger after the meeting is over to ask the therapist if they are making any progress, or they telephone him between meetings. Their behavior during the meetings is often merely an act of compliance, either "sweating out" the hour until they can speak privately to the therapist, or doing what he wants so that later they can say that he didn't help them ("See How Hard I've Tried"). Meanwhile they learn to play a good game of "Psychiatry." This can be turned to advantage in analysing their clinging game. The other patients can be very helpful here, and the patient may end up enjoying himself both in the group and outside. The games should be broken up in the following order: first, the lingering after the hour; next, the game of "Psychiatry" by which they "sweat out" the hour "without learning anything"; third, "See How Hard I've Tried," with its now obvious goal of demonstrating that the therapist is not helping them. These patients are easily lost, however, especially by "effective" therapists, who frighten them by actually doing something for them instead of playing "I'm Only Trying To Help You."

OBSESSIVE BEHAVIOR

This is an ideal situation for symptomatic cure by the exercise of Adult social control. The main task is decontamination of the Adult from Parent and Child elements. Obssessive patients love to play "Psychiatry," particularly the psychoanalytic variety. This must be cut short on the premise, clearly stated to the patient, of symptomatic cure first and analysis later. Incestuous thoughts and fantasies must be recognized as coming from the Child, and hence subject to Adult control. Once this is reasonably well established, the Adult is in condition to deal with the decisive problem, which is usually death, and this subject can then be frankly broached. Even if the rage cannot be effectively linked in the group to its early psychosexual origins, the patient may make a most gratifying social recovery.

REACTIVE DEPRESSION

Structurally, there are three types of "depressive" conditions. Melancholia is due to the influence of a harsh Parent, and despair to the draining away of cathexis from the Adult. Reactive depression is a choice of the Child. The mother or father repeatedly demonstrates this reaction to the actual child: "When the going gets rough, the solution is to feel depressed (or guilty or hurt)." Transactionally, this solution emerges as a hard game of "Ain't It Awful." If the actual child can find no better procedure, he will follow the Parental example. When he presents himself for treatment in later years, the diagnosis is reactive depression. In a transactional group, he is colloquially said to be "in the depression racket" (or the guilt or hurt feelings "racket").

A woman with a blind daughter spent most of her waking hours worrying, although the daughter herself was quite independent and was successful in her studies. From the patient's behavior when a new member came into the group, she was nicknamed "My Name Is I Have A Blind Daughter." The other members used to ask her "What would happen if you dared to enjoy something?" "We were never allowed to enjoy ourselves at home." "What would your neighbors say if they saw you enjoying something?" "Oh, they would be shocked too." At first the patient refused to consider other possible sources for her depression, but after she was partially "divorced" from her mother and her neighbors she began to talk about her miserable sex life. She had resented her husband's attempts at intercourse long before her daughter was born. Some of the women opined that sex could be more fun than playing "Ain't It Awful" or even "Frigid Woman." At this point the patient for the first time became animated; her eyes flashed, and a whole hidden repertoire of facial expressions, gestures, and intonations emerged. Following this meeting, her attitude changed, and "for the first time" in her life she participated in and enjoyed sex (much to the dismay of her husband — something the other members had predicted).*

Reactive depressions are approached transactionally through game analysis: the question is "What are the advantages of feeling depressed (or guilty or hurt) *and* telling people about it?" As a grown-up, the patient learns that there are whole professions whose ethics require them to sit and listen. The prognosis, and the reaction to the tough-minded therapist who does not want to listen, depends on whether it is primarily the patient's Adult who is in the group in order to get better, or whether it is primarily his Child who is there in order to exploit the situation.

The forthright therapist, however, must have a touch of the most delicate sensitivity in order to use this approach effectively; inadequate preparation of the patient, or a mistake in timing or intonation, may result in very undesirable consequences. Above all, the patient must feel that the therapist is "nearby" and hence available, although not necessarily indulgent.

CHARACTER DISORDERS

Character structure is the result of quite conscious decisions made early in childhood: "From now on I will transact my business with other people as follows . . ." This may be an "identification," i.e. a decision to be like someone. As the character becomes more ingrained, the decision and the events leading up to it are forgotten. The decisions are usually made in the first few years of life and are difficult to resurrect. Sometimes a later derivative is accessible. One man decided to spend the rest of his

---

* This case is instructive, but the ultimate result was disappointing. The patient gave up sex, withdrew from the group, and went back to her old way of life, probably in large part at her husband's behest.

life picking fights. The decision was made under the following conditions. His mother deserted him at the age of eight, and he fell sick. During his convalescence he tried to stand and collapsed from weakness. At that moment he said to himself "What's the use anyway, my mother has gone to another country. Never again will I love anyone, and in fact I hate everybody." As soon as he was well, he started to pick fights with all the boys in the neighborhood, and had followed this course ever since. It took a long time to recover this memory, but it convinced him that his "character" was the result of conscious decisions. Since decisions are always subject to revision, it was possible for him to make more headway from that point on.

THE BORDERLINE PATIENT

Structural analysis is almost as specific for borderline conditions as Vitamin C is for scurvy. In these conditions there is confusion between the Adult and the Child, compounded by interference from the Parent. Decontamination of the Adult, and clarification and strengthening of the boundaries between the ego states, often results in rapid improvement.

MANIC-DEPRESSIVE PSYCHOSIS

This psychosis results from gross shifts of cathexis between ego states. The shifts may have a biological basis, but a great deal can be accomplished by psychotherapy. The sequence is as follows. The Child becomes highly cathected at the expense of the Adult and Parent. This gives rise to the familiar symptomatic behavior of the manic phase. The Child has taken over the executive, and also becomes "real self." The Parent meanwhile, although powerless for lack of energy, is "watching." After the Child is exhausted, the Parent becomes powerfully cathected (possibly from biological sources) and takes his revenge on the now hapless Child. This is the depressive phase. The two phases may alternate, or there may be a rest period when the Adult once more takes over the executive, until a new cycle starts. A "gratifying response" in the treatment of a depressive may signify the onset of a manic phase; such patients should therefore be treated on a long-term basis — never for less than one year.

SCHIZOPHRENIA

In full-blown schizophrenia, the Adult is decommissioned and the executive resides in a confused Child. The role of the Parent is variable but is usually not of primary importance because of defects in the actual parents. Hence the therapeutic goal is to "throw a hook into the Adult." The results of transactional treatment in schizophrenia depend on how good a "hook-thrower" the therapist is: how effectively he gets the Child on his side and soothes it, so that the Child permits him to talk to the Adult. Frieda Fromm-Reichmann was an expert at this,[2] although she describes it with a different vocabulary.

PARANOID CONDITIONS

Transactionally, paranoid patients play a hard game of "Ain't It Awful." They spend their hours complaining about the bad treatment they are receiving. After proper preparation, which takes a few months or years, the therapist can start to break the game up by saying, "You've already told me how awful it is. What else is new?" If the timing is correct, the patient will be disconcerted. If the therapist persists in his refusal to play, the patient will try various procedures to fill in the time. It can often be observed that these have a certain ironical quality. The therapist can draw attention to this, and say, in effect, "Knock it off." The object is to leave the patient with no way to structure the hour. When this is successfully accomplished, he falls silent, becomes increasingly uneasy, and finally starts to laugh compulsively. This reveals that it is not the world which is playing tricks on him (as he claims), but he who is playing a trick on the world. If this advantage is properly exploited, the patient will then confess his sadistic fantasies and the deconfusion of the Child can proceed.

This transactional approach to paranoia is a delicate task and can become a dangerous one; a bad slip may precipitate a serious crisis. Therapists without a clear commitment to transactional analysis may easily become discouraged in such a situation, particularly if they are not favorably inclined toward the system to begin with. It should not be attempted by beginners or those without formal training in this approach. A good therapist can do it, if he cares to take the risk, even with patients who are homicidal.[3]

INVOLUTIONAL PSYCHOSES

Depressions of later years ("involutional psychoses") may take the form of melancholia, which may be alleviated in some measure by game analysis. They may be preceded by a hard game of "Harried" played by harassed housewives or busy business executives, in which the patient takes on a sufficient overload to give him a legitimate excuse to "collapse" into a "nervous breakdown from overwork."

More interesting are the "pre-involutional" depressions. Between 35 and 45 years of age many people begin to take stock of how they have spent their prime years. In transactional language, they begin to realize that they have spent the best part of their lives playing games to no good purpose, and that either their scripts are not being fulfilled or that they are not going to yield much satisfaction if they are. They make last minute eccentric or desperate attempts to "find Santa Claus" in some new way. This may be closely connected with the fact that their actual children are now growing up. The man throws away his Homburg and starts to wear a cowboy hat, takes to drink, absconds with the assets and/or his secretary, or gets a divorce. The woman takes a young lover, a hopeful trip to Tahiti, a fling in Las Vegas, or a course in ceramics. The failure of these expedients leads to a state of despair, which must be distinguished from depression by the criteria discussed earlier. Briefly, depression is based on an inner dialogue, while despair results from a failure of the dialogue between the patient and the outside world.

PSYCHOPATHIC STATES

Psychopaths are of two types: those with remorse and those without. Structurally, those who feel remorse about their peccadillos and have a "morning after" go through the same sequence as a manic-depressive. Those without remorse are at peace with their Parents. Hence it is no use appealing to the Parent or Child of such people. The best approach is to "hook" their Adult and decontaminate it. The only effective restraint on their behaviour is reason, e.g. "If you give marijuana to your friends, at least don't take money for it." Usually there are two different elements that must be dissected away from each other. The first is the "psychopathy" itself, the lack of Parental restraint in areas where most people have it, and the compliance of the Adult in dangerous behavior. The second is the heavy overlay of games, resulting from the responses of society to psychopathic behavior. The therapist can suggest "Either smoke marijuana or play 'Cops and Robbers,' but don't do both at the same time." If the "behavior" can be separated from the games, that is an important step. Such people often have an unusual curiosity about, and aptitude for, game analysis, which may be turned to good advantage.

SEXUAL DEVIATIONS

Again, the deviation should be separated from the overlying games. Homosexual sex is one thing, and "playing Homosexual" is another. On one side homosexuals may sidle up to the underworld by playing "Cops and Robbers," and on the other they may merge with the organically disabled by playing "Napoleon." (Napoleon was a homosexual, Napoleon was an epileptic, etc.). A game-free homosexual can lead quite a different life from one who insists on exploiting the game aspects of the situation.

ALCOHOL ADDICTION

Simple alcohol addiction should be differentiated from the game of "Alcoholic." Some people drink ten to twenty ounces of hard liquor every day, or before going to bed at night, but keep a "clean" situation: they are on the job punctually every day and turn out acceptable work, and their drinking does not materially involve or injure other people. It is self-evident that this condition is more common among the unmarried. The drinker who gets himself involved in unpleasant situations at work, at play, or at home, is in a different category, and is playing "Alcoholic." This transactional difference is more significant than a chemical or doctrinaire diagnosis. It is much less important from several points of view whether a man takes a drink before breakfast than whether he gets into altercations as a result of drinking.

The indications are that in many cases the payoff in the game of "Alcoholic" is a hangover. If such an alcoholic can be induced to give up the internal and external advantages of the hangover, he may be able to stop drinking altogether. After his recovery is stabilized, he should then be able to drink socially without being in jeopardy. In this respect, successful transactional treatment has an advantage over some more popular approaches.

DRUG ADDICTION

Part of the attraction of drug addiction is the excellent opportunities it provides for playing secondary games with a variety of people, such as policemen, doctors, judges, and prison personnel. In young people it also involves parents and school authorities. The primary game, the addiction itself, is probably very similar to "Alcoholic," although rescuers are fewer and persecutors more numerous. It is getting harder and harder for "alcoholics" to find persecutors nowadays.

PSYCHOSOMATIC DISORDERS

The favorite game with people suffering from psychosomatic disorders is "Ain't It Awful," and the advantages derived from this game have a strong influence in continuing the disorder. "Obesity" is a special case; it resembles "Alcoholic" in many respects, and the favored game is "Do Me Something." ("I can't stop eating, so what are you going to do about it?")

THE TREATMENT OF ADOLESCENTS

Many of the grown-ups whom adolescents are expected to respect and emulate are sulks, jerks, cowards, hypocrites, fanatics, prudes, bunglers, bigots, and finks. As the patient approaches the twenties he becomes less compliant and gullible and his natural Child emerges with its long-suppressed archaic qualities of awareness, candidness, and capacity for intimacy. For a brief time he sees the world clearly, and what he sees confuses him. As a result of his natural strivings and his fresh view of his betters, what he comes to value above everything is authenticity. The first requirement for therapy with adolescents, therefore, is authenticity on the part of the therapist. The patient will often try to bluff, and if he bluffs back or is taken in, he is lost. The adolescent's love of drama and fear of boredom are the chief temptations to spuriousness. The saving grace is that adolescents do not usually consider themselves fragile, nor do they appreciate being treated as though they were. The main thing for the therapist to be careful about is Parental bluster, which is nearly always an error.

Since the majority of teen-age patients are "sent" or "brought" to treatment, their relationship to the therapist is not an autonomous one, so that there is a strong temptation to rebellion, withdrawal, or sabotage. In effect, the therapist becomes a delegate of their parents which, under the usual contract, puts him at a great disadvantage from the beginning. The sought-for "cure" too often resembles a prescription written by the parents, who visualize the therapeutic relationship as a Parent-Child one, and the patient tends to do the same. The situation can be decisively altered at the social level by explicitly setting up an Adult-Adult (teacher-pupil) contract, whereby the therapist offers to teach the patient transactional analysis, with the proviso that the patient can do as he pleases with what he learns. This procedure has been followed with great success by Kupfer,* who obtained almost perfect attendance records in his adolescent groups (ages 14–16 and 16–18). His youthful patients learned to apply transactional analysis with great adeptness to their inner problems, their family living, and their relationships at school with both teachers and fellow-pupils. In effect, these were set up and described as clinical teaching groups rather than as therapy groups. Many of the patients had the advantage that their parents were also in transactional therapy groups.

MARITAL THERAPY

The three commonest games that have to be broken up in a marital group are "Court-Room," "Sweetheart," and "Further-

* Kupfer has collected some accounts of experiences in such groups, written by the patients themselves. See *Transactional Analysis Bulletin* 4:51–6, July 1965.

more." In "Court-Room" one spouse accuses the other and the therapist is supposed to act as judge with the other members as jury. That is terminated, after a reasonable period of indulgence, when the therapist forbids the use of the grammatical third person, so that a speaker must speak directly to the other person concerned, and cannot act as prosecuting attorney before the group. He may then fall back on "Sweetheart," in which he says outrageous or derogatory things to his spouse, prefacing each statement with "Well, honey," or "But, sweetheart." This is broken up by emphasizing the inconsistency between his endearments and his accusations. "Furthermore" has already been described.

Once these consulting-room games have been eliminated, the analysis of domestic games such as "Uproar" can proceed, and if those can be broken up, the underlying sexual difficulties are laid bare, and the treatment can then proceed along conventional lines.

FAMILY THERAPY

Not all parents are interested in family therapy. The initial assumption that the therapist should make is that any family who consents to this procedure does so because it fits into an already established family game or script. His first task should be to discover what that is. Usually it is some variant of "Mental Health" or "See How Hard We're Trying." The offspring, particularly the adolescent ones, will gladly help him break up such games, and he will earn their gratitude by doing so — gratitude he can put to good use later as therapeutic leverage. The next layer is usually some form of "Uproar" which enables the members of the family to avoid intimacy with each other and the sexual temptation that implies. When the mutual goading becomes apparent to everyone, the situation should begin to quiet down, offering an opportunity to consider more basic problems.

At this point it may be advisable to terminate the family group and separate the children from the parents. There are certain things that children should not know about their parents, such as their sexual fantasies. If a young lady cannot have at least a shred of illusion about her own mother and father, she may find herself without any illusions at all, and in that case she may end up not being a lady.

Satir's book [4] is an enlightening introduction to the adventure of treating families as a whole.

SUGGESTIONS

Some hints or aphorisms are given below which the therapist may sooner or later find useful in his practice:

Psychotherapy is like surgery in that before any decisive intervention is made the patient must be thoroughly prepared. The difference is that in psychotherapy the preparation may take much longer than the intervention.

Preparation of the therapist must precede preparation of the patient.

Until you know what the patient expects you to do, you do not know what you are doing. Until you know what the patient is trying to do to you, you do not know what you are doing to yourself.

A fool defends his mistakes, a wise man learns from them, and a practical man does both.

You will get good results when you are young and good results when you are old, but for different reasons. At first you will be an artist, later a craftsman.

Self-analysis is like giving oneself a haircut: with sufficient care and practice it can be done.

If you want the patient to be your therapist, be sure first that you can afford to pay him your usual fee.

Each intervention must be considered from eight points of view: the patient's resistances, his defenses, the transference, his games, his symptoms, his assets, his therapeutic goals, and your therapeutic goals.

The recumbent patient is more impressed by your competence than by your virtuosity. It does not reassure him to be treated like a violin.

When he is on the couch, a patient will forgive you more quickly for falling asleep than for being too wide awake. Vis à vis, it is the reverse.

If the diagnosis escapes you, the patient is probably paranoid.

If a paranoid smiles compulsively during an interview, he is curable. If his smile is oily, the case is not so good.

A Rorschach is only as good as the practitioner who recommends it.

A schizophrenic is not properly in treatment until he offers voluntarily to discuss his masturbatory fantasies. You cannot know a patient until you know those fantasies.

A dilettante knows what to do; a professional knows what not to do. A mediocre therapist is like a bull, who charges wherever he sees the cape; a good one is like a matador.

Psychotherapy should never be an end in itself; it should be used solely and forthrightly as an instrument toward better living.

REFERENCES

1. Arieti, S. (ed.). *American Handbook of Psychiatry*. Basic Books, New York, 1959.
2. Fromm-Reichmann, F. *Principles of Intensive Psychotherapy*. University of Chicago Press, Chicago, 1950.
3. Concannon, J. P. "An Aggressive Ambulatory Paranoid Treated with Structural and Transactional Analysis." *Transactional Analysis Bulletin* 1:21, 1962.
4. Satir, V. *Conjoint Family Therapy*. (Chap. 9, ref. 18.)

Glossary

Figures in parentheses give the chapter to consult for details.

Absence, Accidental   One clearly and unequivocally due to external contingencies (1).

Absence, Psychological (Resistance Absence)   One not unequivocally due to external contingencies, hence presumably due to psychodynamic factors relating to the group situation (1).

Adaptation   The alteration of a script to make the best use of the facilities at hand (12).

Adult   An ego state oriented toward objective, autonomous data-processing and probability estimating (10).

Archaeopsyche   The hypothetical organ that deals with Child ego states (10).

Authentic Individual   One whose signature on an act is free of external influences irrelevant to the act itself (3).

Authority Principle   The principle that each member of an organizational hierarchy tries to comply with the presumed or fantasied wishes of those above him (6).

Boundaries   Physical or psychological factors that separate relevant regions in the group structure.
External   The boundary separating the group from the external environment.
Major Internal   That which distinguishes the leadership from the membership.

Minor Internal   Those which distinguish subgroups or individual patients from each other (Minor₁), or individuals within a subgroup (Minor₂). There may also be minor boundaries in the leadership if there is more than one therapist present (6).

Child   An ego state which is an archaic relic from an early significant period of life. The adapted Child is influenced by Parental parameters. The expressive Child is more autonomous (10).

Commitment   An operationally ratified decision to follow certain principles of action in order to attain a certain goal (3).

Confirmation   A re-confrontation, which may be undertaken by the patient himself (11).

Confrontation   The use of information to disconcert the patient by pointing out an inconsistency (11).

Consensus   An explicit agreement of several people without a serious examination of motives (3).

Consultant   An expert in a field related to group treatment (7).

Consultant, Independent   One who is not a regular member of the sponsoring organization (2).

Contract   An explicit bilateral commitment to a well-defined course of action (4).

Contract, Administrative   The statement between the administration and the therapist concerning the occasions, purposes, and goals of a treatment group, usually in sociological language (2).

Contract, Organizational   The agreement concerning group treatment between the therapist and his organization (2).

Contract, Professional   A statement of the technical goals of a treatment group, usually in psychiatric language (2).

Contract, Psychological   The therapist's assessment of the ulterior motives of the administration that will influence the fate of his treatment group in the organization (2).

Contract, Therapist-Patient   Administratively, this concerns the relationships between the therapist, the patients, and the organization. Professionally, it states the goals of the therapy. Psychologically, the therapist (inwardly) tries to anticipate which games the patients are likely to play in the group (2).

Conviction   A firm opinion about the OKness or not-OKness of oneself on the one hand, and the rest of the world on the other (12).

Cowboy   A relaxed therapist who knows how to make himself understood by the patient's Child (Foreword).

Crystallization   A statement of the patient's position from the Adult of the therapist to the Adult of the patient (11).

Decision   A childhood commitment to a certain form of behavior; the basis for character formation in the form of a verb absolute (12).

Demonstrator   A nonmedical teacher of group treatment (7).

Depression   The failure of a dialogue between the Child and the Parent (13).

Despair   The failure of a dialogue between the Adult and the outside world (13).

Diagram, Authority   1. A diagram showing the relationships of all individuals, particularly superiors, who might influence the therapist's attitude or determine the scope or fate of his group (2).   2. A diagram showing the four aspects of the group authority:

The Organizational Aspect is shown on the Organization Chart, which gives the administrative relationships of those in the hierarchy.

The Personal Aspect is shown on the Personnel Chart, which gives the name of each individual filling a slot on the Organization Chart.

The Historical Aspect gives the names of past leaders whose influence is still felt.

The Cultural Aspect names the canonical books and manuals that regulate the workings of the organization (6).

Diagram, Dynamics   A diagram that demonstrates the forces acting on the major and minor group boundaries (6).

Diagram, Seating   A diagram showing where each member of a group sits in relation to the others and in relation to the furnishings and layout of the treatment room (6).

Diagram, Structural   1. One which shows the internal structure of a group (6).   2. One which shows the ego-state structure of a personality (10).

Differentiation   The assignment of slots in a group imago to the actual individuals in a group. Thus a group may be under-differentiated (more people than slots), fully differentiated (each individual assigned to a special slot), or over-differentiated (more slots than people). Heteromorphic differentiation corrects under-differentiation by activating new slots; homomorphic differentiation, by assigning several members to the same slot (6).

Ego State   A consistent pattern of feeling and experience directly related to a corresponding consistent pattern of behavior (10).

Embroidery   Idiosyncratic elaboration of a procedure for personal satisfaction (4).

Engram   A trace left by an early experience, influential in later relationships (12).

Explanation   An attempt on the part of the therapist to strengthen, decontaminate, or re-orient the patient's Adult (11).

Exteropsyche   The hypothetical organ that deals with Parental ego states (10).

Extraneous Fantasies   Those concerned with matters outside the actual situation (10).

Game   A series of ulterior transactions with a gimmick, leading to a well-defined payoff (10).

Group Apparatus   Those people who preserve internal order in a group (internal apparatus) and those who deal with the external environment (external apparatus) (6).

Group, Discussion   One that deals with specific problems, in group work (1).

Group, Experimental   One that is set up for the purpose of experimenting with some aspect of group therapy or group dynamics (1).

Group, Heterogeneous   One to which the patients are assigned with whatever degree of randomness is available (1).

Group, Homogeneous   One in which the patients are selected because they have a common characteristic. The homogeneity may be a matter of organizational planning, for patients with the same syndrome, symptom, or condition; or it may be a matter of personal policy, according to idiosyncrasies of the therapist (1).

Group Imago   A mental image of the dynamic relationships between the people in the group, including the therapist; idiosyncratic for each individual present (6).

Group Process   Transactions that are not directly concerned with the group activity.

External Transactions between the group and the external environment.

Major Internal Transactions between the members and the therapist.

Minor Internal Transactions between patients not directly involving the therapist; or transactions between therapists not directly involving the patients (6).

Group, Special One that is set up for the purpose of treating a special category of patients; hence, a less prejudicial name for a planned homogeneous group (2).

Group Treatment 1. The treatment of several psychiatric patients simultaneously by meeting in a room for a specified period of time with a small number of them for the declared purpose of alleviating psychiatric disabilities (1). 2. The treatment by a trained psychotherapist of more than one patient at a time with the object of relieving symptoms or effecting psychodynamic changes in the patients' personalities (5).

Group Work 1. Guidance in group experience without systematic focus on the psychiatry of specific psychopathology (1). 2. A form of group activity in which the leader guides or manipulates the members according to psychodynamic principles withrevealing to them the basis for his actions (5).

Gumdrop Same as marshmallow (3).

Illustration An anecdote, simile, or comparison which reinforces a confrontation or softens its possible undesirable effects. It may be immediate or remote in time and may refer to the external environment or to the internal situation in the group (11).

Institution A set of transactions standardized by consensus and containing elements irrelevant to the material aim of the set (4).

Institutionalization The introduction of irrelevant elements into a procedure, or their retention after their usefulness is past and their maintenance by consensus without serious examination of their relevancy and truth (14).

Interposition A therapeutic operation that interposes something at the boundary between two ego states (11).

Interpretation An operation designed to de-confuse the Child (11).

Interrogation A question designed to document a clinically decisive point of information (11).

Intervention   A therapeutic operation that intervenes in the conflict between two ego states (11).

Intimacy   A game-free exchange of affective expression without covert exploitation (10).

Magic Orb   The mythical reward which the Child spends his life hoping for (12).

Marshmallow   An overly sweet or affected response of encouragement or approval (3).

Martian Viewpoint   The naïvest possible frame of mind for observing earthly phenomena, leaving the intellect free for inquiry without the distraction of preconceptions (4).

Meetings, Alternate   Meetings held by the members of a clinical group without the therapist or leader, between their regular meetings (1).

Meetings, Large Group   Meetings too large to allow for unremitting observation of every patient, as distinguished from a small group of not more than eight members where such observation is possible (1).

Meetings, Informal   Meetings held without the therapist or leader, following after the regular sessions (1).

Meeting, Ward (or Cell-Block or Wing Meeting)   A discussion group attended by the staff and patients (inmates, clients) of a section of an institution (1).

Neopsyche   The hypothetical organ that deals with Adult ego states (10).

Observer   One who observes a group without active participation or duties (2).

Palimpsest   A later version of a script arising from new potentialities as the child enters later phases of development (12).

Parent   An ego state borrowed from a parental figure. It may exert itself as an indirect influence, or be directly exhibited in parental behavior (10).

Pastimes   Semi-stereotyped sets of transactions, usually of a multiple-choice, sentence-completion structure (10).

Patient, Receptive   One who prescribes group therapy for himself (2).

Patient, Reluctant   One who is unwilling to undertake group treatment (2).

Patient, Sophisticated   One who is well trained in the institutionalized aspects of psychotherapy (2).

Patient, Unready   One who in the therapist's judgment is not yet ready for group treatment (2).

Patient, Unsophisticated   One who is not trained in the institutionalized aspects of psychotherapy (2).

Position   A predicate absolute that justifies a decision (12).

Private Interview   Time spent with an individual patient immediately following a group session, usually extemporaneously at the patient's initiative (1).

Procedure   A set of operations all of which are relevant to, and necessary for the stated aim (4).

Protocol   The original dramatic experiences upon which the script is based (12).

Provisional Fantasy (Provisional Group Imago)   The patient's fantasy of what will occur when he enters a group (2).

Psychoanalysis   Individual treatment by a qualified psychoanalyst or by a properly prepared candidate under adequate supervision, by the resolution of infantile conflicts through the systematic use of free association to deal with transference and resistance (1).

Psychodrama   A form of group therapy in which the patient dramatizes his conflicts with the assistance of trained or untrained personnel who take the other roles required for the dramatization (5).

Racket   The sexualization and transactional exploitation of unpleasant feelings (13).

Ratification   The demonstration in operation that a contractual commitment will be carried through in spite of difficulties and unforeseen eventualities (4).

Recorder   One who records what happens in a group without active participation (2).

Research, Hidden   Research done without the patients' knowledge (2).

Research, Open   Research done with full knowledge of the patients (2).

Rituals   Stereotyped sets of transactions (10).

Role   A socially compliant set of transactions played out in any of the three ego states, hence differentiated from an ego state (13).

Role Playing   An imitative form of behavior, not all of which is procedural, designed to meet institutionalized requirements (4).

Santa Claus   The mythical source of the mythical gift which the Child spends his life waiting for; it may be synonymous with death (12).

Schedule   A statement of the time and attendance structure of a treatment group, including the serial number, time, duration, and the actual/possible attendance of the meeting presented, and the gross attendance during the life of the group (6).

Script   An unconscious life plan. In some cases it may be preconscious or conscious (10).

Self-Correction   The therapist's duty to be aware of what games he is likely to be tempted to play in the group, and to apply appropriate corrections to his own behavior at all times (2).

Sequestration   To cut oneself off from society, by going to an institution or by partial or complete social isolation (12).

Slots   Elements of an Organization Chart or a Group Imago (6).

Specification   A declaration on the part of the therapist categorizing certain information. It may be assentive or informative (11).

Stroke   The unit of recognition; e.g. "Hello." (10).

Structural Analysis   Analysis of the personality into its constituent Parent, Adult, and Child ego states (10).

Supervision, Private   When only the therapist and supervisor are present (2).

Supervision, Public   When others besides the therapist and supervisor are present (2).

Supervisor   A clinical expert in group treatment, professionally, administratively, and legally competent to take full responsibility for a program of group treatment and the supervision of other therapists (7).

Termination, Accidental   One clearly and unequivocally due to external contingencies (1).

Termination, Therapeutic   When the patient and therapist agree that the planned therapeutic goals have been attained (1).

Therapeutic Community   An artificial co-operative society under professional guidance and supervision (1).

Therapeutic Hypothesis   A hypothesis concerning the value of an

operation. The psychological or informational aspect is concerned with clarifying the patient's personality structure or
dynamics. The transactional or social aspect is concerned with
the effect of the operation on the patient (11).

Therapist, Assistant A junior, participating colleague who assists a
therapist (2).

Therapist, Co- One of two therapists working in a single group
whose administrative position, professional qualifications, experience, and freedom in the group are equal or complementary
(2).

Therapy, Activity Group A form of group therapy in which the
patient's conflicts are revealed and investigated in the course
of the manipulation of external materials (5).

Therapy, Combined Concurrent individual and group therapy (1).

Therapy, Didactic Group A form of group therapy based on pedagogical activity on the part of the leader (5).

Therapy, Existential A form of group therapy that deals roman-
tically with whither and why rather than classically with
whence and how (5).

Therapy, Individual The treatment of a single patient by a single
therapist in private sessions (1).

Therapy, Group The same as group treatment, except that more
diffuseness of method, focus, and goal is permissible (1).

Therapy, Group-Analytic A form of group therapy based on the
hypothesis that the patient's condition at a given moment is a
product of the condition of the whole group, a holistic approach
which assumes the existence of something like a "group
mentality" (5).

Therapy, Multiple The presence of more than one therapist at an
individual or group session (1).

Therapy, Psychoanalytic Individual or group treatment that attempts
to deal with transference and resistance phenomena (1).

Therapy, Psychoanalytic Group A form of group therapy based
primarily on the use of psychoanalytic principles and techniques (5).

Therapy, Supportive Group Group therapy in which the leader plays
a parental role and, aided by the other members, gives license,
concurrence, or active incitement to the patient (5).

Trading Stamp An incident "collected" for the purpose of justi-
fying pathological feelings or behavior (12).

Transaction   A transactional stimulus plus a transactional response. In a *complementary* transaction, the vectors are parallel. In a *crossed* transaction, they are crossed. An *ulterior* transaction is effective at two levels, the social and the psychological. An ulterior transaction may be *angular* involving three ego states, or *duplex,* involving four (10).

Transaction, Autistic   A transaction carried out mentally rather than overtly. It may be adapted or unadapted (10).

Transactional Analysis   1. A system of psychotherapy based on the analysis of transactions and chains of transactions as they actually occur during treatment sessions (5). Its principal phases are structural analysis, transactional analysis proper, game analysis, and script analysis (10). 2. A theory of personality based on the study of specific ego states (10). 3. A theory of social action based on the rigorous analysis of transactions into an exhaustive but finite number of classes based on the specific ego states involved (10). 4. The analysis of single transactions by means of transactional diagrams. This is transactional analysis proper (10).

Vis medicatrix naturae   The healing powers of nature (3).

Withdrawal   Unexplained, unannounced, or merely plausible termination (1).

Work Workshop   A specially arranged all-day seminar in which more time is devoted to the formal sessions than to coffee-breaks (7).

Name Index

Italic page numbers refer to the bibliographies at the end of each chapter.

Subject Index

374